ST. BARNABAS' EPISCOPAL CHURCH
22 W 415 BUTTERFIELD ROAD
GLEN ELLYN ILLINOIS 60137

Resolutions of the twelve Lambeth Conferences
1867–1988

Resolutions
of the twelve
Lambeth Conferences
1867–1988

Edited by Roger Coleman

With an Introduction by
OWEN CHADWICK

Anglican Book Centre
Toronto, Canada

1992
Anglican Book Centre
600 Jarvis Street
Toronto, Ontario
Canada M4Y 2J6

Typesetting by Jay Tee Graphics Ltd.

Canadian Cataloguing in Publication Data

Lambeth Conference
   Resolutions of the twelve Lambeth Conferences,
1867-1988

Includes index.
ISBN 0-921846-44-4

1. Anglican Communion – Congresses. I. Coleman,
Rogers, 1929-   . II. Title.

BX5021.L35 1992   262'.53   C92-093007-7

Contents

EDITOR'S NOTE

The wording of the Resolutions as first published is given unchanged, but minor adjustments have been made to punctuation, spelling and presentation in the interests of general consistency. Footnotes accompanying the published Resolutions are included where they are not misleading or unintelligible away from their original context. A small number of editorial notes in square brackets has been added, where necessary for clarification. Attention is drawn to the editorial note appearing at the beginning of the 1878 'Recommendations' on page 4.

In the Index, the references in roman figures are to *page numbers* in the Introduction and Chronology; those in arabic figures are to *the year and number of the Resolution* concerned. Churches and dioceses are normally indexed under the name by which they were known when this book was compiled.

R.C.

For Lord Runcie of Cuddesdon
Archbishop of Canterbury 1980–1991

Foreword

This publication originated with the first Archbishop of Nigeria, the Most Reverend Timothy Olufosoye. At a meeting of the Anglican bishops of Africa held in Limuru, Kenya, in 1987 in preparation for the Lambeth Conference 1988, he reminded his brother bishops that many of the topics proposed for the agenda of Lambeth 1988 had been the subject of various Resolutions at previous Lambeth Conferences. A gentle reminder, perhaps, not to reinvent the wheel!

There the concept was born, and with diligent work by the Right Reverend Philip Russell, former Archbishop of Cape Town, and the Reverend Arthur Gosling of Durban a resource book containing all the Resolutions of the eleven Lambeth Conferences 1867–1978 was available for the Steering Committee of the Lambeth Conference 1988.

A considerable amount of revision was required: adding the 1988 Resolutions and full indexing to mention but two aspects.

With the publication of this comprehensive book giving all the Resolutions of the twelve Lambeth Conferences to date and providing an interesting overview of the social and moral concerns of the times, I want to record the thanks of the Anglican Communion to three people in particular:

> To the editor, Roger Coleman, for his meticulous and painstaking work carried out with good grace and much humour;
> to the Reverend Professor Sir Owen Chadwick for the scholarly, provocative and magisterial overview given in his Introduction;
> and lastly to the Reverend Michael Lloyd, Director of the Anglican Book Centre in Toronto, for his constant support and professional guidance. Without his enthusiastic endorsement of the project this book could not be found on our shelves.

I predict that this book will be essential reading for all those who will attend the next Lambeth Conference and that it will be a vital resource for all scholars, researchers, theologians and seminarians interested in a world vision of Anglicanism.

I would like to dedicate this book to Lord Runcie of Cuddesdon who hosted the 1988 Lambeth Conference, and with whom I worked with pleasure, friendship and gratitude. He showed that the Anglican Communion is alive and well and, indeed, growing and developing. As Archbishop of Canterbury he played a positive and predominant role in binding the Anglican Communion together.

SAMUEL VAN CULIN
Secretary, The Lambeth Conference 1988

Introduction

BY OWEN CHADWICK

The Lambeth Conference is a meeting of bishops from all parts of the world who belong to the Anglican Communion. The first Conference was in 1867. Though interrupted by wars it has met more or less every ten years; last in 1988. The last digit moved from 7 to 8 because the second Lambeth Conference could not get ready in time for 1877.

THE ANGLICAN COMMUNION

Who is in the Anglican Communion? The word Anglican is simply the Latin word for English. But in the later meetings a majority of those who met were not English. In the earlier meetings the Americans thought themselves no part of the Anglican Communion, in the fear that if they were they might seem to be part again of some British Empire. They thought that they were in communion with the Anglican Communion, because they had the same ministry and much the same prayer book and the same doctrines. Soon they lost this fear and accepted that they were part of the Anglican Communion. Later on some of the Africans were not happy about the name Anglican Communion because of its suggestion of Englishness, and were afraid that someone would think their Church to be European in its cast of mind and its interests. Still, there did not seem to be any other name to use but Anglican Communion. It meant a body of bishops all in communion with the See of Canterbury, in various parts of the world, not necessarily having English as their first language, some of them unable to speak English; but with their doctrine derived from the Reformed doctrine of the English sixteenth century, and their worship developed out of the English prayer book, and their hymnody using the hymns of all the centuries, and their ways of spirituality the devotions of all the centuries.

Why should the Archbishop of Canterbury invite a lot of *bishops* from across the seas to come and meet at Lambeth? Why did he not invite representative priests or lay people?

COUNCILS OF THE CHURCH

The answer lies in the Acts of the Apostles and then in early Christian history. In Acts 15 there is the description of a meeting of the apostles and apostolic men to settle a difficulty which plagued the Church. From the third century if not before, at least from the earliest

i

time of which we have a sight into the workings of church order, the bishops met with apostolic authority to settle disputes in the Church. They needed to meet, when they could come together despite the persecution, to agree a common policy. Suppose that a Christian under persecution abandoned his faith to save his or her life, and afterwards repented and asked to be taken back into the Church? When that happened some bishops were severe, other bishops were forgiving. It was a necessity to find a common policy. There were many other such questions to determine.

When the Roman Empire became Christian, it was possible for councils to meet which represented the whole Church, even though travelling was arduous and expensive and sometimes dangerous. These great councils won a permanent place in the history of the Church by settling the creeds and the right way to express the doctrines of God and Christ. They not only left a structure of Christian doctrine. They left the memory that the right way to settle the affairs of the Church is by meetings of bishops, that is, by people of apostolic authority who are the representatives of God to their flocks and of their flocks to God.

Throughout the Middle Ages this was accepted as an axiom. In practice it was weakened: first by the sovereigns who saw that decisions by a council of bishops could affect the laws of their land, and therefore wanted to establish some kind of control; secondly by the growth of the Pope in power and in the effectiveness of his rulings. If the Pope could decide, what need of a council to decide? If Rome could decide, no one needed to desert their dioceses and travel a thousand miles. This might be convenient in theory, but in practice it did not work conveniently, because bishops in a dispute still needed to get the right answer out of the Roman courts, and so still needed to travel the thousand miles in order that their case should be properly put.

But at the end of the fourteenth century the Pope's system went very wrong. There were rival Popes, the ills of the Church were incurable by Rome, and a great movement arose to heal the Church by councils. These councils did not only consist of bishops; the theologians were there, and the representatives of sovereigns, or even the sovereigns themselves, and some priests were there to help their bishops. But they were like meetings of the representatives of all Western Europe. Thus the names of Swiss towns—Constance, Basle—were thenceforth and for ever associated with the belief that the supreme authority in healing the ills of the Church and settling its disputes was the Council.

These Councils did not succeed in healing the ills of the Church. Therefore there came the Reformation, and the division of Western Christendom.

BISHOPS AND THE REFORMATION

At first the Protestants had little use for bishops. In Germany the political course of events made it hardly possible for them to survive with any authority, if they survived at all. That did not mean that the idea of a Council was dead. On the contrary, here was the greatest dispute of all Church history; everyone agreed that it could only be settled by a truly representative council. But not everyone was agreed when a council was truly representative, and the Protestants always refused to recognise the Council of Trent (1545–1563) as in any sense representative of Western Christendom. From the end of the Council of Trent, the notion that a council could heal the ills of Christian Europe was in suspense, in the Roman Catholic as well as in the Protestant Church. If the first Lambeth Conference met in 1867, the first Roman Catholic council after the Council of Trent did not meet till two and a half years after that. With no need to take account of the Protestants, Rome could decide the disputes. It did not need a council, or did not seem to. When the dioceses or parish churches or monasteries ran into trouble, the law of Rome was enough.

Most Protestant Churches either did not have bishops or, if they had bishops, treated them at first as a sort of survival or as a useful bit of administration. They did not need councils of bishops, either because there were no bishops or, where they existed, because they would not think the bishops representative enough. The disputes in the Church were settled locally, by a mixture of lay and clerical decision, through some committee or other, usually called a consistory.

But in Sweden, and in England, Wales and Ireland, the Reformation left bishops in office. And in England they came to be particularly valued, as symbols of continuity with the Catholic past and indeed with the English past. Therefore where Anglican Churches came to exist, not in England and Wales but overseas or across the border—in Scotland, then in the United States and Canada, then in Australia and New Zealand and India—the mark which distinguished them among Protestant Churches was the apostolic authority which they attributed to bishops. When Anglicanism had ceased to be seen as a thing of England and Wales and Ireland, and was of the world, it was embodied across the continents by a pattern of episcopal Churches with much the same way of worship and much the same expression of doctrine. And if they attributed apostolic authority to bishops, and had no higher authority like a Pope to settle matters that needed determining, they naturally thought—though at first they thought very hesitantly—that they must have meetings of the bishops from all the various Churches of the Anglican Communion.

iii

AN ANGLICAN EPISCOPAL COUNCIL

Naturally the bishops could not meet until it was physically possible to meet. When a journey from New Zealand could still take three months, it was not sensible to think that the heads of the Churches should all be brought together at Lambeth, for such a plan would have been an invitation to absenteeism and gross neglect of a lot of dioceses. It was during the 1840s that transatlantic travel began to be faster and regular. The word Anglicanism is first found during the 1830s. The Anglican Communion, as an expression to describe a union of episcopal Churches across the world, is first found in 1851. It will be observed that the Anglican Communion was not 'founded'—unlike, say, the Lutheran World Federation. It happened because of a long Catholic tradition within its own past. Like the Lutheran World Federation, and like two modern Vatican Councils, the work of the Lambeth Conference was made possible by the invention of steam power, and later the use of oil and later still the aero-engineer. Technological advances helped not only by improving transport to and from the Conference, but also in speeding the flow of information in preparing and following up the meetings. The development of the international postal system, world-wide telegraph and telephone services, and in the 1980s a computer-based telecommunication network (the Inter-Anglican Information Network) came to provide immediate mutual access between all parts of the Anglican Communion.

By 1860 there was an Anglican Communion called, though not yet widely called, by that new name: of independent Churches, worshipping in the tradition of the Anglican Prayer Book, with a ministry of bishops, priests and deacons, and in communion with the See of Canterbury. It was inevitable that the heads of the various provinces should wish to meet. It was also inevitable that some of those heads should wish for some kind of supreme government for the Anglican Communion, so that it should not be split apart as the provinces developed their own life, or as controversial questions received different answers according to local circumstances.

It was Canadian bishops who first asked the Archbishop of Canterbury to hold such a meeting. Things were happening in England which sounded alarming and controversial. They did not know what was happening. They asked if they could be brought together. Without the long background of the history of councils of bishops through the Christian centuries, this request would have been merely plausible. To find out what was happening they did not need to meet. They could get through the post the information which they needed. But they had the conviction that they also shared in the common experience and common difficulty, and that in such cases it was the right of all the bishops to participate, after prayer and common experience of friendships, in affecting what was to happen.

There was another push behind the coming together of the bishops. Councils had so fallen out of use that they were known only to the historians. The Roman Catholic Church had not held a Council for three hundred years; the last important Council held by the Ortho-dox Church ended in Jerusalem almost two hundred years before. But it happened that in the early 1860s the contemporary Pope Pius IX was under pressure from the Italian government, who wished to con-fiscate his state to make a united Italy. It was evident to him that he could show the support of Catholics from across the world against these local bandits by summoning all the Roman Catholic bishops to meet in Rome. It would be a wonderful demonstration that Rome belonged to the world and not to the Piedmontese. In 1866 he had not proclaimed that there would be a Vatican Council. But he was known to be considering it and was believed to be about to summon it. This revived interest in the nature and function of councils of bishops within Christendom. This was much discussed even in the Protestant communities.

Here then is already an Anglican world-wide Church which needs a government. It cannot be governed by Canterbury because Canter-bury is governed by English law and English tradition, and even York is not governed by Canterbury. The structure of Church government is different in Cape Town and Sydney and Delhi and Auckland and Washington and Edinburgh. On smaller matters the different provinces will go their own way. But suppose some province decides something which others cannot accept—let us imagine that it decides to reunite unconditionally with the Church of Rome, or changes its creed so that no one need accept the doctrine of the Trinity—then is there any government above that local government which can determine that this is wrong and that this province is no longer part of the Anglican Communion? There had to be a meeting of all the Churches. And some people wanted the meeting to turn itself into an umbrella govern-ment for the world-wide Church.

OPPOSITION AND CONTROVERSY

That first Lambeth Conference of 1867 did not meet without much doubt and powerful opposition. The Archbishop of York and the Bishop of Durham, two of the most senior bishops in England, refused to have anything to do with it.

This opposition had various motives.

First, all large meetings are bad. The members are too numerous to have a sensible debate. If they are numerous they divide into parties and behave in a partisan manner which is bad for the Church. The history of councils brings up some important decisions but also a mass of unedifying behaviour. Because they have been consecrated as bishops, human beings are not exempt from the universal experience that in a parliament some of them will behave badly.

Second, is this meeting going to claim to be a government, so that the bishop from Auckland in New Zealand will claim to be able to affect what is done in the Diocese of Durham? Why should he?

Third, the opponents were nervous of a particular decision that might be taken in 1867. Who was the rightful Bishop of Natal?

At that first Lambeth Conference there were several bishops of exceptional stature. The two who counted for most, because of their place overseas, were Selwyn of New Zealand and Gray of Cape Town. Selwyn, as the first bishop of the new world of New Zealand, had a romantic and justified reputation as a pioneer of Christian faith in the Southern Pacific. He caused the idea of a bishop, till then rather static and ceremonious, to be associated with navigating small ships and fording mountainous streams and intervening in war between the Maoris and the settlers. Never was a bishop who carried with him more fresh air. It was not certain that fresh air and the freedom of open spaces created the best of all temperaments for the making of constitutions, on which the Anglican Communion was then, almost without knowing it, engaged. Sometimes they needed precise and crabbed barristers with no desire for elbow-room, rather than evangelists impatient of law. But Selwyn had created a constitution for the Church of New Zealand, he was revered in the English-speaking world, and no one stood more for the independence of Anglicanism as a way of devotion and faith that was not necessarily tied up with the particular form in which it was expressed in the history of England and Wales. He was one who cared more about the Anglican way than the way of the Church of England, and these two ideas were not identical in his mind.

Robert Gray of Cape Town was regarded by some as a kind of St Athanasius of the modern world, standing for the truth of the Christian faith against heretics who tried to corrupt it, against lawyers who backed the heretics, against privy councils, against bishops who compromised with the heresy. And he also had fame as a leader of evangelism in Africa, for under his oversight there developed the first northern expansion of the faith into South-Central Africa.

If it is the object to have an edifying and non-controversial meeting of bishops, then it is not a good idea to invite St Athanasius. But if the meeting is to be nothing but edifying and non-controversial, why have a meeting at all which deprives so many dioceses of their heads?

Gray had a suffragan, Colenso the Bishop of Natal. Colenso was a good mathematician, a pastor who cared about the Zulus, and a person of little judgement. By taking the mathematical figures given in the Old Testament he proved the impossibility of some of them and inferred that the Old Testament could not be true in all its parts, and thought he had discovered something important. Gray ought to have left him alone. But he deposed him from his see on a charge of heresy and finally excommunicated him, and naturally the law-courts held that this deposition was improper and illegal. Therefore Gray needed a council of Anglican bishops. Just as Pope Pius IX needed a council of Roman Catholic bishops to tell Italian politicians that they had no business interfering with the Church, so Gray needed a council of bishops to tell the lawyers that they had no standing to determine whether Colenso was a bishop or not. The question took a pointed form. Should Gray consecrate a new bishop for the See of Natal or not? If he rightly deposed Colenso, yes; if wrongly, no. This was an awkward question for the first Lambeth Conference to face.

And because it was so awkward a question, it was a powerful reason why some people did not want a Lambeth Conference to happen. They were afraid that these bishops from across the world would claim to decide whether a particular person was really the Bishop of Natal; or even worse, that they would claim to say that no one who doubted the history in the early books of the Old Testament could be a proper Christian person. Gray and Selwyn wanted a government for the Anglican Communion. Some were afraid that if such a government existed it would make decisions that they did not want, and even more were afraid that it could be turned into a body which would take narrowing decisions on doctrine.

And some of the English were afraid that it was illegal to have a meeting. For the Thirty-nine Articles of the Church of England laid it down: 'General Councils may not be gathered together without the commandment and will of Princes' (Article XXI). The Act of Henry VIII of 1534 said that no new canon might be made without the royal assent—if the bishops met at Lambeth and decided something, was that a General Council, and was what they decided equivalent to a canon? This had the effect that the Lambeth meeting was not called a Lambeth Council or a Lambeth Synod but a Lambeth Conference. It was made clear by Archbishop Longley in summoning it that it was invited to confer, not to decide.

THE PROBLEM OF AUTHORITY

This basic difficulty about the meeting of 1867 had two grave consequences for the future of the Lambeth Conference.

The first was that, if the meeting was to be acceptable to some of its more moderate opponents, it seemed to be necessary to say that the meeting was only a discussion group, and none of its decisions would have any authority. Archbishop Longley of Canterbury would only summon the meeting, and several bishops would only attend it, if its resolutions were declared beforehand to have no binding force. Some of the American bishops who were determined to take no orders out of England were equally strong that this meeting was 'only' for consultation.

Therefore at this Lambeth Conference, and at various subsequent Lambeth Conferences, several of the leaders went out of their way to point out that the meeting on which they were engaged had no authority and bound no one. 'It should be distinctly understood', said Archbishop Longley, 'that at this meeting . . . no decision [shall be] come to that shall affect generally the interests of the Church, but that we shall meet together for brotherly counsel and encouragement.' Far fewer words or ink were expended in saying that if a group of apostolic ministers, who were specially representative of all the Anglican communities, got together and said some prayers and then made some recommendations, those recommendations carried with them some sort of authority in the Church. There was a real danger in 1867, and also at the next in 1878, that they would be advertised as meetings which could achieve nothing and therefore must be unimportant.

The second danger arose from the nature of a parliament. Large parliaments on average debate badly—it is the nature of the animal—even though the result leads to a change in the law which affects the people. Large parliaments which debate a motion, when everyone knows that the debate can have no practical outcome, are asking for a still worse debate, and for even more numerous sleepers during the discussion. That is, a debate which cannot produce anything is a way to invite a feeling of irresponsibility.

Now the chief makers of the first Lambeth Conference had no idea whatever of a meeting that would produce nothing. Selwyn and Robert Gray were fighting for an absolute principle, that the Church of Christ teaches truth and that it has the freedom to determine what is compatible with that truth. Nothing could be less irresponsible than their Athanasian stance. But the difficulty was that in order to have a meeting at all you must concede it to have no authority, and that necessity produced danger for the future.

THE IMPORTANCE OF LEADERSHIP

Therefore a lot was to depend on the host or President, the Archbishop of Canterbury. A miscellaneous body of humanity from all over the world with all sorts of different local interests, and united by their common faith and common way of worship and common order, needed management if the debates, under these conditions, were not to end in fiasco and frustration. Archbishop Longley (1867) was not much of a chairman. Archbishop Tait (1878) was a goodish chairman, but he wanted to press his own views more forcibly than good chairmen should do. Archbishop Benson (1888) was a bad chairman but chose an excellent manager, Randall Davidson, so the meeting was admirably run. Archbishop Frederick Temple (1897—the 'wrong' digit, not 1898, because it was the thirteenth centenary of St Augustine setting up the See of Canterbury) was a dictator; Davidson (1908; 1920, two years late because of a world war) was a top-class chairman, quiet and wise; Lang (1930) was able and had dignity and chose a good secretary in George Bell, but at times the dignity was a bit too much for the American bishops; William Temple was an excellent chairman, but never had a chance to preside at a Lambeth Conference; Fisher (1948; 1958) could have been a dictator but was not, and things went well; Ramsey (1968) went to sleep in the chair but was a better chairman than that suggests, partly because he was the most trained theologian ever to occupy that seat at a Lambeth Conference, and this won him a respect which would not have been given merely to a skilful manager. The office of chairman, it must be remembered, grew steadily more difficult as the numbers of the meeting rose: 1867, 76; 1897, 194; 1968, 462 plus 26 consultants and 76 observers, total 564. What clergyman of any Church is trained to be a chairman of a meeting of 564 people? When we think of the turmoil which afflicts the Speaker of the British House of Commons, we realise that there must be some very Christian people among the members who attend the meetings of the Lambeth Conference or the job of chairman would be impossible.

In any great meeting there will be others beside the chairman who stand out by reason of their office, or even without their office by reason of their personality. Randall Davidson was one such before he became the chairman: of excellent judgement, gentle, painstaking, uninspiring in speech, wise, a master of detail but never losing sight of a longer perspective. Ramsey was another before he became the chairman, for quite different reasons, with his evident spirituality and humane learning and massive yet attractive personality. William Temple was another, though he never became chairman, for the breadth and range of his insight, one of the real founders of the modern ecumenical movement. George Bell was another, who experienced three Lambeth Conferences and became influential not by his utterances, which were usually convoluted, but because his courage and principle made him the leader in many of the great ethical causes about which the Church cared most: on war, and bombing, and the Jews, and religion and art. From the old Commonwealth some of the most influential were the most theologically instructed: Lowther Clarke of Melbourne, or D'Arcy of Armagh. But often an American bishop, or a Canadian, or an Australian, or a South African, or an Indian or a New Zealander, would make a big difference to a particular motion or a particular piece of drafting. And then there were dervishes who came to the Conference to prophesy and were heard with respect or amusement or embarrassment, and had no influence but somehow injected fresh air: a Frank Weston from Zanzibar, who told all the bishops to go live in the slums, and could hardly bear the contrast between what he knew in his diocese and these apparently complacent prelates meeting in comfort, and denounced the Lambeth Conference to its face. Then there were the leaders in the younger Churches who were heard with deep respect in the earlier Conferences because they were few—for example Samuel Crowther from Nigeria, or Azariah from Dornakal in South India; in the later Conferences they were so numerous that they could claim no special reverence, because they were no longer from younger Churches but simply from other Churches. By then they had become as much a historic part of the Anglican Communion as the Americans.

RESPECT AND INFLUENCE

We have seen that the Lambeth Conference was allowed to be founded only if it had no authority. But meetings start to gather authority if they exist and are seen not to be a cloud of hot air and rhetoric. It was impossible that the leaders of the Anglican Communion should meet every ten years and not start to gather respect; and to gather respect is slowly to gather influence, and influence is on the road to authority. It continued to have that absence of legal authority which some of its founders wanted and which of necessity was denied to them. But in most Churches some of the most important parts of authority are not based upon the law.

The first element in this was the discovery that mere meeting was after all not mere. Some people had said that if the meeting could not decide anything there was no reason for the bishops to neglect their distant dioceses. But, as they met, they discovered that there was virtue in the original Canadian desire to know better what was going on. Here they were at Lambeth, all with an apostolic commission in different parts of the globe and therefore with different social problems and environments of peoples and laws and traditions, with a common gospel and a common way of worship and common attitudes in spirituality and much common ethical agreement. They found that they needed to say some prayers together; that to meet for common worship or quiet days was no minor part of the purpose of the meeting; that they needed to know each other personally so that the name at the foot of the letter was not merely a signature; and that they needed to draw inspiration from their roots in the way of pilgrimage. Samuel Crowther from Nigeria and Azariah from South India had roots that were not British. But in the way in which their faith had reached them there were sacred moments and places and even things—St Augustine's chair at Canterbury, and the steps once stained with the blood of Becket, and the shrines at Westminster Abbey or St Paul's Cathedral, and the historic place of prayer on Holy Island, and the sward among the ruins of the abbey at Glastonbury. They wanted to talk with each other and to say their prayers together and perhaps also to recapture the long historic dimension in their faith. Some of them found that this was what really mattered about the Lambeth Conference. For such visiting bishops it was not important that they could not decide anything. They needed to meet because they needed to meet, not because they needed to determine who was the right Bishop of Natal. They came in from Mozambique or from the Rio Gambia, isolated mission stations in an unfriendly society, and felt themselves part of a world-wide community, and found strength and sustenance in their mutual respect and consultation.

CHRISTIAN REUNION

Probably the meeting could not have lasted, nevertheless, or could not have met so frequently, if its purpose was confined to prayer and personal knowledge. Quite quickly they discovered that they had indeed a function. When the Bishop of Montreal urged Archbishop Longley to summon the first Lambeth Conference, he suggested that there was one function for which such a conference would be indispensable: the question of reunion between the Anglicans and other Churches. At first this was taken up only with politeness. Soon it became a key question to be debated and encouraged by every Lambeth Conference.

The first big impetus to this was not very ecumenical because it was in part anti-papal. The first Lambeth Conference was summoned just as the first Vatican Council was about to be summoned. After the first Vatican Council declared the Pope to be infallible, and it was evident that Roman Catholic assent to this claim was not universal, there was a wave of anti-papal movement across Christendom. Could there not be a Catholicism more faithful to the ancient Church? In South Germany, Catholics set up what came to be called the Old Catholic Church; they looked for assistance to other Churches of a Catholic tradition, in Sweden and in St Petersburg and in Constantinople and in Canterbury and among the more conservative disciples of Luther. The first Vatican Council put Catholic reunion much on the map.

Out of this movement across Christendom arose a definition by the Lambeth Conference of the points which in Anglican opinion were necessary for the restoration of unity among the Churches. This was the Lambeth Quadrilateral, agreed by the Conference of 1888. The Lambeth Conference did not invent the Quadrilateral. It had been suggested by an American evangelical William Reed Huntington and then adopted in 1886 by the American bishops. The Lambeth drafters slightly amended the American version, chiefly by adding a mention of the Apostles' Creed and making certain that reference to Scripture stated that in the matter of faith the Bible contains all things necessary to salvation. The four things necessary to reunion were said to be: (1) the Bible as sufficient rule of faith; (2) the two creeds; (3) the two sacraments instituted by Christ; (4) the historic episcopate, locally adapted to the varying needs of the peoples.

What was soon clear was that the adoption by a Lambeth Conference of this fourfold formula of conditions for reunion gave it an authority which it had not possessed when it was the statement of the American House of Bishops. The Lambeth Conference had begun to gather the influence which its founders wished to deny it. And its resolution made far easier the approaches of friendship to the Old Catholics and to the Swedes, and, paradoxically, to the Roman Catholics.

From 1910 onwards, and especially from 1927 onwards, the ecumenical movement was on the Christian map. Men like William Temple were among the leaders of the movement, and were determined that it should not be a limited federation of Protestant bodies but should reach out to the Roman Catholics as well as the Orthodox. This new openness was stimulated by the horror of the First World War and then by the Bolshevik revolution, which turned towards atheism what had been thought to be a Christian nation. Christian life seemed more at risk than at any time for centuries, and Christians of the various denominations felt their harmony and their need to stand together against a materialist world. The second great document on unity by a Lambeth Conference, the Lambeth Appeal, dated from shortly after the First World War and the Bolshevik revolution.

The second big area where the Conference gained an influence which proved indispensable was on ethical questions. In some parts of the world polygamy was no sin, in Christendom monogamy was an absolute rule—what was to be done with the Christian wife of a polygamist, or a polygamist who wished to be a Christian? In some parts of Christendom divorce was accepted much more easily than in other parts—all the Anglicans ought to work together on the attitude to marriage and the family, and the Lambeth Conference was the only instrument capable of settling such a crucial matter in the ethics of society. It played a crucial role also in the acceptance of contraception by the Churches.

IDENTITY OF THE ANGLICAN COMMUNION

As the Lambeth Conference came to exist and be accepted, it created a consciousness of the Anglican Communion in the general mind. This did not happen until the twentieth century. Even in the Conference itself some members felt that the Anglican tie across the world developed into something closer between the end of the First World War and the end of the 1960s. George Bell went to four Lambeth Conferences. He testified that the sense of an Anglican Communion was far deeper and stronger in 1958 than earlier, and this though he disliked the way in which the business was conducted in 1958. He did not ask himself whether there was any relation between this closer sense of brotherhood and the new invention of the modern airline, or link it with the ability of Archbishops of Canterbury to travel round the world without neglecting their job at home, and then of a Pope to become an evangelist across the world while he remained Bishop of Rome.

This consciousness of an Anglican Communion produced a desire for instruments to embody it. One or two bishops wanted it to meet more frequently, even every five years. This did not win favour, because everyone knew that meetings should not be encouraged beyond necessity. This meeting was now so regular a part of the scene that it needed to become more regular; there needed to be an office and a secretary general (first called prosaically the Executive Officer) of the Anglican Communion. Then it was felt that since it met only once in ten years, there needed to be a representative committee to give advice between Conferences, and in 1968 the Anglican Consultative Council was created and had an influence on events more controversial than anyone involved in its creation had expected. The primates of the various provinces held meetings (from 1979) which became an equally or still more important source of knowledge and decision during the years between the Conferences. The 1988 Conference expected that this meeting of primates could become an effective guide in doctrinal, moral and pastoral matters, and be a symbol or focus of apostolic leadership in the mission of the Church. This body was also charged with caring about the variety of liturgies, how they should be within a recognised Anglican ethos. Between 1948 and 1966 a college was set up in the historic buildings at St Augustine's, Canterbury, which was the college of the Anglican Communion, and trained clergy, and allowed the future leaders of the distant Churches to know each other at a formative stage in their Christian growth. But in 1966 the primates came to the conclusion that this college did not work quite as they wished and allowed it to close, and though the decision was probably forced on them this was a pity, since it was one important little centre for the consciousness of the Anglican Communion which the Lambeth Conference had created. Another little focus was the Anglican Centre in Rome, created in 1966–67 to provide representation at the Vatican of the entire Anglican Communion. By 1991 its long future was uncertain.

The bishops had refused the Archbishop of Canterbury the title of Patriarch, which some of the early makers of the Conference had wanted him to hold. The Archbishop was much more really a patriarch of the Anglican Communion by 1967 than he had been in 1867. In 1867 he was the senior bishop, and the bishop with the most ancient see, and therefore possessed of a primacy of honour. As the Anglican Communion moved across the world his real power grew. A young Church, not yet fully constituted, needed his authority to choose bishops or to guide the new structure or to settle disputes. A hundred years after 1867 he had lost a lot of this direct power among the Churches as the provinces became independent. Yet the see lost nothing of stature but gained it. For the Archbishop was now the key to the unity of the Anglican Communion, so that one definition of an Anglican diocese was that it was in communion with the See of Canterbury. To the outside world, to Popes and Patriarchs or the World Council or the heads of other Churches, he was felt to be the visible symbol of a world-wide communion. The Oecumenical Patriarch Athenagoras insisted in his communications on giving Archbishop Ramsey the title of Patriarch. After the 1988 Conference two instruments of the Conference in a joint meeting, the Primates and the Anglican Consultative Council, affirmed this wider function for the office in direct language:

> The Archbishop of Canterbury . . . serves as the principal focus of unity in the Communion. Initiatives are often taken by him with the concurrence, encouragement and understanding of other bodies. This involvement, and initiatives undertaken in his own right and later reported to the various appropriate bodies, are of vital importance. Through the experience of Lambeth 1988 the Archbishop of Canterbury's role has been warmly appreciated and affirmed.

Thus the Conference, though still without any technical legal or canonical authority, acquired an influence which at times was so close to authority as hardly to be distinguishable from it. This was of necessity. The situation demanded the instrument. It was caused by the growth of independent Churches across the world, especially but not only as Central and Southern Africa became a largely Christian continent. The Anglican Communion was always a federation. By 1960 it was a federation with many different bodies participating. Yet this federation had no federal government. This meant tension, as some provinces went ahead with changes that they believed to be right, such as the ordination of women to the priesthood, while other provinces believed the changes wrong. If it meant tension it also meant a liberty for wider experiment. But whether tension or experiment, the situation clamoured for a body to surround the See of Canterbury in making the federation workable as a federation. By 1960 the only possible claimant for this office was the Lambeth Conference. Therefore the question began to arise whether the structure of the Lambeth Conference itself was best adapted to this function that was being forced upon it.

LEGISLATION IN THE CHURCH

All bodies of law are confusing, because each law is passed to meet a particular situation, and then the code grows little by little, even century by century, and is interpreted by judges to meet hard cases, and the resolutions of the judges become precedents. By that stage, whereas everyone agrees that law ought to be easy to understand by the simplest citizen, all experience shows that this is impossible and that after a long time a big body of law requires high expertise and training to present it clearly, and then judges and advocates in the courts rightly address one another as 'my learned friend'. The law of the medieval Church, derived from the decisions of numerous Councils and Popes, became a huge and confused body of church law. From 1499 onwards it was printed as a vast corpus of legal knowledge, but you needed to be an expert to penetrate its meanings, and it was made no less confusing, and no less of a trial to the ignorant, by the Counter-Reformation. The weight, and the confusion, and sometimes the amazing stupidities which all legal systems produce in ever-changing circumstances, were the reasons why the Protestants of the Reformation resented church law and wanted as little to do with it as possible. And some of them were not quite sure that law and Gospel went hand in hand, for to them the word gospel was very close to the word freedom; and although law is the safeguard of freedom for the individual, there are many circumstances in which it does not feel to be compatible with a proper freedom. Because church lawyers worked closely with state lawyers, their methods and conclusions, all over Europe, were affected by the methods and conclusions of secular law; this was true in Catholic Europe, and more emphatically true in Protestant

Europe, where they suspected church law as a clergy-preserve and liked to have their church laws incorporated in the main body of state laws.

In modern times various attempts were made to codify the mass of church laws into systems. The most famous of these were the codifications of its law by the Church of Rome, the first published in 1917 and the second in 1983. These books made a big improvement in the sense of making church law more accessible to the educated lay person as well as to the church lawyers. But all states refused to incorporate church laws into their own state laws unless their own parliaments approved them. Thus modern church laws took the form of resolutions without legal force in the state; though the state would recognise their validity as it recognised the validity of the rules of private clubs, except in so far as in some Catholic countries there were concordats, agreements about law between the state and the See of Rome, and in Protestant countries where, as in Scandinavia or England, the Church was established and church laws, or some church laws at least, still needed to be approved by the state.

The perception came very early that the world-wide nature of the Anglican Church changed the conditions under which law could be made. It was essential to get representatives of all the Anglican Churches to meet together—not to make law but to take resolutions which should be a guide to the various far-flung Churches in their making of law. Since they were all brought up on a knowledge of the system in the early Church, where in difficult cases the bishops of an area or even of the whole Church met to take a resolution, it was natural that the representatives of the different Churches who came to these Conferences were their bishops.

The Oxford Dictionary of the Christian Church ends its article on 'Lambeth Conferences' with the sentence: 'The resolutions, though not binding, are significant expressions of the opinions of the Anglican episcopate.' That is the minimum that can be said. These resolutions are not legally binding on the provincial Churches because all those Churches have systems by which their clergy and their laity share with the bishops in the taking of the resolutions which are to have the force of a church law. The first Conference of 1867 (Resolution 4) proposed that each of the provincial synods be in 'due and canonical subordination' to a higher synod. But that was not, at least at first, practicable. A resolution taken at Lambeth had to be brought home and considered by the legislative bodies in each province before it could have the force of local law. In that sense these resolutions were not 'binding'. But they were as binding as many of the resolutions taken by councils of bishops in primitive Christianity, and as many of the decrees laid down in the Roman Catholic code of canon law. They might only be advice, by the law of the land or even by the customs of the local Church, but they were of such weight that they were more than 'not binding'. The consciences of many bishops felt the resolution to lay down a decision which they ought to follow or at least try to follow. It was a resolution taken after due debate and after prayer by the ministers who represented the apostles to their Churches. Where two or three were gathered together, there the Spirit was likely to be, they thought, and they hoped that they acted therefore in accordance with what they took to be the providential government of the world.

That did not mean that the resolution was infallible, because none of them believed in the infallibility of bishops, singly or taken together. They were all agreed that wrong or out-of-date decisions could be reversed without a qualm. But they hoped that they decided as the Spirit led them, and left the results to be what they might be.

In this way the Lambeth Conference started to make a new body of legislation. Every ten years or so it considered the circumstances of that day and took what decisions it thought best on advising the Churches what to do. Sometimes the circumstances were much the same ten years later and then two Conferences might resolve almost the same thing, or might vary their advice. But always some of the circumstances would be different, and therefore decade by decade there came to be built up a substantial body of resolutions which touched many aspects of church life. Like all other bodies of church law they became complicated by time, and were sometimes contradictory, and there were so many of them that it started to need an expert to give advice on what they had resolved. Therefore, as with all other bodies of resolutions built up over a long period, they began to need codification, so that they would be easier to apprehend and much easier to use.

After each of the first few Conferences reports were published which accumulated the principal papers and resolutions of the previous Conferences. By 1930 this had grown to a volume of almost unmanageable size, and the sectional reports, resolutions and encyclical letters of each subsequent Conference were published as a separate book. Reference to a number of books made for more difficulty. Therefore a collected text of the resolutions of all the earlier Conferences was compiled by Bishop Philip Russell and Arthur Gosling and duplicated for the use of bishops attending the Conference of 1988. The value of such a complete and accessible text was plain. At the instance of the Secretary General of the Anglican Communion, Canon Samuel van Culin, the present volume is published in printed form with a fuller index, can be updated by computer techniques, and may be republished with the resolutions of future Lambeth Conferences incorporated.

Printed as they are they have another value beside the use to which they will be put by the leaders of the various Churches. Like all bodies of church law or church resolutions from past centuries, they make a tool for the student of history. A Church is set always in a changing world, and it is always adapting its language and its practice to the new needs and the new ideas of the time, while it seeks to enshrine an unchanging gospel to deliver to the nations. A body of such resolutions is interwoven with the public and private life of the peoples, their politics and their wars and their inventions and their hatreds and their wealth or poverty.

Therefore some resolutions must touch only temporary situations. The first Lambeth Conference took two resolutions about the state of the Church in Natal which was divided and a public scandal. A division arising from this situation has persisted to this day; but it became a minor matter which could be dealt with by local pastoral sense and charity and did not need the attention or the legislation or the consideration of the central representative body. It was not the business of the Lambeth Conference to crack walnuts with sledgehammers or trespass on the proper pastoral care of local authorities, who were more likely to understand a situation and its varied complexities.

In law it is decisions that matter, not the debates by which they are reached. Sometimes the drafting of a resolution, which may look odd, can be better understood by reading the debates out of which it came. But the intention in the debates has no force like the wording of the result. Behind resolutions of the Lambeth Conference lie discussions in committees, and a report of a committee. From the first the Conferences were aware that large assemblies are incapable of drafting, and therefore that much of the preparation of business must be done in committee. Consequently the materials of these committees formed in time valuable records, and sometimes the report of a committee was more valuable than the debate of the full Conference on that report. From time to time a Conference, unwilling to take a resolution on an issue, commended the study of the report of its committee. Such committee reports may be taken as useful guides but cannot have the authority of the formal resolutions of the Conference.

Here it is fitting to point to certain threads which run through the Conferences 1867 to 1988.

THE NATURE OF ANGLICANISM

The first Conference was summoned at the request of the Canadians, who wanted to understand what was happening in other provinces. We are a world-wide Church; we must know what the other branches are doing. This theme is often repeated. One instance only: the resolution of 1978 that on major issues none of the provinces should take action without first consulting the Lambeth Conference or a meeting of the primates, that is, a meeting of the presiding archbishops or bishops from each province.

Such a stress on the world-wide nature of the Church carried with it definition, in various aspects and at diverse times, of the nature of Anglicanism as historic Christian faith. It was agreed that those Churches of many different lands and far-sundered peoples have a common faith and order. In old Anglicanism the two historic statements of faith were the Thirty-nine Articles of 1571 and the Book of Common Prayer of 1662. But in Britain itself, by the time the first Lambeth Conference opened, the Book of Common Prayer was much more weighty than the Thirty-nine Articles; partly because the Articles were more 'dated', as bearing within their drafting the signs of the time in which they were framed; and partly because it is classical Anglican thinking that the way of worship is the key to the way of belief. The non-English Churches, whose interest in the special circumstances of 1571 was negligible, saw no reason why their ordinands should pay particular attention to the Articles; and when some of the English bishops agreed, it was easy for the Lambeth Conference, as early as 1920, to recommend that candidates for ministerial office should no longer need to assent to the Articles.

The Prayer Book was another matter. Its teaching was part of the being of Anglicanism. But it was also a way of worship in a language which was not the first language of many Anglicans. And as it was translated and used, so it was adapted, until the way of worship (that is, the way of doctrine) was seen to be in accordance with the spirit and intention of the Prayer Book, not necessarily by close adherence to all of its words.

In 1930 the Lambeth Conference defined Anglicanism laconically:

> It is part of the one Holy Catholic and Apostolic Church. Its centre of unity is the see of Canterbury. To be Anglican it is necessary to be in communion with that see. It upholds and propagates the Catholic and Apostolic faith as they are *generally* [italics not original] set forth in the Book of Common Prayer as authorised in their several Churches.

Within the definition of the faith of the Catholic Church which Anglicans profess were three pillars: the uniqueness and sufficiency of the Bible; the authority of the early Church in understanding the Bible; the value of the study of the Bible in each generation, whether by further study or by new insights into its truth and its implications.

The Bible

More than once the Lambeth Conference asserted the sufficiency of Scripture as the guide to Christian truth; so that nothing may be taught as necessary to salvation that cannot be warranted by Scripture. It welcomed the large place that the words of the Bible take in the way of Anglican worship.

The members were always convinced of the need for freedom of enquiry. As they thanked God for the work of students of the Bible, so they asserted that the Bible in no way interferes with the freedom of the scientists; and that we thank God for the work of the scientists in disclosing more of the truth about the physical world.

They did not regard the Bible as of fixed interpretation. Each generation may have new insights into its meaning or application. The Conference always took a high view of the work of the theologians who studied the Bible—'not least by facing with intellectual integrity the questions raised by modern knowledge and modern criticism'.

Being a Church of many different peoples, they wanted good modern translations. They showed no sign of wanting to keep the King James Version framed as being sacrosanct for ever.

They were aware how a people of a different culture or different religious background expressed its faith, not only with a new language but sometimes with a new insight; so that as once the Greek people as they entered the Church affected the words of the apostolic faith with its Jewish background and gave it new expression, so later the Romans, and then the Germans, and then the Slavs, and then the peoples of Africa and of Asia. Thus the Lambeth Conference expected some form of 'development' in Christian doctrine as the Church moves down from generation to generation.

The early Church

The Prayer Book contains three creeds: (a) The Apostles' Creed, which is not used in the Orthodox Churches of the East. In its original form it was a short statement of faith used when a convert was baptized at Rome as early as the end of the second century AD. (b) The Nicene Creed, agreed by the Council of Constantinople in 381, based upon a creed adopted by the Council of Nicaea in 325. (c) The Athanasian Creed or Quicunque Vult, a western creed of the fifth century AD, but also used in modern times by some Orthodox Churches in Eastern Europe.

The last of these three creeds is a theological statement unsuitable for use in worship; and from the time of the first Lambeth Conference some Anglicans tried to change the rule of the Prayer Book that it should be recited in church on thirteen days of the year. The Lambeth Conference of 1908 agreed that no one need use the Athanasian Creed. Therefore the two creeds remaining are the Apostles' and the Nicene, which are very similar in their words.

The first Lambeth Conference of 1867 had a curious dispute about the councils of the early Church. Prompted by Bishop Fulford of Montreal, Archbishop Longley proposed a declaration which began:

> We, the bishops of Christ's Holy Catholic Church, professing the faith of the primitive and undivided Church, as based upon the Scriptures, and defined by the first four General Councils . . .

This question of the first four General Councils came near the essence of a Lambeth Conference. Four General Councils—at Nicaea 325, Constantinople 381, Ephesus 431 and Chalcedon 451—had made precise the language in which the Church expressed the doctrines of the Trinity and the Incarnation. John Henry Hopkins, the Presiding Bishop of the American Episcopal Church, an office which was steadily respected in all Lambeth Conferences, wanted the wording to be 'the first six General Councils'—that is, to include Constantinople II of 553, and Constantinople III of 680–681. In the debate he lost more than the fifth and sixth General Councils. The majority of bishops thought that their declaration needed to be based upon the Bible and the Reformation, not the definitions of the faith during the first four centuries. Also, they were not sure that they were *the* bishops of the Catholic Church, as though there were no others. They did not think much of the formula based upon Scripture, as though there might be developments of doctrine arising out of Scripture. So the declaration became:

> We, bishops of Christ's Holy Catholic Church . . . , professing the faith delivered to us in Holy Scripture, maintained by the primitive Church, and reaffirmed by the Fathers of the English Reformation . . .

So the first great council of the Anglican Communion lost its reference to the first great Councils of Christian history, though not its reference to the early Christians.

This rewording did not represent the real attitude of the bishops as the Conferences succeeded one another. How important the Councils were to the Conference may be shown by the resolution of 1908 which affirmed that the historical statements within the Creeds are an essential part of the faith of the Church.

This sense of their importance was dramatically proved by the Conferences of 1978 and 1988. The original text of the Nicene Creed had the words 'proceeding from the Father', and this is the text which the

Orthodox Churches still use. During the sixth century, in the struggle to cope with local heresy, the Western Church began to adopt the phrase 'proceeding from the Father and the Son', and this was then canonised in Western tradition. Prolonged discussions between Anglicans and Orthodox had proved that there was no difference of theological meaning between the two forms of the Creed. Since the Western formula was by then much valued in Western ways of worship, there was no reason in diplomacy or in truth to go back to the original text—except the desire to follow correctly what the early General Councils had determined. Both the Conferences of 1978 and 1988 recommended that Anglican use should go back to the original text. The 1988 Conference even recommended that future liturgies should be printed in the form 'proceeding from the Father'.

Nothing could give a stronger expression to the bishops' conviction of the importance of the first great Christian Councils in the interpretation of the Bible. Simultaneously they showed their conviction that Christians ought to adhere to the faith in the Triune God as the earliest Christians formulated its doctrine.

Upon the sacraments they were equally clear. It was of the essence of their faith that they administered the two sacraments of the Gospel, baptism and the Lord's supper, with Christ's words of institution and the elements ordained by him. (They came in modern times to allow the custom of intinction in the administration of the sacrament—dipping the bread into the chalice and receiving the two elements as one—but they rejected the use of one kind only, and the use of unfermented wine to help teetotallers).

The later Middle Ages numbered seven sacraments, and the traditional Anglican teaching always accepted that the other five, not having a warrant from the mouth of Christ, were not in the same way of the essence of their faith. Nevertheless we shall see how momentous they felt the sacrament of marriage to be; they asked that the possibility of confession be taught; they regarded due ordination, at the hands of a bishop, as constitutive of the Anglican ministry; they preserved the rite of confirmation and attached much importance to it in the religious training of the young. They refused to condemn priests who anointed the dying.

UNITY

Because they believed that their ministry must indispensably be a ministry of persons ordained by bishops in succession from the apostles, the sacrament of ordination lay at the heart of their practical concern for Christian unity. On the one side they welcomed every friendly act by other episcopal Churches, especially the Roman Catholic and the

Orthodox, and they approved intercommunion with the Old Catholic Church and with the Lutheran Church of Sweden. On the other side they were concerned at various times with schemes to unite them with Churches which had no apostolic succession of bishops, and with the extent to which they could wholeheartedly recognise the ministries of non-episcopal Churches to be in the fullest sense apostolic ministries. They welcomed such plans where they were successful (especially South India, North India and Pakistan, and Sri Lanka) and encouraged them where they were promising (as with the plans to unite Anglicans and Methodists in England and in Nigeria).

This had practical consequences which must concern them. When may a non-Anglican minister or lay person preach in an Anglican pulpit? They allowed it, with the bishop's leave. They disapproved the celebration of the sacrament by a non-Anglican minister in an Anglican church; they allowed the bishop to sanction the coming of persons to the Lord's supper when they were baptized but not confirmed; they allowed the bishop to grant leave for Anglicans to receive the sacrament from non-Anglicans, provided that they know they are welcome and if the two Churches are seeking unity. They warmly recommended the use of the Week of Prayer for Christian Unity.

As part of this concern for world-wide Christendom, they looked out upon the persecuted Churches and demanded prayer for them and aid sent to them: the Armenians massacred in Asia Minor, the Assyrians massacred in northern Iraq and its environs, the Russian churchmen under Lenin and then under Stalin, the Greek churchmen suffering in northern Greece during the civil war of 1948, the southern Sudanese in their civil war; and prisoners like the hostages in broken Lebanon, or Nelson Mandela in South Africa; and refugees from all over the world, especially in the aftermath of the Second World War, and in the Middle East after the Six Days War.

THE MINISTRY

A constant concern of the Conference was to get priests educated enough and with a true vocation to serve God. They kept insisting on the need for a high standard at ordination. They wished for as many as possible to be graduates of universities. They wanted them trained in theology as well as blessed with a general education. The 1930 Conference laid down as necessary a formidable syllabus:

the Bible; a competent knowledge of Christian worship, history, theology (= doctrine and why), morals and pastoral work; training in the devotional life, reading, and preaching; some knowledge of elementary psychology, how to teach, and social economics.

'We are anxious', said the bishops who ordered this, 'not to overload the curriculum.'

With initial reluctance, but later with full acceptance, they allowed 'worker-priests' and 'auxiliary priests'—those who on ordination did not give up their secular job—provided that they were auxiliary and not a substitute for the full-time priest.

During the last half-century they needed to consider the ministry of women: at first as church officers and as deaconesses; then as conductors of retreats. They were asked in 1948 whether the South China Diocese could ordain a deaconess as priest for an experimental period of 20 years, and replied that this would be contrary to Anglican tradition and order; then by 1968 they accepted that deaconesses or other women could be made deacon, presumably so that no one could challenge (as had happened) that deaconesses were in a holy order; they allowed duly qualified women to conduct worship and preach and baptize and read and help in the distribution of the sacrament; recognised in 1978 that three provinces had women priests and that eight other provinces saw no objection to women priests but that some provinces objected—and asked that this big difference in ministry should not mean any break in the communion between the provinces; and ten years later asked that provinces which disapproved the consecration of a woman as bishop should respect provinces which consecrated a woman as bishop, and should maintain courtesy to any woman who was consecrated bishop.

DEVOTION

The Conference cared both about preaching as an instrument of the word of God to humanity, and about private prayer within the Church. In 1968 the Conference called upon all their people to join with them in a determination to deepen and strengthen their life of prayer. They commended periods of withdrawal for prayer, as preparation for fuller service in the world. The resolution had a sentence unusual in the history of great Christian meetings: 'The Church should pay more attention to the development of that capacity for silent prayer which exists in all her members, and should encourage corporate and personal waiting upon God.'

The Conference formally welcomed the existence of monks and nuns within the Anglican tradition. Three times it expressed gratitude for the contribution of these religious, because they were people of prayer and because some of them worked in the mission field; and asked that more people should consider this special vocation even while it recognised that it is the vocation of most Christians to work in the world. In 1958 it went so far as to ask that all traditions in the Church—that is, not only the more Catholic tradition within Anglicanism—should find forms of this special vocation. The Conference of 1968 expressed its sense of the value of their witness 'to the absolute character of the claim of God on the life of man, to the fruitfulness of a life given to prayer and service, and to the unity of the Church across the divisions which at present exist'.

The Conference agreed that commemorations of saints were right so long as there were not too many, and that there should be a 'Kalendar' in which Christian heroes besides those of the New Testament are remembered. It recognised that the persons commemorated would vary with country and province. It resolved that they should only commemorate persons about whose historical character and devotion there was no doubt; and that a new name proposed should be allowed to mature until anything controversial could be seen in the perspective of history, and until the extent of the local demand to remember that person could be tested.

THE MORAL LAW

Another big area for resolution was guidance in ethics. The Conference was against drugs (except in medicine), alcoholism, gambling; capital punishment; torture; imprisonment without trial; secularist education.

The most difficult part of this concerned sex. The Conference condemned abortion. At first it hesitated about contraception, but then accepted fully that it is right to plan families, and that the purpose of sexual intercourse is ill defined if it is seen solely as a way of making babies. It agreed that the sex instinct is a holy thing. It did not like couples living together when not legally married. It held high the Christian ideal of marriage and the home and the family. Like the Protestant Reformation it condemned brothels, and rejected the plea that in the constitution of humanity brothels are necessary evils. It condemned pornography.

Faced with new knowledge about humanity the Conference asked for a deep and dispassionate study of homosexuality.

The Christian ideal of the family shrank from divorce. The Conference did not like states to enact laws which made divorce easy to get. At first it preferred that the biblical exception, divorce only on account of adultery, should be preserved in modern law. It hesitated whether 'innocent parties' in a divorce should be able to be remarried in church, but in the end came down against it, though it allowed them back to the sacrament.

A big change, in consequence of new evidence and new moral reflection, occurred in the Conference's attitude to polygamy. All traditional Christianity only allowed monogamous marriage, and the Conference agreed wholeheartedly. But as more and more Africans, or Mohammedans, became Christians, the moral problem was agony. If a man with four wives became a Christian, the Church insisted that he put away three wives—and then their lot in their society was unhappy. This difficulty perplexed the Conference more than once. Finally in 1988 it resolved that a polygamist might be baptized with his believing wives, on condition that he did not marry again, and that the local community was content with the situation; and that he should not be compelled to put away any of his wives because of the deprivation they would suffer.

POLITICS

The Conference knew that its vocation was ethical, not political; yet that often an ethical judgement had political results.

This was easiest when the resolution could be practical rather than general. As Christians the members wanted peace. Therefore:

(1) They backed the institutions of international law—the Hague Conference of 1905 enthusiastically, the League of Nations in 1920 fervently, the United Nations in 1948 with only moderate enthusiasm, hoping that it might be improved.

(2) They condemned certain weapons of war: nuclear, chemical, bacteriological.

But (3) what of war itself? They were sure that war was not a Christian way of settling international disputes, and that all violence ultimately contradicts the gospel. They repeated this several times. But they could not rule out all war because their experience of Hitler and of the struggles of the peoples for freedom convinced them that armed struggles for justice *as a last resort* were justified. Therefore there is such a thing as a war in which a Christian may rightly fight; even though if possible civil disobedience should be tried as a better way against a tyrant.

(4) What of political systems? Christianity is freedom for humanity through Christ. Does that conviction give a Christian the recognition that some forms of constitution are more moral than others? Are there certain forms of constitution which a Christian *qua* Christian ought to try to create or work to preserve? Traditional Christianity always asserted that the Church works with any kind of political constitution; it accepts whatever the people of the region concerned decide is for the best, and does its work within various different structures, and these structures will vary from time to time according to political or economic or social need. This ancient doctrine was restated by the Lambeth Conference of 1958. And it was generally thought to be neces-

sary to the prosperity of a Church. For if the people of (for example) Uganda or the Sudan decided that in the crisis of their society they needed a dictator, the Church of that country still had to get its sacraments to the people, and it helped not at all to declare that dictatorships are always wrong, and so be accused of disloyalty or even treason.

And yet, most Conferences took a different attitude. The liberalism of the nineteenth century came after hesitation to accept that democracy is the most moral form of government because it allows the human personality most freedom. As early as 1908 the Conference expressed its approval of democracy because of the inestimable value of each human being in the sight of God. Its experience of Fascism and Nazism confirmed it in this opinion, and in 1948 it condemned any form of totalitarianism, Marxist Communist or Fascist. It especially condemned the doctrine that the aim of the state is the welfare of the corporate state irrespective of the welfare of the individuals which compose that society.

As the phrase 'human rights' came into international discussion, the Lambeth Conference warmly accepted the idea as moral: freedom of speech, movement, worship; the right to be housed and educated, to eat and to work. It accepted 'the welfare state' as morally good.

The Conference of 1988 went further. It declared that among fundamental human rights is the right of self-determination, 'to which every person, nation and region is entitled'. Mostly Lambeth Conferences were very clear in their resolutions. 'It is doubtful', wrote the historian Stephen Neill after reading the records (*Anglicanism* p 365—he was writing in 1958), 'whether any similar assembly has put on record so much sense and so little nonsense.' But this last is one of the rare resolutions where the meaning is far from plain.

In modern times the political judgements went into more detail. The Christian tradition has generally shrunk from political judgements of detail by synods, partly because lay persons are more likely to have political experience than bishops, and if bishops have political expertise they are thought to have neglected their real apostolic work; and partly because of the feeling that all politics by its nature can corrupt the judgement. The Lambeth Conference of modern times came to regard this axiom as a refusal of responsibility. It was always strongly against racialism, which was a Christian ethical judgement, and went on to propose a unified state for South Africa with a democratic constitution—which partly depended on facts which were not ethical. It asked for sanctions against South Africa, and for no sanctions against Cuba and Nicaragua and Panama. It accepted that the state of Israel has a right to exist with recognised and secure boundaries, and affirmed that the Palestinians have the right of self-determination. It condemned violence in or over Northern Ireland. The old caution of Christian councils—speak on ethical issues but leave politics to the laity—was thrown aside in the modern generation as morality was always more directly engaged within the political strife of the peoples.

This record shows something of the breadth and variety of the tasks which the Lambeth Conference has undertaken, and the way in which it has become an indispensable organ of the Anglican Communion, an organ which may continue to confront, advise upon, and regulate a range of situations and needs as yet unknown.

Chronology of Events 1862–1991

Anglican Affairs	*Other Events*
1862	
C.T. Longley Archbishop of Canterbury.	
1863	
Deposition of Bishop J.W. Colenso of Natal by Archbishop Gray of Cape Town.	Abolition of slavery in the USA.
The Church Times first published.	
1864	
Consecration of Samuel Crowther as the first black African bishop of the Anglican Communion.	
1865	
Successful appeal of Bishop Colenso to the Privy Council.	Conclusion of the American Civil War.
General council of the Anglican Communion urged by Canadian provincial synod.	Foundation of the Salvation Army. Foundation of the China Inland Mission.
1866	
J.W. Colenso excommunicated.	
Office of Lay Reader introduced in England.	
Foundation of the Society of St John the Evangelist (Cowley Fathers).	
1867	
The first Lambeth Conference.	Establishment of the Dominion of Canada.
1868	
A.C. Tait Archbishop of Canterbury.	
1869	
Passage of legislation to disestablish the Church of Ireland.	Inauguration of the First Vatican Council. Opening of the Suez Canal.
1870	
Committee including non-Anglican scholars appointed by Convocation of Canterbury to revise the Authorized Version of the Bible.	Conclusion of the First Vatican Council.
Formation of the Province of South Africa.	
1874	
Passage of the Colonial Clergy Act and Public Worship Regulation Act in England.	First Bonn Reunion Conference of the Old Catholic Churches.

Chronology of Events 1862–1991

Anglican Affairs	*Other Events*
1875	
Establishment of mission in Masasi, Nyasaland, by Universities Mission to Central Africa (UMCA).	Second Bonn Reunion Conference. Foundation of the Alliance of Reformed Churches.
1878	
The second Lambeth Conference.	Election of Pope Leo XIII.
1881	
Publication of the New Testament of the (English) Revised Version of the Bible.	
1882	
Foundation of the Church Army.	
1883	
Formation of the Province of the Church in the West Indies. E.W. Benson Archbishop of Canterbury.	
1884	
	Formation of Zion Watch Tower Society (Jehovah's Witnesses) in USA.
1885	
Publication of the Revised Version Old Testament. Murder of Bishop James Hannington in Uganda.	
1886	
First version of the 'Lambeth Quadrilateral' propounded at the Chicago Convention of the Protestant Episcopal Church.	Formation of the National Christian Science Association in the USA.
1887	
Formation in Japan of Nippon Sei Ko Kai.	
1888	
The third Lambeth Conference.	
1889	
Establishment of mission in southern Brazil by Protestant Episcopal Church of the USA.	Declaration of Utrecht by bishops of the Old Catholic Church, establishing its doctrinal basis.
1890	
Inauguration of SPG mission in Korea.	
1891	
Foundation of the Society of the Sacred Mission.	

Anglican Affairs

Other Events

1894
Church of England Newspaper first published (as *Church Family Newspaper*).

1896
F. Temple Archbishop of Canterbury.

Issue of papal encyclicals *Satis cognitum* and *Apostolicae curae*, seeking reunion of the Churches but rejecting the validity of Anglican orders.

1897
The fourth Lambeth Conference.
Issue of the Response of the Archbishops of Canterbury and York to *Apostolicae curae*.

1899

Establishment of a court of international arbitration by the first Hague Conference.
Outbreak of the Boer War.

1901
Publication of the American Standard Version of the Bible.

Inauguration of the Commonwealth of Australia.
Accession of King Edward VII.

1902

Conclusion of the Boer War.
Inauguration of the Philippine Independent Church.

1903
R.T. Davidson Archbishop of Canterbury.

Election of Pope Pius X.
Declaration of independence of Panama.

1905

Formation of the Baptist World Alliance.

1906
First publication of *The English Hymnal*.
Foundation of the Anglican and Eastern Orthodox Churches Union (later Anglican and Eastern Churches Association).
Issue of 'Letters of Business' authorising revision of the Book of Common Prayer.

Chronology of Events 1862–1991

Anglican Affairs	Other Events
1907	
	The second Hague Conference.
	Designation of New Zealand as Dominion.
	Papal decree *Ne temere*, restricting Roman Catholic recognition of mixed marriages.
1908	
The fifth Lambeth Conference, preceded by a Pan-Anglican Congress.	
1909	
	Constitution of the Union of South Africa.
1910	
	World Missionary Conference at Edinburgh.
1911	
	Accession of King George V.
1912	
Consecration of V.S. Azariah, the first indigenous Indian bishop of the Anglican Communion.	
1913	
A federation of missionary Churches in East Africa proposed by the Kikuyu Conference.	
1914	
	Colonial status for Nigeria.
	Outbreak of the First World War.
	Election of Pope Benedict XV.
1916	
Publication in England of the *Report on the Relations of Church and State*.	
1917	
	Revolution in Russia.
	Publication of canon law of the Roman Catholic Church.
1918	
Industrial Christian Fellowship formed in England.	Conclusion of the First World War.
1919	
Passage in England of Church of England Assembly (Powers) Act, enabling the Church to prepare ecclesiastical legislation.	

Anglican Affairs	*Other Events*
1920	
The sixth Lambeth Conference. The Church in Wales disestablished and independent of the Church of England. Establishment of intercommunion with the Church of Sweden.	Foundation of the League of Nations. Prohibition instituted in the USA.
1921	
Opening of the Malines Conversations between Anglican and Roman Catholic theologians.	
1922	
Establishment of the Church of England Commission on Doctrine. Introduction of revised Canadian Prayer Book.	Election of Pope Pius XI. Establishment of the Irish Free State.
1925	
Conclusion of the Malines Conversations.	Stockholm Conference of 'Life and Work' movement.
1926	
Approval of the revised Irish Prayer Book.	General strike in Britain.
1927	
	Lausanne Conference of 'Faith and Order'.
1928	
Approval of the revised Book of Common Prayer of the Protestant Episcopal Church in the USA. British parliament's refusal to sanction proposed Revised Prayer Book in England. C.G. Lang Archbishop of Canterbury.	Issue of papal encyclical *Mortalium animos,* forbidding Roman Catholic participation in ecumenical conferences.
1929	
Approval of revised Scottish Prayer Book.	Recognition by Italy of the Vatican as a sovereign state. Beginning of the Depression (Wall Street crash).
1930	
Church of India, Burma and Ceylon constituted as an autonomous province.	
1931	
The seventh Lambeth Conference. Bonn agreement on full communion between Anglican and Old Catholic Churches.	

Anglican Affairs	*Other Events*

1932

Formation of united Methodist Church in Britain.

1933

Assumption of power in Germany by Hitler.
End of prohibition in the USA.

1934

Barmen Declaration by the Confessing Church in Germany.

1935

War between Italy and Abyssinia.

1936

Conquest of Abyssinia by Italy.
Outbreak of Spanish Civil War.
Accession of King Edward VIII and then King George VI.

1937

Oxford Conference of 'Life and Work'.
Edinburgh Conference of 'Faith and Order'.
Entry into force of Irish republican constitution.
Issue of papal encyclicals *Divini Redemptoris* condemning atheistic communism and *Mit brennender Sorge* condemning Nazism.

1938

Publication of *Doctrine in the Church of England* (Report of the 1922 Commission).

German annexation of Austria.
World Missionary Conference at Tambaram, India.

1939

Conclusion of Spanish Civil War.
Outbreak of Second World War.
Election of Pope Pius XII.
Formation of Free Church Federal Council in England.

1941

Malvern (England) Conference on the crisis of civilisation.

USA entered Second World War following Japanese attack on Pearl Harbor.

1942

W. Temple Archbishop of Canterbury.

Formation of British Council of Churches.

Anglican Affairs	*Other Events*
1945 G.F. Fisher Archbishop of Canterbury.	Atomic bombing of Hiroshima and Nagasaki. Conclusion of Second World War.
1946 Archbishop Fisher's Cambridge sermon on reunion.	Inauguration of UN General Assembly. Political independence of the Philippines. Publication of Revised Standard Version New Testament.
1947 Inauguration of the United Church of South India.	Political independence of: India; Pakistan. Referral of Palestine question to UN. First discoveries of the Dead Sea Scrolls.
1948 The eighth Lambeth Conference.	Constitution of World Council of Churches (WCC) at Amsterdam Assembly. Proclamation of the state of Israel. Political independence of: Burma; Ceylon. Assassination of Mahatma Gandhi.
1949	Establishment of People's Republic of China.
1950	Outbreak of Korean War.
1951 Foundation of the Province of West Africa.	
1952	Conference of Faith and Order at Lund, Sweden. Accession of Queen Elizabeth II.
1953	Conclusion of Korean War. Death of Joseph Stalin. Publication of complete Revised Standard Version of the Bible.
1954 Anglican Congress in Minneapolis, USA. Publication of the South African Book of Common Prayer.	Evanston Assembly of WCC.

Anglican Affairs	*Other Events*
1955 Foundation of the Province of Central Africa.	
1956	The Suez crisis. Pakistan an Islamic republic. Political independence of Sudan.
1957	Political independence of Ghana.
1958 The ninth Lambeth Conference.	Election of Pope John XXIII.
1960 Foundation of the Province of East Africa. Appointment of Bishop S.F. Bayne as first Executive Officer of the Anglican Communion. Visit of Archbishop Fisher to Rome.	Political independence of: Nigeria; Zaire.
1961 A.M. Ramsey Archbishop of Canterbury. Inauguration of the Province of Uganda, Rwanda, Burundi and Boga-Zaire.	Political independence of: Sierra Leone; Tanganyika. Declaration of Republic of South Africa. New Delhi Assembly of WCC. Publication of New English Bible New Testament.
1962 Publication of revised Canadian Prayer Book.	Inauguration of Second Vatican Council. Political independence of: Burundi; Jamaica; Rwanda; Uganda; Trinidad and Tobago.
1963 Anglican Congress, Toronto, Canada. Publication of the Book of Common Worship of the Church of South India.	Assassination of President J.F. Kennedy. Election of Pope Paul VI. Promulgation of Vatican decree on ecumenism (*Unitatis redintegratio*). Political independence of: Kenya; Zanzibar. Inauguration of Malaysia. Commitment of US forces in Vietnam.
1964 Appointment of Bishop R.S. Dean as Executive Officer.	Political independence of: Malawi; Zambia. Tanzania formed by union of Tanganyika with Zanzibar and Pemba.

Anglican Affairs	*Other Events*

1965

Episcopal Church of Brazil constituted as an autonomous province.

Conclusion of Second Vatican Council. Declaration of independence by Rhodesia. Independence of Singapore from Malaysia.

1966

Visit of Archbishop Ramsey to the Pope, and issue of the 'Common Declaration'. Establishment of the Anglican Centre in Rome.

Political independence of Guyana. Publication of the Jerusalem Bible.

1967

Meeting of joint Anglican/Roman Catholic Preparatory Commission.

Outbreak of civil war in Nigeria. The Six Days War between Israel and the Arab states.

1968

The tenth Lambeth Conference. Publication of the 'Malta Report' of the Anglican/Roman Catholic Preparatory Commission.

Uppsala Assembly of WCC. Issue of papal encyclical *Humanae vitae*. Political independence of Mauritius.

1969

Appointment of Bishop J. Howe as Executive Officer.

First landing on the moon.

1970

Inauguration of the Church of the Province of Burma (Myanmar). Start of Anglican/Lutheran International Conversations.

Political independence of Fiji. End of civil war in Nigeria. Publication of the complete New English Bible.

1971

First meeting of Anglican Consultative Council (ACC) at Limuru (Kenya). Women ordained as priests in Hong Kong. *Anglican Information* first published.

Assumption of power in Uganda by Idi Amin. Political independence in Bangladesh.

1972

Conclusion of first Anglican/Lutheran International Conversations and publication of Pullach Report.

1973

Second meeting of ACC in Dublin, Ireland. Foundation of the Province of the Indian Ocean.

Final withdrawal of US forces from Vietnam. Israel-Arab conflict: the 'Yom Kippur' war.

Chronology of Events 1862–1991

Anglican Affairs	*Other Events*

1974

F.D. Coggan Archbishop of Canterbury.

Inauguration of the Province of Consejo Anglicano Sud Americano (later refounded as Iglesia Anglicano del Cono Sur).

Lausanne Congress on World Evangelism.

1975

Foundation of the autonomous Province of Melanesia.

Nairobi Assembly of WCC.
Political independence of: Mozambique; Papua New Guinea; the Seychelles.

1976

Third meeting of ACC in Trinidad.

Death of Mao Zedong.

Inauguration of the Episcopal Church of the Sudan as an independent province.

Inauguration of the Province of Jerusalem and the Middle East.

First publication of *The Anglican Cycle of Prayer*.

1977

Visit of Archbishop Coggan to the Pope.

Assassination of Archbishop Janani Luwum in Uganda.

Inauguration of the Province of Papua New Guinea.

1978

The eleventh Lambeth Conference.

Publication of the Australian Prayer Book.

Election of Pope John Paul I.
Election of Pope John Paul II.

1979

Primates Meeting in Ely, England.

Fourth meeting of ACC in London, Ontario.

Inauguration of the Church of the Province of Nigeria.

Publication of revised Book of Common Prayer of the Episcopal Church in the USA.

Overthrow of Idi Amin in Uganda.
Overthrow of the Shah of Iran and return from exile of Ayatollah Khommeini.

1980

R.A. Runcie Archbishop of Canterbury.

Separation of the Province of Burundi, Rwanda and Zaire from the Province of Uganda.

Formation of the Council of Churches of China.

Inauguration of the Republic of Zimbabwe.

Anglican Affairs	*Other Events*

1980 (cont'd)

Accession to the Anglican Communion of the Lusitanian Church of Portugal and the Spanish Reformed Episcopal Church.

Publication in England of *The Alternative Service Book*.

1981

Fifth meeting of ACC in Newcastle, England.

Primates Meeting in Washington, USA.

Inaugural meeting of the Commission of the Anglican and Reformed Churches.

Publication in USA of *Lutheran-Episcopal Dialogue: Report and Recommendations*.

1982

Publication of report of ARCIC-1.

Publication by WCC of *Baptism, Eucharist and Ministry*.

1983

Primates Meeting in Nairobi, Kenya.

Appointment of Dr S. Van Culin as Secretary General of ACC.

Publication of *Anglican-Lutheran Dialogue: The Report of the European Commission*.

Refounding of the Iglesia Anglicano del Cono Sur de America.

First meeting of ARCIC-2.

Vancouver Assembly of WCC.

Promulgation of revised code of Roman Catholic canon law.

1984

Sixth meeting of ACC in Badagry, Nigeria.

Award of Nobel Peace Prize to Bishop Desmond Tutu.

Publication of: Book of Common Prayer for use in the Church in Wales; *The Alternative Prayer Book* of the Church of Ireland; *God's Reign and our Unity* (report of Anglican-Reformed Commission).

Assassination of Indira Gandhi in India.

1985

Publication in Canada of *Book of Alternative Services*.

Publication of J. Howe, *Highways and Hedges*.

Publication of The New Jerusalem Bible.

Chronology of Events 1862-1991

Anglican Affairs	Other Events
1986 Primates Meeting in Toronto, Canada. Publication of *For the sake of the Kingdom: a Report of the Inter-Anglican Theological and Doctrinal Commission.*	Overthrow of President Marcos in the Philippines.

1987
Seventh meeting of ACC in Singapore.
Terry Waite taken hostage in Lebanon.
Publication of *The Emmaus Report* (Anglican Ecumenical Commission); S.W. Sykes (ed.), *Authority in the Anglican Communion;* A. Nichols, J. Clarke & T Hogan, *Transforming Families and Communities.*

1988
The twelfth Lambeth Conference.
First International Conference of Young Anglicans.
Consecration of Barbara Harris (ECUSA) as first Anglican woman (suffragan) bishop.
Appointment of Commission on Communion and Women in the Episcopate (Eames Commission).
Publication of *The Niagara Report* (Anglican-Lutheran Consultation on Episcope).

| **1989**
Primates Meeting in Cyprus.
Consecration of Penelope Jamieson (New Zealand) as first Anglican woman diocesan.
Publication of *A New Zealand Prayer Book—He Karakia Mikinare O Aotearoa.* | Reversal of government policy on apartheid in South Africa.
Fall of communist governments in eastern Europe, and demolition of the Berlin Wall.
Death of Ayatollah Khommeini.
Massacre of demonstrators in Tienanmen Square, Beijing, China.
Publication of The Revised English Bible. |
| **1990**
Eighth meeting of ACC in Wales.
Constitution of Philippine Episcopal Church as an autonomous province.
Publication of R.C. Craston, *Anglicanism and the Universal Church.* | World Convention on Justice, Peace and the Integrity of Creation in Seoul, Korea.
Political independence of Namibia.
Release from prison of Nelson Mandela in South Africa.
Occupation of Kuwait by Iraq.
Publication of New Revised Standard Version of the Bible. |

Anglican Affairs	*Other Events*
1991 G.L. Carey Archbishop of Canterbury. Sir Paul Reeves first UN representative of ACC and the Archbishop of Canterbury. Primates Meeting in Ireland. Inauguration of the Decade of Evangelism. Inter-Anglican Theological and Doctrinal Consultation, Virginia Seminary, USA.	The Gulf War. Canberra Assembly of WCC. Assassination of Rajiv Gandhi in India. Opening of negotiations for general settlement in Middle East, and release of hostages including Terry Waite.

Resolutions
of the Lambeth Conference
1867

Resolution 1
That it appears to us expedient, for the purpose of maintaining
brotherly intercommunion, that all cases of establishment of new sees,
and appointment of new bishops, be notified to all archbishops and
metropolitans, and all presiding bishops of the Anglican Communion.

Resolution 2
That, having regard to the conditions under which intercommunion
between members of the Church passing from one distant diocese to
another may be duly maintained, we hereby declare it desirable:
(1) That forms of letters commendatory on behalf of clergymen
visiting other dioceses be drawn up and agreed upon.
(2) That a form of letters commendatory for lay members of the
Church be in like manner prepared.
(3) That His Grace the Lord Archbishop of Canterbury be pleased
to undertake the preparation of such forms.

Resolution 3
That a committee be appointed to draw up a pastoral address to all
members of the Church of Christ in communion with the Anglican
branch of the Church Catholic, to be agreed upon by the assembled
bishops, and to be published as soon as possible after the last sitting
of the Conference.

Resolution 4
That, in the opinion of this Conference, unity in faith and discipline
will be best maintained among the several branches of the Anglican
Communion by due and canonical subordination of the synods of the
several branches to the higher authority of a synod or synods above
them.

Resolution 5
That a committee of seven members (with power to add to their number, and to obtain the assistance of men learned in ecclesiastical and
canon law) be appointed to inquire into and report upon the subject
of the relations and functions of such synods, and that such report
be forwarded to His Grace the Lord Archbishop of Canterbury, with

a request that, if possible, it may be communicated to any adjourned meeting of the Conference.

Resolution 6
That, in the judgement of the bishops now assembled, the whole Anglican Communion is deeply injured by the present condition of the Church in Natal; and that a committee be now appointed at this general meeting to report on the best mode by which the Church may be delivered from the continuance of this scandal, and the true faith maintained. That such report be forwarded to His Grace the Lord Archbishop of Canterbury, with the request that he will be pleased to transmit the same to all the bishops of the Anglican Communion, and to ask for their judgement thereupon.

Resolution 7
That we who are here present do acquiesce in the Resolution of the Convocation of Canterbury, passed on 29 June 1866, relating to the Diocese of Natal, to wit:

If it be decided that a new bishop should be consecrated: As to the proper steps to be taken by the members of the Church in the Province of Natal for obtaining a new bishop, it is the opinion of this House:

first, that a formal instrument, declaratory of the doctrine and discipline of the Church of South Africa should be prepared, which every bishop, priest and deacon to be appointed to office should be required to subscribe;

secondly, that a godly and well-learned man should be chosen by the clergy, with the assent of the lay communicants of the Church;

and thirdly, that he should be presented for consecration, either to the Archbishop of Canterbury—if the aforesaid instrument should declare the doctrine and discipline of Christ as received by the United Church of England and Ireland—or to the bishops of the Church of South Africa, according as hereafter may be judged to be most advisable and convenient.

Resolution 8
That, in order to the binding of the Churches of our colonial empire and the missionary Churches beyond them in the closest union with the Mother-Church, it is necessary that they receive and maintain without alteration the standards of faith and doctrine as now in use in that Church. That, nevertheless, each province should have the right to make such adaptations and additions to the services of the Church as its peculiar circumstances may require. Provided, that no change

or addition be made inconsistent with the spirit and principles of the Book of Common Prayer, and that all such changes be liable to revision by any synod of the Anglican Communion in which the said province shall be represented.

Resolution 9
That the committee appointed by Resolution 5, with the addition of the names of the Bishops of London, St David's, and Oxford, and all the colonial bishops, be instructed to consider the constitution of a voluntary spiritual tribunal, to which questions of doctrine may be carried by appeal from the tribunals for the exercise of discipline in each province of the colonial Church, and that their report be forwarded to His Grace the Lord Archbishop of Canterbury, who is requested to communicate it to an adjourned meeting of this Conference.

Resolution 10
That the Resolutions submitted to this Conference relative to the discipline to be exercised by metropolitans, the Court of Metropolitans, the scheme for conducting the election of bishops, when not otherwise provided for, the declaration of submission to the regulation of synods, and the question of what legislation should be proposed for the colonial Churches, be referred to the committee specified in the preceding Resolution.

Resolution 11
That a special committee be appointed to consider the Resolutions relative to the notification of proposed missionary bishoprics, and the subordination of missionaries.

Resolution 12
That the question of the bounds of the jurisdiction of different bishops, when any question may have arisen in regard to them, the question as to the obedience of chaplains of the United Church of England and Ireland on the continent, and the Resolution submitted to the Conference relative to their return and admission into home dioceses, be referred to the committee specified in the preceding Resolution.

Resolution 13
That we desire to render our hearty thanks to Almighty God for the blessings vouchsafed to us in and by this Conference; and we desire to express our hope that this our meeting may hereafter be followed by other meetings to be conducted in the same spirit of brotherly love.

1878

[*NOTE. The Lambeth Conference of 1878 did not adopt any formal Resolutions as such. The mind of the Conference was recorded by incorporating the Reports of its five Committees, received by the plenary Conference with almost complete unanimity, into an Encyclical Letter which was duly published. Recommendations embodied in the Committee Reports were evidently accorded equivalent status to formal Resolutions, and they are reproduced here as they appeared in the course of the Encyclical Letter, under appropriate reference.*]

UNION AMONG THE CHURCHES OF
THE ANGLICAN COMMUNION

[Recommendation 1] *Encyclical Letter 1.5*
There are certain principles of church order which, your Committee consider, ought to be distinctly recognised and set forth, as of great importance for the maintenance of union among the Churches of our Communion.

1   First, that the duly certified action of every national or particular Church, and of each ecclesiastical province (or diocese not included in a province), in the exercise of its own discipline, should be respected by all the other Churches, and by their individual members.

2   Secondly, that when a diocese, or territorial sphere of administration, has been constituted by the authority of any Church or province of this Communion within its own limits, no bishop or other clergyman of any other Church should exercise his functions within that diocese without the consent of the bishop thereof.*

3   Thirdly, that no bishop should authorise to officiate in his diocese a clergyman coming from another Church or province, unless such clergyman present letters testimonial, countersigned by the bishop of the diocese from which he comes; such letters to be, as nearly as possible, in the form adopted by such Church or province in the case of the transfer of a clergyman from one diocese to another.

* This does not refer to questions respecting missionary bishops and foreign chaplaincies, which have been entrusted to other Committees.

[Recommendation 2] *Encyclical Letter 1.6: Of Church organisation*
Inasmuch as the sufficient and effective organisation of the several parts of the Church tends to promote the unity of the whole, your Committee would, with this view, repeat the recommendation in the sixth Report of the first Lambeth Conference, that those dioceses which still remain isolated should, as circumstances may allow, associate

4

themselves into a province or provinces, in accordance with the ancient laws and usages of the Catholic Church.

[Recommendation 3] *Encyclical Letter 1.7: Of common work*
Believing that the unity of our Churches will be especially manifested and strengthened by their uniting together in common work, your Committee would call attention to the great value of such co-operation wherever the opportunity shall present itself; as, for example, in founding and maintaining, in the missionary field, schools for the training of a native ministry, such as that which is now contemplated in Shanghai, and, generally, as far as may be possible, in prosecuting missionary work, such as that which the Churches in England and Scotland are maintaining together in Kaffraria.

[Recommendation 4] *Encyclical Letter 1.8: Of commendatory letters*
1   This Committee would renew the recommendation of the first Lambeth Conference, that letters commendatory should be given by their own bishops to clergymen visiting for a time other Churches than those to which they belong.
2   They would urge yet more emphatically the importance of letters commendatory being given by their own clergymen to members of their flocks going from one country to another. And they consider it desirable that the clergy should urge on such persons the duty of promptly presenting these letters, and should carefully instruct them as to the oneness of the Church in its apostolical constitution under its varying organisation and conditions.

It may not, perhaps, be considered foreign to this subject to suggest here the importance of impressing upon our people the extent and geographical distribution of our Churches, and of reminding them that there is now hardly any part of the world where members of our Communion may not find a Church one with their own in faith, order and worship.

[Recommendation 5] *Encyclical Letter 1.9: Of circulating*
information as to the Churches
It appears that the want has been much felt of some centre of communication among the Churches in England, Ireland, Scotland, America, India, the colonies, and elsewhere, through which ecclesiastical documents of importance might be mutually circulated, and in which copies of them might be retained for reference. Your Committee would suggest that the Society for Promoting Christian Knowledge might be requested to maintain a department for this purpose, supported by special contributions; and also that provision might be made for the more general dissemination, in each Church, of information

respecting the acts and current history of all the rest. They recommend that the Reports and other proceedings of this Conference, which it may think fit to publish, should be communicated through this channel. They further think it desirable that the official acts and other published documents of each representative body of this Communion should be interchanged among the respective bishops and the officers of such bodies.

[Recommendation 6] *Encyclical Letter 1.10: Of a Day of Intercession*
Remembering the blessing promised to united intercession, and believing that such intercession ever tends to deepen and strengthen that unity of his Church for which our Lord earnestly pleaded in his great intercessory prayer, your Committee trust that this Conference will give the weight of its recommendation to the observance, throughout the Churches of this Communion, of a season of prayer for the unity of Christendom. This recommendation has been, to some extent, anticipated by the practice adopted of late years of setting apart a Day of Intercession for Missions. Your Committee would by no means wish to interfere with an observance which appears to have been widely accepted, and signally blessed of God. But, as our divine Lord has so closely connected the unity of his followers with the world's belief in his own mission from the Father, it seems to us that intercessions for the enlargement of his Kingdom may well be joined with earnest prayer that all who profess faith in him may be one flock under one Shepherd. With respect to the day, your Committee have been informed that the Festival of St Andrew, hitherto observed as the Day of Intercession for Missions, is found to be unsuitable to the circumstances of the Church in many parts of the world. They, therefore, venture to suggest that, after the present year, the time selected should be the Tuesday before Ascension Day (being a Rogation Day), or any of the seven days after that Tuesday; and they hope that all the bishops of the several Churches will commend this observance to their respective dioceses.

[Recommendation 7] *Encyclical Letter 1.11-12: Of diversities in worship*
Your Committee, believing that, next to oneness in 'the faith once delivered to the saints', communion in worship is the link which most firmly binds together bodies of Christian men, and remembering that the Book of Common Prayer, retained as it is, with some modifications, by all our Churches, has been one principal bond of union among them, desire to call attention to the fact that such communion in worship may be endangered by excessive diversities of ritual. They believe

that the internal unity of the several Churches will help greatly to the union of these one with another. And, while they consider that such large elasticity in the forms of worship is desirable as will give wide scope to all legitimate expressions of devotional feeling, they would appeal, on the other hand, to the apostolic precept that 'all things be done unto edifying', and to the Catholic principle that order and obedience, even at the sacrifice of personal preferences and tastes, lie at the foundation of Christian unity, and are even essential to the successful maintenance of the faith.

They cannot leave this subject without expressing an earnest hope that churchmen of all views, however varying, will recognise the duty of submitting themselves, for conscience' sake, in matters ritual and ceremonial, to the authoritative judgements of that particular or national Church in which, by God's providence, they may be placed; and that they will abstain from all that tends to estrangement or irritation, and will rather daily and fervently pray that the Holy Spirit may guide every member of the Church to 'think and do always such things as be rightful', and that he may unite us all in that brotherly charity which is 'the very bond of peace and of all virtues'.

VOLUNTARY BOARDS OF ARBITRATION

[Recommendation 8] *Encyclical Letter 2.4-6*
(a)   Every ecclesiastical province, which has constituted for the exercise of discipline over its clergy a tribunal for receiving appeals from its diocesan courts, should be held responsible for its own decisions in the exercise of such discipline; and your Committee are not prepared to recommend that there should be any one central tribunal of appeal from such provincial tribunals.
(b)   If any province is desirous that its tribunal of appeal should have power to obtain, in matters of doctrine, or of discipline involving a question of doctrine, the opinion of some council of reference before pronouncing sentence, your Committee consider that the conditions of such reference must be determined by the province itself; but that the opinion of the council should be given on a consideration of the facts of the case, sent up to it in writing by the tribunal of appeal, and not merely on an abstract question of doctrine.
(c)   In dioceses which have not yet been combined into a province, or which may be geographically incapable of being so combined, your Committee recommend that appeals should lie from the diocesan courts to the Archbishop of Canterbury, to be heard by His Grace with such assistance as he may deem best. The circumstances of each diocese must determine how much consensual jurisdiction could be enforced.

[Recommendation 9] *Encyclical Letter 2.7-11*

As regards the very grave question of the trial of a bishop, inasmuch as any tribunal, constituted for this purpose by a province, is necessarily a tribunal of first instance, it would, in the opinion of your Committee, be expedient that, when any such provisions can be introduced by voluntary compact into the constitutions or canons of any Church, the following conditions should be observed:

(a) When any bishop shall have been sentenced by the tribunal constituted for the trial of a bishop in any ecclesiastical province, if no bishop of the province, other than the accused, shall dissent from the judgement, there should be no appeal; provided that the case be heard by not fewer than five bishops, who shall be unanimous in their judgement.

(b) If, in consequence of the small number of bishops in a province, or from any other sufficient cause, a tribunal of five comprovincial bishops cannot be formed, your Committee would suggest that the province should provide for the enlargement of the tribunal by the addition of bishops from a neighbouring province.

(c) In the event of the provincial tribunal not fulfilling the conditions indicated in paragraph 8 of this Report*, your Committee would suggest that, whenever an external tribunal of appeal is not provided in the canons of that province, it should be in the power of the accused bishop, if condemned, to require the provincial tribunal to refer the case to at least five metropolitans or chief bishops of the Anglican Communion, to be named in the said canons, of whom the Archbishop of Canterbury should be one; and that, if any three of these shall require that the case, or any portion of it, shall be re-heard or reviewed, it should be so re-heard or reviewed.

(d) In cases in which an ecclesiastical province desires to have a tribunal of appeal from its provincial tribunal for trying a bishop, your Committee consider that such tribunal should consist of not less than five bishops of the Churches of the Anglican Communion, under the presidency of the Archbishop of Canterbury, if His Grace will consent thereto, with the assistance of laymen learned in the law.

* [That is, sub-paragraph (a) above.]

MISSIONARY BISHOPS AND MISSIONARIES OF VARIOUS BRANCHES OF THE ANGLICAN COMMUNION, ACTING IN THE SAME COUNTRY

[Recommendation 10]   *Encyclical Letter 3.2-7*

Your Committee have had before them the question of providing Books of Common Prayer for converts from heathenism, suitable to the special wants of various countries, and they recommend as follows:

They think it very important that such books should not be introduced or multiplied without proper authority; and, since grave inconvenience might follow the use of different Prayer Books in the same district, in English and American missions, they recommend that, whenever it is possible, one Prayer Book only should be in use.

It is expedient that Books of Common Prayer, suitable to the needs of native congregations in heathen countries, should be framed; that the principles embodied in such books should be identical with the principles embodied in the Book of Common Prayer; and that the deviations from the Book of Common Prayer in point of form should only be such as are required by the circumstances of particular Churches.

In the case of heathen countries not under English or American rule, any such book should be approved by a board consisting of the bishop or bishops under whose authority the book is intended to be used, and of certain clergymen, not less than three where possible, from the diocese or dioceses, or district, and should then be communicated by such bishop or bishops, or by the metropolitan of the province to which any such bishop belongs, to a board in England, consisting of the Archbishops of England and Ireland, the Bishop of London, the Primus of the Scottish Episcopal Church, together with two bishops and four clergymen selected by them, and also to a board appointed by the General Convention of the Protestant Episcopal Church in the United States of America.

No such book should be held to have been authorised for use in public worship, unless it have received the sanction of these two boards.

In any diocese of a country under English rule, all such new books, being modifications or versions of the Book of Common Prayer, should be submitted, after approval by local authority, to the board in England only.

[Recommendation 11]   *Encyclical Letter 3.8-14*

Your Committee have considered the case of missions in countries not under English or American rule, and they recommend as follows:

In cases where two bishops of the Anglican Communion are ministering in the same country, as in China, Japan, and Western Africa at

9

the present time, your Committee are of opinion that under existing circumstances each bishop should have control of his own clergy, and their converts and congregations.

The various bishops in the same country should endeavour, as members of the same Communion, to keep up brotherly intercourse with each other on the subject of their missionary work.

In countries not under English or American rule, the English or American Church would not ordinarily undertake to establish dioceses with strictly defined territorial limits; although either Church might indicate the district in which it was intended that the missionary bishop should labour.

Bishops in the same country should take care not to interfere in any manner with the congregations or converts of each other.

It is most undesirable that either Church should for the future send a bishop or missionaries to a town or district already occupied by a bishop of another branch of the Anglican Communion.

When it is intended to send forth any new missionary bishop, notification of such an intention should be sent beforehand to the Archbishop of Canterbury, to the Presiding Bishop of the Protestant Episcopal Church in the United States of America, and to the metropolitan of any province near which the missionary bishop is to minister.

ANGLICAN CHAPLAINS AND CHAPLAINCIES

[Recommendation 12]   *Encyclical Letter 4.1-5*
Your Committee have to report that they have agreed the following recommendations:
1   That it is highly desirable that Anglican congregations, on the continent of Europe and elsewhere, should be distinctly urged not to admit the stated ministrations of any clergyman without the written licence or permission of the bishop of the Anglican Communion who is duly authorised to grant it; and that the occasional assistance of strangers should not be invited or permitted without some satisfactory evidence of their ordination and character as clergymen.
2   That it is desirable, as a general rule, that two chapels shall not be established where one is sufficient for the members of both Churches, American and English; also that where there is only one church or chapel the members of both Churches should be represented on the committee, if any.
3   That it be suggested to the societies which partly support continental chaplaincies that, in places where English and American churchmen reside or visit, and especially where Americans out-

number the English, it may be desirable to appoint a properly accredited clergyman of the American Church.

4   That your Committee, having carefully considered a Memorial addressed to the archbishops and bishops of the Church of England by four priests and certain other members of 'the Spanish and Portuguese Reformed Episcopal Church', praying for the consecration of a bishop, cannot but express their hearty sympathy with the memorialists in the difficulties of their position; and, having heard a statement on the subject of the proposed extension of the episcopate to Mexico by the American Church, they venture to suggest that, when a bishop shall have been consecrated by the American Church for Mexico, he might be induced to visit Spain and Portugal, and render such assistance, at this stage of the movement, as may seem to him practicable and advisable.

1888

Resolution 1
That this Conference, without pledging itself to all the statements and opinions embodied in the Report of the Committee on Intemperance, commends the Report to the consideration of the Church.

Resolution 2
That the bishops assembled in this Conference declare that the use of unfermented juice of the grape, or any liquid other than true wine diluted or undiluted, as the element in the administration of the cup in Holy Communion, is unwarranted by the example of our Lord, and is an unauthorised departure from the custom of the Catholic Church.

Resolution 3
That this Conference earnestly commends to all those into whose hands it may come the Report on the subject of Purity, as expressing the mind of the Conference on this great subject.

Voting: Carried unanimously.

Resolution 4
(a)   That, inasmuch as our Lord's words expressly forbid divorce, except in the case of fornication or adultery, the Christian Church cannot recognise divorce in any other than the excepted case, or give any sanction to the marriage of any person who has been divorced contrary to this law, during the life of the other party.

11

(b)   That under no circumstances ought the guilty party, in the case of a divorce for fornication or adultery, to be regarded, during the lifetime of the innocent party, as a fit recipient of the blessing of the Church on marriage.

(c)   That, recognising the fact that there always has been a difference of opinion in the Church on the question whether our Lord meant to forbid marriage to the innocent party in a divorce for adultery, the Conference recommends that the clergy should not be instructed to refuse the sacraments or other privileges of the Church to those who, under civil sanction, are thus married.

Resolution 5

(a)   That it is the opinion of this Conference that persons living in polygamy be not admitted to baptism, but that they be accepted as candidates and kept under Christian instruction until such time as they shall be in a position to accept the law of Christ.

Voting: For 83; Against 21.

(b)   That the wives of polygamists may, in the opinion of this Conference, be admitted in some cases to baptism, but that it must be left to the local authorities of the Church to decide under what circumstances they may be baptized.

Voting: For 54; Against 34.

Resolution 6

(a)   That the principle of the religious observance of one day in seven, embodied in the Fourth Commandment, is of divine obligation.

(b)   That, from the time of our Lord's resurrection, the first day of the week was observed by Christians as a day of worship and rest, and, under the name of 'the Lord's Day', gradually succeeded, as the great weekly festival of the Christian Church, to the sacred position of the sabbath.

(c)   That the observance of the Lord's Day as a day of rest, of worship, and of religious teaching, has been a priceless blessing in all Christian lands in which it has been maintained.

(d)   That the growing laxity in its observance threatens a great change in its sacred and beneficent character.

(e)   That especially the increasing practice, on the part of some of the wealthy and leisurely classes, of making Sunday a day of secular amusement is most strongly to be deprecated.

(f)   That the most careful regard should be had to the danger of any encroachment upon the rest which, on this day, is the right of servants as well as their masters, and of the working classes as well as their employers.

Resolution 7
That this Conference receives the Report drawn up by the Committee on the subject of Socialism, and submits it to the consideration of the Churches of the Anglican Communion.

Resolution 8
That this Conference receives the Report drawn up by the Committee on the subject of Emigration, and commends the suggestions embodied in it to the consideration of the Churches of the Anglican Communion.

Resolution 9
(a)   That this Conference receives the Report drawn up by the Committee on the subject of the Mutual Relation of Dioceses and Branches of the Anglican Communion, and submits it to the consideration of the Church, as containing suggestions of much practical importance.
(b)   That the Archbishop of Canterbury be requested to give his attention to the Appendix attached to the Report, with a view to action in the direction indicated, if, upon consideration, His Grace should think such action desirable.

Resolution 10
That, inasmuch as the Book of Common Prayer is not the possession of one diocese or province, but of all, and that a revision in one portion of the Anglican Communion must therefore be extensively felt, this Conference is of opinion that no particular portion of the Church should undertake revision without seriously considering the possible effect of such action on other branches of the Church.

Resolution 11
That, in the opinion of this Conference, the following articles supply a basis on which approach may be by God's blessing made towards home reunion:
(a)   The Holy Scriptures of the Old and New Testaments, as 'containing all things necessary to salvation', and as being the rule and ultimate standard of faith.
(b)   The Apostles' Creed, as the baptismal symbol; and the Nicene Creed, as the sufficient statement of the Christian faith.
(c)   The two sacraments ordained by Christ himself—Baptism and the Supper of the Lord—ministered with unfailing use of Christ's words of institution, and of the elements ordained by him.
(d)   The historic episcopate, locally adapted in the methods of its administration to the varying needs of the nations and peoples called of God into the unity of his Church.

Resolution 12
That this Conference earnestly requests the constituted authorities of the various branches of our Communion, acting, so far as may be, in concert with one another, to make it known that they hold themselves in readiness to enter into brotherly conference (such as that which has already been proposed by the Church in the United States of America) with the representatives of other Christian communions in the English-speaking races, in order to consider what steps can be taken, either towards corporate reunion, or towards such relations as may prepare the way for fuller organic unity hereafter.

Resolution 13
That this Conference recommends as of great importance, in tending to bring about reunion, the dissemination of information respecting the standards of doctrine and formularies in use in the Anglican Church; and recommends that information be disseminated, on the other hand, respecting the authoritative standards of doctrine, worship, and government adopted by the other bodies of Christians into which the English-speaking races are divided.

Resolution 14
That, in the opinion of this Conference, earnest efforts should be made to establish more friendly relations between the Scandinavian and Anglican Churches; and that approaches on the part of the Swedish Church, with a view to the mutual explanation of differences, be most gladly welcomed, in order to the ultimate establishment, if possible, of intercommunion on sound principles of ecclesiastical polity.

Resolution 15
(a)   That this Conference recognises with thankfulness the dignified and independent position of the Old Catholic Church of Holland, and looks to more frequent brotherly intercourse to remove many of the barriers which at present separate us.
(b)   That we regard it as a duty to promote friendly relations with the Old Catholic community in Germany, and with the 'Christian Catholic Church' in Switzerland, not only out of sympathy with them, but also in thankfulness to God who has strengthened them to suffer for the truth under great discouragements, difficulties, and temptations; and that we offer them the privileges recommended by the Committee under the conditions specified in its Report.
(c)   That the sacrifices made by the Old Catholics in Austria deserve our sympathy, and that we hope, when their organisation is sufficiently tried and complete, a more formal relation may be found possible.

(d)   That, with regard to the reformers in Italy, France, Spain, and Portugal, struggling to free themselves from the burden of unlawful terms of communion, we trust that they may be enabled to adopt such sound forms of doctrine and discipline, and to secure such Catholic organisation as will permit us to give them a fuller recognition.

(e)   That, without desiring to interfere with the rights of bishops of the Catholic Church to interpose in cases of extreme necessity, we deprecate any action that does not regard primitive and established principles of jurisdiction and the interests of the whole Anglican Communion.

Voting: All parts of this Resolution were carried nemine contradicente.

Resolution 16
That, having regard to the fact that the question of the relation of the Anglican Church to the Unitas Fratrum, or Moravians, was remitted by the last Lambeth Conference to a Committee, which has hitherto presented no Report on the subject, the Archbishop of Canterbury be requested to appoint a committee of bishops who shall be empowered to confer with learned theologians, and with the heads of the Unitas Fratrum, and shall report to His Grace before the end of the current year, and that His Grace be requested to take such action on their Report as he shall deem right.

Resolution 17
That this Conference, rejoicing in the friendly communications which have passed between the Archbishops of Canterbury and other Anglican bishops, and the Patriarchs of Constantinople and other Eastern patriarchs and bishops, desires to express its hope that the barriers to fuller communion may be, in course of time, removed by further intercourse and extended enlightenment. The Conference commends this subject to the devout prayers of the faithful, and recommends that the counsels and efforts of our fellow Christians should be directed to the encouragement of internal reformation in the Eastern Churches, rather than to the drawing away from them of individual members of their Communion.

Resolution 18
That the Archbishop of Canterbury be requested to take counsel with such persons as he may see fit to consult, with a view to ascertaining whether it is desirable to revise the English version of the Nicene Creed or of the Quicunque Vult.

Voting: For 57; Against 20.

Resolution 19
That, as regards newly constituted Churches, especially in non-Christian lands, it should be a condition of the recognition of them as in complete intercommunion with us, and especially of their receiving from us episcopal succession, that we should first receive from them satisfactory evidence that they hold substantially the same doctrine as our own, and that their clergy subscribe articles in accordance with the express statements of our own standards of doctrine and worship; but that they should not necessarily be bound to accept in their entirety the Thirty-nine Articles of Religion.

1897

Resolution 1
That, recognising the advantages which have accrued to the Church from the meetings of the Lambeth Conferences, we are of opinion that it is of great importance to the wellbeing of the Church that there should be from time to time meetings of the bishops of the whole Anglican Communion for the consideration of questions that may arise affecting the Church of Christ.

Resolution 2
That whereas the Lambeth Conferences have been called into existence by the invitation of the Archbishop of Canterbury, we desire that similar Conferences should be held, at intervals of about ten years, on the invitation of the Archbishop, if he be willing to give it.

Resolution 3
That the Resolutions adopted by such Conferences should be formally communicated to the various national Churches, provinces, and extra-provincial dioceses of the Anglican Communion for their consideration, and for such action as may seem to them desirable.

Resolution 4
That the conditions of membership of the Lambeth Conferences, as described in the opening sentences of the Official Letter of 1878 and the Encyclical Letter of 1888, should remain unaltered.

Resolution 5
That it is advisable that a consultative body should be formed to which resort may be had, if desired, by the national Churches, provinces,

and extra-provincial dioceses of the Anglican Communion either for information or for advice, and that the Archbishop of Canterbury be requested to take such steps as he may think most desirable for the creation of this consultative body.

Resolution 6
We desire to record our satisfaction at the progress of the acceptance of the principle of provincial organisation since the date of its formal commendation to the Anglican Communion in the Official Letter of 1878. We would also express a hope that the method of association into provinces may be carried still further as circumstances may allow.

Resolution 7
Recognising the almost universal custom in the Western Church of attaching the title of Archbishop to the rank of Metropolitan, we are of opinion that the revival and extension of this custom among ourselves is justifiable and desirable. It is advisable that the proposed adoption of such a title should be formally announced to the bishops of the various Churches and provinces of the Communion with a view to its general recognition.

Resolution 8
We are of opinion that the archiepiscopal or primatial title may be taken from a city or from a territory, according to the discretion of the province concerned.

Resolution 9
Where it is intended that any bishop-elect, not under the metropolitan jurisdiction of the See of Canterbury, should be consecrated in England under the Queen's mandate, it is desirable, if it be possible, that he should not be expected to take an oath of personal obedience to the Archbishop of Canterbury, but rather should, before his consecration, make a solemn declaration that he will pay all due honour and deference to the Archbishop of Canterbury, and will respect and maintain the spiritual rights and privileges of the Church of England, and of all Churches in communion with her. In this manner the interests of unity would be maintained without any infringement of the local liberties or jurisdiction.

Resolution 10
If such bishop-elect be designated to a see within any primatial or provincial jurisdiction, it is desirable that he should at his consecration take the customary oath of canonical obedience to his own primate or metropolitan.

Resolution 11
That this Conference recognises with thankfulness the revival alike of brotherhoods and sisterhoods and of the office of deaconess in our branch of the Church, and commends to the attention of the Church the Report of the Committee appointed to consider the Relation of Religious Communities to the Episcopate.

Resolution 12
In view of the importance of the further development and wise direction of such communities, the Conference requests the Committee to continue its labours, and to present a further Report to His Grace the Archbishop of Canterbury in July 1898.

Resolution 13
That this Conference receives the Report drawn up by the Committee upon the Critical Study of Holy Scripture, and commends it to the consideration of all Christian people.

Resolution 14
That while we heartily thank God for the missionary zeal which he has kindled in our Communion, and for the abundant blessing bestowed on such work as has been done, we recommend that prompt and continuous efforts be made to arouse the Church to recognise as a necessary and constant element in the spiritual life of the Body, and of each member of it, the fulfilment of our Lord's great commission to evangelise all nations.

Resolution 15
That the tendency of many English-speaking Christians to entertain an exaggerated opinion of the excellences of Hinduism and Buddhism, and to ignore the fact that Jesus Christ alone has been constituted Saviour and King of mankind, should be vigorously corrected.

Resolution 16
That a more prominent position be assigned to the evangelisation of the Jews in the intercessions and almsgiving of the Church, and that the various boards of missions be requested to take cognisance of this work; and particularly to see that care be taken for the due training of the missionary agents to be employed in the work.

Resolution 17
That in view (1) of the success which has already attended faithful work among the Mohammedans, (2) of the opportunity offered at the present time for more vigorous efforts, especially in India and in the

Hausa district*, and (3) of the need of special training for the work, it is desirable:
(a) that men be urged to offer themselves with a view to preparation by special study for mission work among Mohammedans;
(b) that attention be called to the importance of creating or maintaining strong centres for work amongst Mohammedans, as, for instance, in the cities of Delhi, Lucknow, and Hyderabad (Deccan), and elsewhere.
* [Central Sudan]

Resolution 18
That while we feel that there is much to encourage us in what has been done, and is now in progress, for the establishment and development of native Churches, we consider it to be of the utmost importance that from the very beginning the idea that the Church is their own and not a foreign Church should be impressed upon converts, and that a due share of the management and financial support of the Church should be theirs from the first. But we hold that the power of independent action, which is closely connected with the establishment of a native episcopate, ought not as a rule to be confided to native Churches until they are also financially independent.

Resolution 19
That it is important that, so far as possible, the Church should be adapted to local circumstances, and the people brought to feel in all ways that no burdens in the way of foreign customs are laid upon them, and nothing is required of them but what is of the essence of the faith, and belongs to the due order of the Catholic Church.

Resolution 20
That while the converts should be encouraged to seek independence of foreign financial aid, and to look forward to complete independence, care should be taken to impress upon them the necessity of holding the Catholic faith in its integrity, and of maintaining at all times that union with the great body of the Church which will strengthen the life of the young Church, and prevent any departure from catholic and apostolic unity, whether through heresy or through schism.

Resolution 21
That due care should be taken to make the diocese the centre of unity, so that, while there may be contained in the same area under one bishop various races and languages necessitating many modes of administra-

tion, nothing shall be allowed to obscure the fact that the many races form but one Church.

Resolution 22
That bishops and clergy engaged in missionary work should give to those of their flock who may travel to other countries letters of commendation in each case, to persons who will interest themselves in the spiritual welfare of such travellers.

Resolution 23
That this Conference desires to give expression to its deep sense of the evils resulting from the drink traffic on the west coast of Africa and elsewhere, and of the hindrance which it presents not only to the development of native Churches, but also to the acceptance of Christianity by heathen tribes.

Resolution 24
That, while it is the duty of the whole Church to make disciples of all nations, yet, in the discharge of this duty, independent Churches of the Anglican Communion ought to recognise the equal rights of each other when establishing foreign missionary jurisdictions, so that two bishops of that Communion may not exercise jurisdiction in the same place, and the Conference recommends every bishop to use his influence in the diocesan and provincial synods of his particular Church to gain the adhesion of the synods to these principles, with a view to the framing of canons or resolutions in accord therewith. Where such rights have, through inadvertence, been infringed in the past, an adjustment of the respective positions of the bishops concerned ought to be made by an amicable arrangement between them, with a view to correcting as far as possible the evils arising from such infringement.

Resolution 25
That when any particular Church contemplates creating a new foreign missionary jurisdiction, the recommendation contained in Resolution 1 of the Conference of 1867 ought always to be followed before any practical steps are taken.

Resolution 26
That this Conference earnestly commends to the consideration of the Churches of the Anglican Communion the suggestions contained in the Report of the Committee on Foreign Missions as to the relation of missionary bishops and clergy to missionary societies.

Resolution 27
That in the foreign mission field of the Church's work, where signal spiritual blessings have attended the labours of Christian missionaries not connected with the Anglican Communion, a special obligation has arisen to avoid, as far as possible without compromise of principle, whatever tends to prevent the due growth and manifestation of that 'unity of the Spirit' which should ever mark the Church of Christ.

Resolution 28
That in accordance with the sentiments expressed by the bishops who met in the last Conference, we regard it as our duty to maintain and promote friendly relations with the Old Catholic community in Germany, and with the Christian Catholic Church in Switzerland, assuring them of our sympathy, of our thankfulness to God who has held them steadfast in their efforts for the preservation of the primitive faith and order, and who, through all discouragements, difficulties, and temptations, has given them the assurance of his blessing, in the maintenance of their principles, in the enlargement of their congregations, and in the increase of their Churches. We continue the offer of the religious privileges by which the clergy and faithful laity may be admitted to Holy Communion on the same conditions as our own communicants.

Resolution 29
That we renew the expression of hope for a more formal relation with the Old Catholics in Austria, when their organisation shall have been made more complete.

Resolution 30
That we recognise thankfully the movement for the formation of an autonomous Church in Mexico, organised upon the primitive lines of administration, and having a liturgy and Book of Offices approved by the Presiding Bishop of the Church in the United States and his Advisory Committee as being framed after the primitive forms of worship.

Resolution 31
That we express our sympathy with the reformation movement in Brazil, and trust that it may develop in accordance with sound principles.

Resolution 32
That we repeat the expressions of sympathy (contained in the Report of the Lambeth Conference of 1888) with the brave and earnest men

of France, Italy, Spain, and Portugal who have been driven to free themselves from the burden of unlawful terms of communion imposed by the Church of Rome; and continue to watch these movements with deep and anxious interest, praying that they may be blessed and guided by Almighty God.

Resolution 33
That we recommend to the Archbishop of Canterbury and the primates and presiding bishops of other Churches in communion with the Church of England the appointment of at least one representative of each Church to attend the International Congress which is to meet in Vienna on 30 August 1897; and we express the hope that there may be a revival of such Conferences as those held at Bonn in 1874 and 1875 to which representatives may be invited and appointed from the Church of England and the Churches in communion with her.

Resolution 34
That every opportunity be taken to emphasise the divine purpose of visible unity amongst Christians as a fact of revelation.

Resolution 35
That this Conference urges the duty of special intercession for the unity of the Church in accordance with our Lord's own prayer.

Resolution 36
That the Archbishops of Canterbury and York and the Bishop of London be requested to act as a committee with power to add to their number, to confer personally or by correspondence with the Orthodox Eastern patriarchs, the 'Holy Governing Synod' of the Church of Russia, and the chief authorities of the various Eastern Churches with a view to consider the possibility of securing a clearer understanding and of establishing closer relations between the Churches of the East and the Anglican Communion; and that under the direction of the said Committee arrangements be made for the translation of books and documents setting forth the relative positions of the various Churches, and also of such catechisms and forms of service as may be helpful to mutual understanding.

Resolution 37
That this Conference, not possessing sufficient information to warrant the expression of a decided opinion upon the question of the orders of the Unitas Fratrum or Moravians, must content itself with expressing a hearty desire for such relations with them as will aid the cause of Christian unity, and with recommending that there should be on the

part of the Anglican Communion further consideration of the whole subject, in the hope of establishing closer relations between the Unitas Fratrum and the Churches represented in this Conference.

Resolution 38
That the Archbishop of Canterbury be requested to appoint a committee to conduct the further investigation of the subject, and for such purpose to confer with the authorities or representatives of the Unitas Fratrum.

Resolution 39
That this Conference, being desirous of furthering the action taken by the Lambeth Conference of 1888 with regard to the validity of the orders of the Swedish Church, requests the Archbishop of Canterbury to appoint a committee to inquire into the question, and to report to the next Lambeth Conference; and that it is desirable that the committee, if appointed, should confer with the authorities or representatives of the Church of Sweden upon the subject of the proposed investigation.

Resolution 40
That the bishops of the several Churches of the Anglican Communion be urged to appoint committees of bishops, where they have not been already appointed, to watch for opportunities of united prayer and mutual conference between representatives of different Christian bodies, and to give counsel where counsel may be asked in this matter. That these committees confer with and assist each other, and regard themselves as responsible for reporting to the next Lambeth Conference what has been accomplished in this respect.

Resolution 41
That this Conference, while disclaiming any purpose of laying down rules for the conduct of international arbitration, or of suggesting the special methods by which it should proceed, desires to affirm its profound conviction of the value of the principle of international arbitration, and its essential consistency with the religion of Jesus Christ.

Resolution 42
That this Conference welcomes the indications of a more enlightened public conscience on the subject of international arbitration, and desires to call the attention of all Christian people to the evidence of the healthier state of feeling afforded by the action of legislatures, and in the increasing literature on the subject.

Resolution 43

That this Conference, believing that nothing more strongly makes for peace than a healthy and enlightened public opinion, urges upon all Christian people the duty of promoting by earnest prayer, by private instruction, and by public appeal, the cause of international arbitration.

Resolution 44

That this Conference receives the Report of the Committee on the duty of the Church in regard to industrial problems, and commends the suggestions embodied in it to the earnest and sympathetic consideration of all Christian people.

Resolution 45

That this Conference recognises the exclusive right of each bishop to put forth or sanction additional services for use within his jurisdiction, subject to such limitations as may be imposed by the provincial or other lawful authority.

Resolution 46

That this Conference also recognises in each bishop within his jurisdiction the exclusive right of adapting the services in the Book of Common Prayer to local circumstances, and also of directing or sanctioning the use of additional prayers, subject to such limitations as may be imposed by provincial or other lawful authority, provided also that any such adaptation shall not affect the doctrinal teaching or value of the service or passage thus adapted.

Resolution 47

That the Archbishop of Canterbury be requested to take such steps as may be necessary for the retranslation of the Quicunque Vult.

Resolution 48

That in the opinion of this Conference it is of much importance that in all cases of infant baptism the clergyman should take all possible care to see that provision is made for the Christian training of the child, but that, unless in cases of grave and exceptional difficulty, the baptism should not be deferred.

Resolution 49

That the baptismal promises of repentance, faith, and obedience should be made either privately or publicly by those who, having been baptized without those promises, are brought by our clergy to confirmation by the bishop.

Resolution 50
Where difficulties arise in regard to the administration of Holy Communion to the sick, we recommend that these difficulties should be left to be dealt with by the bishop of each diocese in accordance with the direction contained in the preface to the Prayer Book of the Church of England 'Concerning the Service of the Church':
> And forasmuch as nothing can be so plainly set forth, but doubts may arise in the use and practice of the same; to appease all such diversity (if any arise) and for the resolution of all doubts, concerning the manner how to understand, do, and execute the things contained in this Book; the parties that so doubt, or diversely take any thing, shall alway resort to the Bishop of the Diocese, who by his discretion shall take order for the quieting and appeasing of the same; so that the same order be not contrary to any thing contained in this Book. And if the Bishop of the Diocese be in doubt, then he may send for the resolution thereof to the Archbishop.

Resolution 51
That this Conference welcomes heartily the proposal for the temporary employment of younger clergy in service abroad as likely to lead to the great benefit of the Church at home, of the Church in the colonies, and of the Church at large.

Resolution 52
That the Conference requests the bishops of the Church of England to grant the same privilege to clergymen temporarily serving in any of the missionary jurisdictions of the United States, with the consent of their diocesan, which they accord to clergymen serving in the colonies.

Resolution 53
That it is the duty of Church people in England to give aid to education in the colonies, whether generally or in the training for the ministry and for the work of teaching:
(a) in the establishment and strengthening of Church schools and colleges;
(b) in the establishment of studentships in England and in the colonies tenable by men living in the colonies, and under preparation for colonial Church work.

Resolution 54
That the endowment of new sees wherever needed, and the augmentation of the endowment of existing sees wherever inadequate, deserve the attention and support of the Church at home.

Resolution 55
That, in the judgement of this Conference, it is the bounden duty of those who derive income from colonial property or securities to contribute to the support of the Church's work in the colonies.

Resolution 56
That while the principle of gradual withdrawal of home aid to the Church in the colonies, according to its growth, is sound policy, the greatest circumspection should be used, and the special circumstances of each case most carefully examined before aid is withdrawn from even long-established dioceses.

Resolution 57
That this Conference desires to draw renewed attention to the recommendation of the Committee of the Lambeth Conference, 1888, on the subject of Emigrants, and recommends that every care should be taken, by home teaching, by commendatory letters, and by correspondence between the home dioceses and the dioceses to which emigrants go, to prevent them from drifting from the Church of their fathers when they leave their old homes.

Resolution 58
That this Conference desires that every care should be taken by the Church at home to impress upon emigrants the duty of helping to provide for the maintenance of the Church in the country to which they emigrate.

Resolution 59
That it is the duty of the Church to aid in providing for the moral and spiritual needs of our seamen of the mercantile service, who in vast numbers visit colonial ports, by means of Sailors' Homes and like institutions, and by ministrations of clergy specially set apart for this work.

Resolution 60
That it is the duty of the Church to give all possible assistance to the bishops and clergy of the colonies in their endeavour to protect native races from the introduction among them of demoralising influences and from every form of injustice or oppression, inasmuch as these, wherever found, are a discredit to Christian civilisation and a hindrance to the spread of the Gospel of Christ our Lord.

Resolution 61
That this Conference commends to the consideration of the duly

constituted authorities of the several branches of the Anglican Communion, the Report of the Committee on Degrees in Divinity with a view to their taking such steps as to them may seem fit, to meet the need of encouraging, especially among the clergy, the study of theology; and that the Archbishop of Canterbury be requested to consider the recommendations contained in the Report, with a view to action in the directions indicated, if His Grace should think such action desirable.

Resolution 62
That this Conference is of opinion that, failing any consent on the part of existing authorities to grant degrees or certificates in divinity without requiring residence, and under suitable conditions, to residents in the colonies and elsewhere, it is desirable that a board of examinations in divinity, under the archbishops and bishops of the Anglican Communion, should be established, with power to hold local examinations, and confer titles and grant certificates for proficiency in theological study.

Resolution 63
Several causes have combined to create a desire for information on the history of the Anglican Church, especially in the early and mediaeval times, but, while recognising with thankfulness the interest now shown in the history of the Church, we think it necessary to call attention to the inadequate and misleading character of the teaching on this point incidentally contained in some of the 'historical readers' which are put into the hands of the young. We recommend that the bishops in all dioceses should inquire into the nature of the books used, and should take steps to effect improvements; and that manuals written in a non-controversial spirit should be prepared to enable teachers to give correctly the oral explanation of the elementary readers.

1908

Resolution 1
The Conference commends to Christian people and to all seekers after truth the Report of the Committee on The Faith and Modern Thought, as a faithful attempt to show how that claim of our Lord Jesus Christ, which the Church is set to present to each generation, may, under the characteristic conditions of our time, best command allegiance.

Resolution 2
The Conference, in view of tendencies widely shown in the writings of the present day, hereby places on record its conviction that the historical facts stated in the Creeds are an essential part of the faith of the Church.

Resolution 3
Whereas our Lord Jesus Christ and his Apostles made it of first importance that the Church's ministers should be men of spiritual character and power, full of faith and of the Holy Ghost; and whereas our Lord has taught us to pray to the Lord of the harvest that he will send forth labourers into his harvest; this Conference desires to emphasise the need of more earnest prayer on the part of the Church generally, especially at the Ember seasons, that God would call and send forth such men to the work of the ministry.

Resolution 4
Whereas, in view of the serious decline in the number of candidates for Holy Orders, it is clear that some do not recognise that call and others are either unwilling or unable to offer themselves for the ministry, we recommend that Christian parents be urged to encourage signs of vocation in their sons, and to count it a privilege to dedicate them for the ministry, and parish priests and teachers in schools and universities to foster such vocations.

Resolution 5
Inasmuch as there are many young men who appear to have a vocation for the ministry and to be hindered from realising it only by lack of means to provide their training, this Conference urges that an ordination candidates fund and committee, or some similar organisation, should form part of the normal equipment of the Church, to assist bishops in discovering such men and enabling them to respond to their call; and that all churchmen should be taught to regard it as their duty to contribute to this object.

Resolution 6
So far from the standard for ordination being lowered to meet the existing deficiency in the number of candidates, the time has now come when, in view of the development of education and of the increased opportunities afforded for university training, a serious effort should be made to secure that candidates for Holy Orders should normally be graduates of some recognised university.

Resolution 7
While rules must of necessity vary to suit the varying conditions in different parts of the world, the principle ought everywhere to be maintained that, in addition to general education, all candidates should be required to receive special theological and practical training under some recognised supervision.

Resolution 8
It is of the greatest importance that the conscience of the Church at large should be awakened as to its primary responsibility for providing for the training, maintenance, and superannuation of the clergy; and we recommend that united action to this end should be taken, where possible, by the provinces or national Churches of our Communion.

Resolution 9
Since it is generally acknowledged that the system of encouraging men to work abroad for a period of three or five years has proved successful, it should be continued and carried out more thoroughly and systematically, and a greater reciprocity of service might be established to the benefit of all concerned.

Resolution 10
In view of the embarrassment arising from the lack of uniform usage regulating the transfer of clergymen from one diocese to another, it is necessary that none should be received into a diocese or missionary jurisdiction of the Anglican Communion until the bishop of the diocese into which he goes has received concerning him, in addition to whatever other letters testimonial may be required, a direct communication or a letter of transfer from the bishop of the diocese from which he comes.

Resolution 11
In the judgement of the Conference it is our duty as Christians to make it clear to the world that purely secular systems of education are educationally as well as morally unsound, since they fail to co-ordinate the training of the whole nature of the child, and necessarily leave many children deficient in a most important factor for that formation of character which is the principal aim of education.

Resolution 12
It is our duty as Christians to maintain that the true end of Bible teaching is a sound and definite Christian faith, realising itself in a holy life of obedience and love, and of fellowship in the Church of Christ

through the sanctifying grace of the Holy Ghost; and no teaching can be regarded as adequate religious teaching which limits itself to historical information and moral culture.

Resolution 13
It is our duty as Christians to be alert to use in all schools every opportunity which the state affords us for training our children in the faith of their parents, and to obtain adequate opportunities for such teaching in countries where they do not already exist.

Resolution 14
There is urgent need to strengthen our Sunday school system, and the Archbishop of Canterbury is respectfully requested to appoint a committee to report to him on the best methods of improving Sunday school instruction, and on the right relations between Sunday schools and the various systems of catechising in church.

Resolution 15
It is of vital importance that the Church should establish and maintain secondary schools, wherever they are needed, for children of the English-speaking race in all parts of the Anglican Communion; and the Conference earnestly supports the plea which reaches it for the establishment of such schools.

Resolution 16
The Conference draws attention to the pressing need of the services of men and women who will consecrate their lives to teaching as a call from the great Head of the Church.

Resolution 17
The religious training of teachers should be regarded as a primary duty of the Church, especially in view of the right use to be made of the light thrown on the Bible by modern research; and teachers should be encouraged in all their efforts to associate themselves for the promotion of their spiritual life.

Resolution 18
The Church should endeavour to promote and cultivate the spiritual life of the students in secondary schools and universities, and should show active sympathy with all wisely directed efforts which have this end in view.

Resolution 19
The Conference desires to lay special stress on the duty of parents in

all conditions of social life to take personal part in the religious instruction of their own children, and to show active interest in the religious instruction which the children receive at school.

Resolution 20
All races and peoples, whatever their language or conditions, must be welded into one Body, and the organisation of different races living side by side into separate or independent Churches, on the basis of race or colour, is inconsistent with the vital and essential principle of the unity of Christ's Church.

Resolution 21
Every effort should be made to train native churches and congregations in self-support and self-government; and in view of the great importance of the establishment of a native episcopate in all countries where the Church is planted, this Conference urges the necessity of providing an advanced theological and practical training for the ablest of the native clergy in the mission field.

Resolution 22
This Conference reaffirms Resolution 24 of the Conference of 1897 and further resolves that, though it may be desirable to recognise, in some cases and under certain special circumstances, the episcopal care of a bishop for his own countrymen within the jurisdiction of another bishop of the Anglican Communion, yet the principle of one bishop for one area is the ideal to be aimed at as the best means of securing the unity of all races and nations in the Holy Catholic Church.

Resolution 23
The Conference commends to the consideration of the Church the suggestions of the Committee on Foreign Missions, contained in their Report, for correlation and co-operation between missions of the Anglican Communion and those of other Christian bodies.

Resolution 24
While the educative value of the Book of Common Prayer and the importance of retaining it as a bond of union and standard of devotion should be fully recognised, every effort should be made, under due authority, to render the forms of public worship more intelligible to uneducated congregations and better suited to the widely diverse needs of the various races within the Anglican Communion.

Resolution 25
National and local Churches are at liberty to adopt native forms of marriage and consecrate them to a Christian use, provided that:
    (a) the form used explicitly states that the marriage is life-long and exclusive;
    (b) the form is free from all heathen and idolatrous taint;
    (c) provision is made for the due registration of the marriage, and for other formalities according to the law of the land.

Resolution 26
This Conference also desires to express its deep sense of the missionary value of the recent Pan-Anglican Congress; and commends to the careful study of the whole Anglican Communion the solemn facts of duty, opportunity, and responsibility, in regard to the non-Christian world, which that Congress elicited and affirmed.

Resolution 27
In any revision of the Book of Common Prayer which may hereafter be undertaken by competent authority the following principles should be held in view:
    (a) the adaptation of rubrics in a large number of cases to present customs as generally accepted;
    (b) the omission of parts of the services to obviate repetition or redundancy;
    (c) the framing of additions to the present services in the way of enrichment;
    (d) the fuller provision of alternatives in our forms of public worship;
    (e) the provision for greater elasticity in public worship;
    (f) the change of words obscure or commonly misunderstood;
    (g) the revision of the Calendar and Tables prefixed to the Book of Common Prayer.

Resolution 28
The Conference requests the Archbishop of Canterbury to take counsel with such persons as he may see fit to consult, with a view to the preparation of a Book containing special forms of service, which might be authorised by particular bishops for use in their dioceses, so far as they may consider it possible and desirable.

Resolution 29
Without in any sense precluding the further consideration by the several Churches of our Communion of the mode of dealing with the Quicunque Vult, it is desirable that a new translation be made, based upon

the best Latin text; and the Archbishop of Canterbury is requested to take such steps as are necessary for providing such a translation.

Resolution 30
The Conference, having had under consideration the liturgical use of the Quicunque Vult, expresses its opinion that, inasmuch as the use or disuse of this hymn is not a term of communion, the several Churches of the Anglican Communion may rightly decide for themselves what in their varying circumstances is desirable; but the Conference urges that, if any change of rule or usage is made, full regard should be had to the maintenance of the Catholic faith in its integrity, to the commendation of that faith to the minds of men, and to the relief of disquieted consciences.

Resolution 31
For reasons given in the Report on the Administration of Holy Communion, as well as for other reasons, the Conference is convinced that it is not desirable to make, on the ground of alarm as to the possible risk of infection, any change in the manner of administering the Holy Communion. Special cases involving exceptional risk should be referred to the bishop and dealt with according to his direction.

Resolution 32
The Conference declares that the only elements which the Church can sanction for use in the administration of the Holy Communion are bread and wine, according to the institution of our Lord. While declaring this, the Conference does not pronounce judgement upon such a course as in cases of absolute necessity may be in particular regions adopted by those bishops on whom falls the responsibility of dealing with an imperative need. But it would insist that any such divergence from the practice of the Church, if it is to be justified by actual necessity, ought to cease as soon as the conditions of necessity are over.

Resolution 33
With regard to ministries of healing, this Conference, confident that God has infinite blessings and powers in store for those who seek them by prayer, communion, and strong endeavour, and conscious that the clergy and laity of the Church have too often failed to turn to God with such complete trust as will draw those powers into full service, desires solemnly to affirm that the strongest and most immediate call to the Church is to the deepening and renewal of her spiritual life; and to urge upon the clergy of the Church so to set forth to the people Christ, the incarnate Son of God, and the truth of his abiding presence in the Church and in Christian souls by the Holy Spirit, that all

may realise and lay hold of the power of the indwelling Spirit to sanctify both soul and body, and thus, through a harmony of man's will with God's will, to gain a fuller control over temptation, pain, and disease, whether for themselves or others, with a firmer serenity and a more confident hope.

Resolution 34

With a view to resisting dangerous tendencies in contemporary thought, the Conference urges the clergy in their dealings with the sick to teach as clearly as possible the privilege of those who are called, through sickness and pain, to enter especially into the fellowship of Christ's sufferings and to follow the example of his patience.

Resolution 35

The Conference recommends the provision for use in pastoral visitation of some additional prayers for the restoration of health more hopeful and direct than those contained in the present Office for the Visitation of the Sick, and refers this recommendation to the committee to be appointed by the President under the Resolution on the subject of Prayer Book enrichment.

Resolution 36

The Conference, having regard to the uncertainty which exists as to the permanence of the practice commended by St James (5.14), and having regard to the history of the practice which professes to be based upon that commendation, does not recommend the sanctioning of the anointing of the sick as a rite of the Church.

It does not, however, advise the prohibition of all anointing, if anointing be earnestly desired by the sick person. In all such cases the parish priest should seek the counsel of the bishop of the diocese. Care must be taken that no return be made to the later custom of anointing as a preparation for death.

Resolution 37

The growing prevalence of disregard of the sanctity of marriage calls for the active and determined co-operation of all right-thinking and clean-living men and women, in all ranks of life, in defence of the family life and the social order, which rest upon the sanctity of the marriage tie.

Resolution 38

The influence of all good women in all ranks of life should be specially applied to the remedying of the terrible evils which have grown up from the creation of facilities for divorce.

Resolution 39
This Conference reaffirms the Resolution of the Conference of 1888 as follows:
(a) That, inasmuch as our Lord's words expressly forbid divorce, except in the case of fornication or adultery, the Christian Church cannot recognise divorce in any other than the excepted case, or give any sanction to the marriage of any person who has been divorced contrary to this law, during the life of the other party.
(b) That under no circumstances ought the guilty party, in the case of a divorce for fornication or adultery, to be regarded, during the lifetime of the innocent party, as a fit recipient of the blessing of the Church on marriage.
(c) That, recognising the fact that there always has been a difference of opinion in the Church on the question whether our Lord meant to forbid marriage to the innocent party in a divorce for adultery, the Conference recommends that the clergy should not be instructed to refuse the sacraments or other privileges of the Church to those who, under civil sanction, are thus married.

Resolution 40
When an innocent person has, by means of a court of law, divorced a spouse for adultery, and desires to enter into another contract of marriage, it is undesirable that such a contract should receive the blessing of the Church.
Voting: For 87; Against 84.

Resolution 41
The Conference regards with alarm the growing practice of the artificial restriction of the family, and earnestly calls upon all Christian people to discountenance the use of all artificial means of restriction as demoralising to character and hostile to national welfare.

Resolution 42
The Conference affirms that deliberate tampering with nascent life is repugnant to Christian morality.

Resolution 43
The Conference expresses most cordial appreciation of the services rendered by those medical men who have borne courageous testimony against the injurious practices spoken of, and appeals with confidence to them and to their medical colleagues to co-operate in creating and maintaining a wholesome public opinion on behalf of the reverent use of the married state.

Resolution 44
The Conference recognises the ideals of brotherhood which underlie the democratic movement of this century; and, remembering our Master's example in proclaiming the inestimable value of every human being in the sight of God, calls upon the Church to show sympathy with the movement, in so far as it strives to procure just treatment for all and a real opportunity of living a true human life, and by its sympathy to commend to the movement the spirit of our Lord Jesus Christ, in whom all the hopes of human society are bound up.

Resolution 45
The social mission and social principles of Christianity should be given a more prominent place in the study and teaching of the Church, both for the clergy and the laity.

Resolution 46
The ministry of the laity requires to be more widely recognised, side by side with the ministry of the clergy, in the work, the administration, and the discipline of the Church.

Resolution 47
A committee or organisation for social service should be part of the equipment of every diocese, and, as far as practicable, of every parish.

Resolution 48
The Church should teach that the Christian who is an owner of property should recognise the governing principle that, like all our gifts, our powers, and our time, property is a trust held for the benefit of the community, and its right use should be insisted upon as a religious duty.

Resolution 49
The Conference urges upon members of the Church practical recognition of the moral responsibility involved in their investments. This moral responsibility extends to:
(a) the character and general social effect of any business or enterprise in which their money is invested;
(b) the treatment of the persons employed in that business or enterprise;
(c) the due observance of the requirements of the law relating thereto;
(d) the payment of a just wage to those who are employed therein.

Resolution 50
The Conference holds that it is the duty of the Church to press upon governments the wrong of sanctioning for the sake of revenue any forms of trade which involve the degradation or hinder the moral and physical progress of the races and peoples under their rule or influence.

Resolution 51
The Conference, regarding the non-medicinal use of opium as a grave physical and moral evil, welcomes all well-considered efforts to abate such use, particularly those of the government and people of China, and also the proposal of the government of the United States to arrange an International Commission on Opium. It thankfully recognises the progressive reduction by the Indian government of the area of poppy cultivation, but still appeals for all possible insistence on the affirmation of the House of Commons that the Indian opium traffic with China is morally indefensible. It urges a stringent dealing with the opium vice in British settlements, along with due precautions against the introduction of narcotic substitutes for opium. Finally, it calls upon all Christian people to pray for the effectual repression of the opium evil.

Resolution 52
The Conference, while frankly acknowledging the moral gains sometimes won by war, rejoices in the growth of higher ethical perceptions which is evidenced by the increasing willingness to settle difficulties among nations by peaceful methods; it records, therefore, its deep appreciation of the services rendered by the conferences at The Hague, its thankfulness for the practical work achieved, and for the principles of international responsibility acknowledged by the delegates; and, finally, realising the dangers inseparable from national and commercial progress, it urges earnestly upon all Christian peoples the duty of allaying race prejudice, of reducing by peaceful arrangements the conflict of trade interests, and of promoting among all races the spirit of brotherly co-operation for the good of all mankind.

Resolution 53
The Conference desires to call attention to the evidence supplied from every part of Christendom as to the grave perils arising from the increasing disregard of the religious duties and privileges which are attached to a due observance, both on the social and spiritual side, of the Christian Sunday. In consequence of this, the Conference records its solemn conviction that strong and co-ordinated action is urgently demanded, with a view to educating the public conscience and forming

a higher sense of individual responsibility alike on the religious and humanitarian aspects of the question.

The Conference further, in pursuance of the Resolutions passed upon this subject in former Conferences, calls upon Christian people to promote by all means in their power the better observance of the Lord's Day, both on land and sea, for the worship of God and for the spiritual, mental, and physical health of man.

Resolution 54
The existing Central Consultative Body shall be reconstructed on representative lines as follows:

(a) It shall consist of the Archbishop of Canterbury (ex officio) and of representative bishops appointed as follows: Province of Canterbury 2, Province of York 1, the Church of Ireland 1, the Episcopal Church in Scotland 1, the Protestant Episcopal Church in the United States of America 4, the Church of England in Canada 1, the Church of England in the Dioceses of Australia and Tasmania 1, the Church of the Province of New Zealand 1, the Province of the West Indies 1, the Church of the Province of South Africa 1, the Province of India and Ceylon 1, the Dioceses of China and Corea and the Church of Japan 1, the missionary and other extra-provincial bishops under the jurisdiction of the Archbishop of Canterbury 1. Total 18.

(b) The foregoing scheme of representation shall be open to revision from time to time by the Lambeth Conference.

(c) The mode of appointing these representative bishops shall be left to the Churches that appoint. A representative bishop may be appointed for one year or for any number of years, and need not be a member of the body which appoints him. Each member shall retain office until the election of his successor has been duly notified to the Archbishop of Canterbury.

(d) For the purpose of appointing the bishop who is to represent the body of missionary and other extra-provincial bishops under the jurisdiction of the Archbishop of Canterbury, each of those bishops shall be requested by the Archbishop of Canterbury to nominate a bishop to him. The list of bishops so nominated shall be then sent to all the bishops entitled to vote, and each of them shall, if he thinks fit to vote, send to the Archbishop the name of the one in that list for whom he votes. The largest number of votes shall carry the election.

Resolution 55
The Central Consultative Body shall be prepared to receive consultative communications from any bishop, but shall, in considering them,

have careful regard to any limitations upon such references which may be imposed by provincial regulation.

Resolution 56
The Consultative Body shall not at any meeting come to a decision on any subject not named in the notice summoning the meeting.

Resolution 57
That the Archbishop of Canterbury be requested to transmit to every diocesan bishop in the Anglican Communion a copy of the Final Report of the Committee appointed by the Conference of 1897 to consider the Relation of Religious Communities within the Church to the Episcopate, accompanying it with a request that it may be duly considered, and that each province of the Anglican Communion will, if it consents to do so, send to him, through its metropolitan, before 31 July 1910, a statement of the judgement formed in that province upon the subject dealt with in the Report.

Resolution 58
This Conference reaffirms the Resolution of the Conference of 1897 that 'every opportunity should be taken to emphasise the divine purpose of visible unity amongst Christians as a fact of revelation.' It desires further to affirm that in all partial projects of reunion and intercommunion the final attainment of the divine purpose should be kept in view as our object; and that care should be taken to do what will advance the reunion of the whole of Christendom, and to abstain from doing anything that will retard or prevent it.

Resolution 59
The Conference recognises with thankfulness the manifold signs of the increase of the desire for unity among all Christian bodies; and, with a deep sense of the call to follow the manifest guiding of the Holy Spirit, solemnly urges the duty of special intercession for the unity of the Church, in accordance with our Lord's own prayer.

Resolution 60
This Conference resolves that a letter of greeting be sent from the Lambeth Conference to the National Council of the Russian Church about to assemble, and that the letter should be conveyed to the Council by two or more bishops if possible; and that His Grace the Archbishop of Canterbury be respectfully requested to cause such a letter to be written, and to sign it on behalf of the Conference, and to nominate bishops to convey it to the Council.

Resolution 61
The Conference respectfully requests the Archbishop of Canterbury to appoint a committee to take cognisance of all that concerns our relations with the Churches of the Orthodox East, and desires that this committee should be on a permanent basis.

Resolution 62
The Conference is of opinion that it should be the recognised practice of the Churches of our Communion:

(1) at all times to baptize the children of members of any Church of the Orthodox Eastern Communion in cases of emergency, provided that there is a clear understanding that baptism should not be again administered to those so baptized;

(2) at all times to admit members of any Church of the Orthodox Eastern Communion to communicate in our churches, when they are deprived of the ministrations of a priest of their own Communion, provided that

(a) they are at that time admissible to communion in their own Churches, and

(b) are not under any disqualification so far as our own rules of discipline are concerned.

Resolution 63
The Conference would welcome any steps that might be taken to ascertain the precise doctrinal position of the ancient separate Churches of the East with a view to possible intercommunion, and would suggest to the Archbishop of Canterbury the appointment of commissions to examine the doctrinal position of particular Churches, and (for example) to prepare some carefully framed statement of the faith as to our Lord's person, in the simplest possible terms, which should be submitted to each of such Churches, where feasible, in order to ascertain whether it represents their belief with substantial accuracy. The conclusions of such commissions should in our opinion be submitted to the metropolitans or presiding bishops of all the Churches of the Anglican Communion.

Resolution 64
In the event of doctrinal agreement being reached with such separate Churches, the Conference is of opinion that it would be right (1) for any Church of the Anglican Communion to admit individual communicant members of those Churches to communicate with us when they are deprived of this means of grace through isolation, and conversely, for our communicants to seek the same privileges in similar circumstances; (2) for the Churches of the Anglican Communion to

permit our communicants to communicate on special occasions with these Churches, even when not deprived of this means of grace through isolation, and conversely, that their communicants should be allowed the same privileges in similar circumstances.

Resolution 65
We consider that any more formal and complete compact between us and any such Church, seeing that it might affect our relations with certain other Churches, should not take place without previous communication with any other Church which might be affected thereby.

Resolution 66
The Conference is of opinion that it is of the greatest importance that our representatives abroad, both clerical and lay, whilst holding firmly to our own position, should show all Christian courtesy towards the Churches of the lands in which they reside and towards their ecclesiastical authorities; and that the chaplains to be selected for work on the continent of Europe and elsewhere should be instructed to show such courtesy.

Resolution 67
We desire earnestly to warn members of our Communion against contracting marriages with Roman Catholics under the conditions imposed by modern Roman canon law, especially as these conditions involve the performance of the marriage ceremony without any prayer or invocation of the divine blessing, and also a promise to have their children brought up in a religious system which they cannot themselves accept.

Resolution 68
The Conference desires to maintain and strengthen the friendly relations which already exist between the Churches of the Anglican Communion and the ancient Church of Holland and the Old Catholic Churches, especially in Germany, Switzerland, and Austria.

Resolution 69
With a view to the avoidance of further ecclesiastical confusion, the Conference would earnestly deprecate the setting up of a new organised body in regions where a Church with apostolic ministry and Catholic doctrine offers religious privileges without the imposition of uncatholic terms of communion, more especially in cases where no difference of language or nationality exists; and, in view of the friendly relations referred to in the previous Resolution, it would respectfully request the Archbishop of Canterbury, if he thinks fit, to bring this Resolution to the notice of the Old Catholic bishops.

Resolution 70

For the sake of unity, and as a particular expression of brotherly affection, we recommend that any official request of the Unitas Fratrum for the participation of Anglican bishops in the consecration of bishops of the Unitas should be accepted, provided that:

(i) such Anglican bishops should not be less than three in number, and should participate both in the saying of the prayers of consecration and in the laying-on of hands, and that the rite itself is judged to be sufficient by the bishops of the Church of our Communion to which the invited bishops belong;

(ii) the synods of the Unitas (a) are able to give sufficient assurance of doctrinal agreement with ourselves in all essentials (as we believe that they will be willing and able to do); and (b) are willing to explain its position as that of a religious community or missionary body in close alliance with the Anglican Communion; and (c) are willing to accord a due recognition to the position of our bishops within Anglican dioceses and jurisdictions; and (d) are willing to adopt a rule as to the administration of confirmation more akin to our own.

Resolution 71

After the conditions prescribed in the preceding Resolution have been complied with, and a bishop has been consecrated in accordance with them, corresponding invitations from any bishop of the Unitas Fratrum to an Anglican bishop and his presbyters to participate in the ordination of a Moravian presbyter should be accepted, provided that the Anglican bishop should participate both in the saying of the prayers of ordination and in the laying-on of hands, and that the rite itself is judged to be sufficient by the bishops of the Church of our Communion to which the invited bishop belongs.

Resolution 72

Any bishop or presbyter so consecrated or ordained should be free to minister in the Anglican Communion with due episcopal licence; and, in the event of the above proposals—i.e. Resolutions 1 and 2*—being accepted and acted upon by the synods of the Unitas, during the period of transition some permission to preach in our churches might on special occasions be extended to Moravian ministers by bishops of our Communion.

* [Conference Resolutions 70 and 71; the numbers in the text of Resolution 72 refer to the draft Resolutions as proposed by the Committee concerned.]

Resolution 73

We recommend that the Archbishop of Canterbury be respectfully requested to name a committee to communicate, as need arises, with representatives of the Unitas, and also to direct that the decisions of the present Conference be communicated to the Secretarius Unitatis.

Resolution 74
This Conference heartily thanks the Archbishop of Upsala for his letter of friendly greeting, and for sending his honoured colleague, the Bishop of Kalmar, to confer with its members on the question of the establishment of an alliance of some sort between the Swedish and Anglican Churches. The Conference respectfully desires the Archbishop of Canterbury to appoint a commission to correspond further with the Swedish Church through the Archbishop of Upsala on the possibility and conditions of such an alliance.

Resolution 75
The Conference receives with thankfulness and hope the Report of its Committee on Reunion and Intercommunion, and is of opinion that, in the welcome event of any project of reunion between any Church of the Anglican Communion and any Presbyterian or other non-episcopal Church, which, while preserving the faith in its integrity and purity, has also exhibited care as to the form and intention of ordination to the ministry, reaching the stage of responsible official negotiation, it might be possible to make an approach to reunion on the basis of consecrations to the episcopate on lines suggested by such precedents as those of 1610.* Further, in the opinion of the Conference, it might be possible to authorise arrangements (for the period of transition towards full union on the basis of episcopal ordination) which would respect the convictions of those who had not received episcopal orders, without involving any surrender on our part of the principles of Church order laid down in the Preface to the Ordinal attached to the Book of Common Prayer.

* [When the episcopate was restored temporarily in the Church of Scotland through the agency of three bishops consecrated in England.]

Resolution 76
Every opportunity should be welcomed of co-operation between members of different Communions in all matters pertaining to the social and moral welfare of the people.

Resolution 77
The members of the Anglican Communion should take pains to study the doctrines and position of those who are separated from it and to promote a cordial mutual understanding; and, as a means towards this end, the Conference suggests that private meetings of ministers

and laymen of different Christian bodies for common study, discussion, and prayer should be frequently held in convenient centres.

Resolution 78
The constituted authorities of the various Churches of the Anglican Communion should, as opportunity offers, arrange conferences with representatives of other Christian Churches, and meetings for common acknowledgment of the sins of division, and for intercession for the growth of unity.

1920

CHRISTIANITY AND INTERNATIONAL RELATIONS

Resolution 1
We rejoice that in these times of peril God is giving to his Church a fresh vision of his purpose to establish a Kingdom in which all the nations of the earth shall be united as one family in righteousness and peace. We hold that this can only come through the acceptance of the sovereignty of our Lord Jesus Christ and of his teaching, and through the application of the principles of brotherhood, justice, and unselfishness, to individuals and nations alike.

Resolution 2
The Conference calls upon the citizens of all nations to promote in every way the resumption of the efforts, interrupted by the war, to increase international comity and goodwill, and to secure expression for these by an increased recognition of international law and custom.

Resolution 3
The Conference, heartily endorsing the views of its Committee as to the essential Christian basis of the League of Nations, is of opinion that steps should immediately be taken, whether by co-operation or concurrent action, whereby the whole Church of Christ may be enabled with one voice to urge the principles of the League of Nations upon the peoples of the world.

Resolution 4
We hold that the peace of the world, no less than Christian principle, demands the admission of Germany and other nations into the League of Nations at the earliest moment which the conditions render possible.

Resolution 5
The Conference commends the Report of its Committee on International Relations to the careful consideration of the Churches of the Anglican Communion, both in their assemblies and in other ways, and urges upon all Church members the importance of supporting the League of Nations Union.

Resolution 6
It is the duty of all supporters of the League of Nations to set their face against injustice to the indigenous or native races, and particularly in regard to such matters as the tenure of land, forced labour, and the trade in intoxicating liquors, and also the morphia traffic in China and other abuses.

Resolution 7
The Conference records its protest against the colour prejudice among the different races of the world, which not only hinders intercourse, but gravely imperils the peace of the future.

Resolution 8
The Conference, believing that nations no less than individuals are members one of another, expresses its grave concern at the evidence as to the disease and distress from which the populations in large tracts of Europe and Asia are suffering. It therefore calls upon all Christian men and women to support by every means in their power the action which is being taken, both by governments and by voluntary associations, for the relief of this suffering.

REUNION OF CHRISTENDOM

Resolution 9
The Conference adopts and sends forth the following Appeal to all Christian people:

An Appeal To All Christian People
from the Bishops Assembled in the Lambeth Conference of 1920

We, Archbishops, Bishops Metropolitan, and other Bishops of the Holy Catholic Church in full communion with the Church of England, in Conference assembled, realising the responsibility which rests upon us at this time, and sensible of the sympathy and the prayers of many, both within and without our own Communion, make this appeal to all Christian people.

We acknowledge all those who believe in our Lord Jesus Christ, and have been baptized into the name of the Holy Trinity, as sharing with us membership in the universal Church of Christ which is his Body. We believe that the Holy Spirit has called us in a very solemn and special manner to associate ourselves in penitence and prayer with all those who deplore the divisions of Christian people, and are inspired by the vision and hope of a visible unity of the whole Church.

I   We believe that God wills fellowship. By God's own act this fellowship was made in and through Jesus Christ, and its life is in his Spirit. We believe that it is God's purpose to manifest this fellowship, so far as this world is concerned, in an outward, visible, and united society, holding one faith, having its own recognised officers, using God-given means of grace, and inspiring all its members to the world-wide service of the Kingdom of God. This is what we mean by the Catholic Church.

II   This united fellowship is not visible in the world today. On the one hand there are other ancient episcopal Communions in East and West, to whom ours is bound by many ties of common faith and tradition. On the other hand there are the great non-episcopal Communions, standing for rich elements of truth, liberty and life which might otherwise have been obscured or neglected. With them we are closely linked by many affinities, racial, historical and spiritual. We cherish the earnest hope that all these Communions, and our own, may be led by the Spirit into the unity of the faith and of the knowledge of the Son of God. But in fact we are all organised in different groups, each one keeping to itself gifts that rightly belong to the whole fellowship, and tending to live its own life apart from the rest.

III   The causes of division lie deep in the past, and are by no means simple or wholly blameworthy. Yet none can doubt that self-will, ambition, and lack of charity among Christians have been principal factors in the mingled process, and that these, together with blindness to the sin of disunion, are still mainly responsible for the breaches of Christendom. We acknowledge this condition of broken fellowship to be contrary to God's will, and we desire frankly to confess our share in the guilt of thus crippling the Body of Christ and hindering the activity of his Spirit.

IV   The times call us to a new outlook and new measures. The faith cannot be adequately apprehended and the battle of the Kingdom cannot be worthily fought while the body is divided, and is thus unable to grow up into the fullness of the life of Christ. The time has come, we believe, for all the separated groups of Christians to agree in forgetting the things which are behind and reaching out towards the goal of a reunited Catholic Church. The removal of the barriers which have arisen between them will only be brought about by a new comradeship of those whose faces are definitely set this way.

The vision which rises before us is that of a Church, genuinely

Catholic, loyal to all truth, and gathering into its fellowship all 'who profess and call themselves Christians', within whose visible unity all the treasures of faith and order, bequeathed as a heritage by the past to the present, shall be possessed in common, and made serviceable to the whole Body of Christ. Within this unity Christian Communions now separated from one another would retain much that has long been distinctive in their methods of worship and service. It is through a rich diversity of life and devotion that the unity of the whole fellowship will be fulfilled.

V   This means an adventure of goodwill and still more of faith, for nothing less is required than a new discovery of the creative resources of God. To this adventure we are convinced that God is now calling all the members of his Church.

VI   We believe that the visible unity of the Church will be found to involve the wholehearted acceptance of:

The Holy Scriptures, as the record of God's revelation of himself to man, and as being the rule and ultimate standard of faith; and the Creed commonly called Nicene, as the sufficient statement of the Christian faith, and either it or the Apostles' Creed as the baptismal confession of belief;

the divinely instituted sacraments of Baptism and the Holy Communion, as expressing for all the corporate life of the whole fellowship in and with Christ;

a ministry acknowledged by every part of the Church as possessing not only the inward call of the Spirit, but also the commission of Christ and the authority of the whole body.

VII   May we not reasonably claim that the episcopate is the one means of providing such a ministry? It is not that we call in question for a moment the spiritual reality of the ministries of those Communions which do not possess the episcopate. On the contrary we thankfully acknowledge that these ministries have been manifestly blessed and owned by the Holy Spirit as effective means of grace. But we submit that considerations alike of history and of present experience justify the claim which we make on behalf of the episcopate. Moreover, we would urge that it is now and will prove to be in the future the best instrument for maintaining the unity and continuity of the Church. But we greatly desire that the office of a bishop should be everywhere exercised in a representative and constitutional manner, and more truly express all that ought to be involved for the life of the Christian family in the title of Father-in-God. Nay more, we eagerly look forward to the day when through its acceptance in a united Church we may all share in that grace which is pledged to the members of the whole body in the apostolic rite of the laying-on of hands, and in the joy and fellowship of a eucharist in which as one family we may together, without any doubtfulness of mind, offer to the one Lord our worship and service.

VIII   We believe that for all, the truly equitable approach to union is by way of mutual deference to one another's consciences. To this end, we who send forth this appeal would say that if the authorities of other Communions should so desire, we are persuaded that, terms of union having been otherwise satisfactorily adjusted, bishops and clergy of our Communion would willingly accept from these authorities a form of commission or recognition which would commend our ministry to their congregations, as having its place in the one family life. It is not in our power to know how far this suggestion may be acceptable to those to whom we offer it. We can only say that we offer it in all sincerity as a token of our longing that all ministries of grace, theirs and ours, shall be available for the service of our Lord in a united Church.

It is our hope that the same motive would lead ministers who have not received it to accept a commission through episcopal ordination, as obtaining for them a ministry throughout the whole fellowship.

In so acting no one of us could possibly be taken to repudiate his past ministry. God forbid that any man should repudiate a past experience rich in spiritual blessings for himself and others. Nor would any of us be dishonouring the Holy Spirit of God, whose call led us all to our several ministries, and whose power enabled us to perform them. We shall be publicly and formally seeking additional recognition of a new call to wider service in a reunited Church, and imploring for ourselves God's grace and strength to fulfil the same.

IX   The spiritual leadership of the Catholic Church in days to come, for which the world is manifestly waiting, depends upon the readiness with which each group is prepared to make sacrifices for the sake of a common fellowship, a common ministry, and a common service to the world.

We place this ideal first and foremost before ourselves and our own people. We call upon them to make the effort to meet the demands of a new age with a new outloook. To all other Christian people whom our words may reach we make the same appeal. We do not ask that any one Communion should consent to be absorbed in another. We do ask that all should unite in a new and great endeavour to recover and to manifest to the world the unity of the Body of Christ for which he prayed.

Resolution 10
The Conference recommends to the authorities of the Churches of the Anglican Communion that they should, in such ways and at such times as they think best, formally invite the authorities of other

Churches within their areas to confer with them concerning the possibility of taking definite steps to co-operate in a common endeavour, on the lines set forth in the above Appeal, to restore the unity of the Church of Christ.

Resolution 11
The Conference recognises that the task of effecting union with other Christian Communions must be undertaken by the various national, regional, or provincial authorities of the Churches within the Anglican Communion, and confidently commits to them the carrying out of this task on lines that are in general harmony with the principles underlying its Appeal and Resolutions.

Resolution 12
The Conference approves the following statements as representing the counsel which it is prepared to give to the bishops, clergy and other members of our own Communion on various subjects which bear upon the problems of reunion, provided that such counsel is not to be regarded as calling in question any canons or official declarations of any synod or House of Bishops of a national, regional, or provincial Church which has already dealt with these matters.

A   *In view of prospects and projects of reunion:*
(i) A bishop is justified in giving occasional authorisation to ministers, not episcopally ordained, who in his judgement are working towards an ideal of union such as is described in our Appeal, to preach in churches within his diocese, and to clergy of the diocese to preach in the churches of such ministers.
(ii) The bishops of the Anglican Communion will not question the action of any bishop who, in the few years between the initiation and the completion of a definite scheme of union, shall countenance the irregularity of admitting to Communion the baptized but unconfirmed communicants of the non-episcopal congregations concerned in the scheme.
(iii) The Conference gives its general approval to the suggestions contained in the Report of the Sub-Committee on Reunion with Non-Episcopal Churches in reference to the status and work of ministers who may remain after union without episcopal ordination.

B   *Believing, however, that certain lines of action might imperil both the attainment of its ideal and the unity of its own Communion, the Conference declares that:*
(i) It cannot approve of general schemes of intercommunion or exchange of pulpits.
(ii) In accordance with the principle of Church order set forth in the Preface to the Ordinal attached to the Book of Common Prayer,

it cannot approve the celebration in Anglican churches of the Holy Communion for members of the Anglican Church by ministers who have not been episcopally ordained; and that it should be regarded as the general rule of the Church that Anglican communicants should receive Holy Communion only at the hands of ministers of their own Church, or of Churches in communion therewith.

C   *In view of doubts and varieties of practice which have caused difficulties in the past, the Conference declares that*:

(i) Nothing in these Resolutions is intended to indicate that the rule of confirmation as conditioning admission to Holy Communion must necessarily apply to the case of baptized persons who seek Communion under conditions which in the bishop's judgement justify their admission thereto.

(ii) In cases in which it is impossible for the bishop's judgement to be obtained beforehand the priest should remember that he has no canonical authority to refuse Communion to any baptized person kneeling before the Lord's Table (unless he be excommunicate by name, or, in the canonical sense of the term, a cause of scandal to the faithful); and that, if a question may properly be raised as to the future admission of any such person to Holy Communion, either because he has not been confirmed or for other reasons, the priest should refer the matter to the bishop for counsel or direction.

Resolution 13

The Conference recommends that, wherever it has not already been done, councils representing all Christian Communions should be formed within such areas as may be deemed most convenient, as centres of united effort to promote the physical, moral, and social welfare of the people, and the extension of the rule of Christ among all nations and over every region of human life.

Resolution 14

It is important to the cause of reunion that every branch of the Anglican Communion should develop the constitutional government of the Church and should make a fuller use of the capacities of its members for service.

Resolution 15

The Conference urges on every branch of the Anglican Communion that it should prepare its members for taking their part in the universal fellowship of the reunited Church, by setting before them the loyalty which they owe to the universal Church, and the charity and understanding which are required of the members of so inclusive a society.

Resolution 16
We desire to express our profound thankfulness for the important movements towards unity which, during the last twelve years, have taken place in many parts of the world, and for the earnest desire for reunion which has been manifested both in our own Communion and among the Churches now separated from us. In particular, the Conference has heard with sympathetic and hopeful interest of the preliminary meeting of the proposed World Conference on Faith and Order about to be held at Geneva, and earnestly prays that its deliberations may tend towards the reunion of the Christian Church.

Resolution 17
We desire to express our deep sympathy with the Church of Russia in the terrible persecution which it has in many places suffered. We earnestly trust that in the providence of God its difficulties may speedily be removed, and that it may be enabled in renewed life and strength so to carry on its work unhindered as to further, in the life of the Russian people, whatsoever things are true and just, whatsoever things are lovely and of good report.

Resolution 18
The Conference heartily thanks the Oecumenical Patriarchate for the mission of the Metropolitan of Demotica and others to confer with its members on questions concerning the relations between the Anglican and Eastern Churches, and expresses its grateful appreciation of the great help given to its Committee by the delegation.

Resolution 19
The Conference welcomes the appointment by the Archbishop of Canterbury of an 'Eastern Churches Committee' on a permanent basis, in pursuance of Resolution 61 of the Conference of 1908; and looks forward hopefully to the work of that Committee, in conjunction with similar committees appointed in Constantinople and Athens, as helping greatly to forward the cause of reunion with the Orthodox Church.

Resolution 20
The Conference expresses its heartfelt sympathy with the Armenian, Assyrian, and Syrian Jacobite Christians in the persecutions which they have been called upon to endure, deploring with indignation the terrible massacres that have taken place among them both before and during the Great War; and earnestly prays that in the rearrangement of the political affairs of the East they may be granted a righteous government and freedom from oppression in the future.

Resolution 21
The Conference has received with satisfaction its Committee's report of the investigations that have been made during the last twelve years with regard to the present doctrinal position of the Separated Churches of the East; and, without expressing an opinion as to the past, believes that these investigations have gone far towards showing that any errors as to the incarnation of our Lord, which may at some period of their history have been attributed to them, have at any rate now passed away.

Resolution 22
The Conference repeats the proposal made by the Conference of 1908 that, when any of the Separated Churches of the East desire closer relations with us, and wish for the establishment of occasional inter-communion, and give satisfactory assurances as to their faith, such relations should at once be established.

Resolution 23
The Conference respectfully requests the Archbishop of Canterbury to take advantage of any opportunity that may arise to enter into friendly relations with these Churches, and to inform the authorities of the Orthodox Eastern Church of any steps that may be taken in the direction of intercommunion with them. Similar action should be taken with regard to informing the metropolitans of our own Communion.

Resolution 24
The Conference welcomes the Report of the Commission appointed after the last Conference entitled 'The Church of England and the Church of Sweden', and, accepting the conclusions there maintained on the succession of the bishops of the Church of Sweden and the conception of the priesthood set forth in its standards, recommends that members of that Church, qualified to receive the sacrament in their own Church, should be admitted to Holy Communion in ours. It also recommends that on suitable occasions permission should be given to Swedish ecclesiastics to give addresses in our churches.

If the authorities of any province of the Anglican Communion find local irregularities in the order or practice of the Church of Sweden outside that country, they may legitimately, within their own region, postpone any such action as is recommended in this Resolution until they are satisfied that these irregularities have been removed.

Resolution 25
We recommend further that in the event of an invitation being extended to an Anglican bishop or bishops to take part in the consecration of

a Swedish bishop, the invitation should, if possible, be accepted, subject to the approval of the metropolitan. We also recommend that, in the first instance, as an evident token of the restoration of closer relations between the two Churches, if possible more than one of our bishops should take part in the consecration.

Resolution 26
The Conference thanks the Old Catholic bishops for their explanation, in response to the letter of the Archbishop of Canterbury, of their action in consecrating the Revd A.H. Mathew to the episcopate in 1908, and repeats the desire expressed at previous Conferences to maintain and strengthen the friendly relations which exist between the Churches of the Anglican Communion and the ancient Church of Holland and the Old Catholic Churches, especially in Germany, Switzerland and Austria.

Resolution 27
We regret that on a review of all the facts we are unable to regard the so-called Old Catholic Church in Great Britain (under the late Bishop Mathew and his successors), and its extensions overseas, as a properly constituted Church, or to recognise the orders of its ministers, and we recommend that, in the event of any of its ministers desiring to join our Communion, who are in other respects duly qualified, they should be ordained *sub conditione* in accordance with the provisions suggested in the Report of our Committee.

Resolution 28
The Conference recommends that the same course be followed, as occasion may require, in the case of persons claiming to have received consecration or ordination from any *'episcopi vagantes'*, whose claims we are unable to recognise.

Resolution 29
The Conference, while welcoming the Report of the Committee appointed by the Conference of 1908 on the Unitas Fratrum or Moravians, regrets that it is unable to recommend any such action being taken as is suggested in Resolutions 70-72 of that Conference so long as the Unitas retains its practice of the administration of confirmation and the celebration of Holy Communion by deacons, but hopes that, in the event of the Unitas changing its rules in these matters, negotiations with individual provinces of the Unitas may be resumed, and believes that in this case there would be good prospect of such negotiations being brought to a satisfactory conclusion.

Resolution 30
We recommend with a view to this end that the Archbishop of Canterbury be respectfully requested to reappoint with additional members the Committee appointed at the last Conference; and we hope that, in the event of all the remaining difficulties being removed to his satisfaction, with the concurrence of the Central Consultative Body of the Lambeth Conference, the action suggested in the Resolutions of the Conference of 1908 may take place without further delay.

Resolution 31
The Conference regrets that it is unable to recommend the acceptance of the proposals of the 'Southern Synod' of the 'Reformed Episcopal Church' in England for reunion with the Church of England, and, while unable to advise the acceptance of other proposals for corporate union with the Reformed Episcopal Church, recommends that, if applications for admission into the English Church are made by individual ministers of that Communion, such applications should be sympathetically received, and the ministers, if in all respects equal to the standard and requirements of the Church of England, be ordained *sub conditione.*

MISSIONARY PROBLEMS

Resolution 32
The Conference declares its conviction that the present critical position of the world calls, as perhaps never before, for the presentation of Jesus Christ and his redemption to every race and individual; and, in view of the urgent need for workers in many dioceses overseas, earnestly appeals to men, both clerical and lay, and to women, to dedicate themselves to the service of the Church in those dioceses.

Resolution 33
The normal method of missions is that in which the whole Church, within any area, acts as a missionary body expressly organised for that function, and the principle which underlies this method is capable of universal application. While we humbly thank God for the work of the missionary societies, we consider that these societies, where they exist, should not stand outside the one organisation, but should be elements in it, co-ordinated, whether by a central advisory council or otherwise, under the supreme synodical authority, but retaining severally such degrees of independence as the conditions of their efficiency demand.

Resolution 34

The Conference thankfully recognises the practical steps which missionary societies and boards have taken towards the realisation of the ultimate aim of all mission work, namely, the establishment of self-governing, self-supporting, and self-extending Churches, from which outside control has been withdrawn at the earliest moment, so as to allow the free expression of their national character.

It would urge further that the call for such action is in the present day more insistent than ever before, and believes that, generally speaking, the societies and boards can best achieve their purpose by making their work centre from the first in the Church rather than in the mission organisation, and in particular:

(1) by the establishment of councils which shall be fully representative of the congregations, and have real responsibilities of government;

(2) by substituting for committees and councils representative chiefly of the mission and its subscribers, diocesan boards and committees, and in general associating all their work with the diocesan organisation;

(3) by entrusting to these local bodies a real share in the financial control and general direction of the work of the mission;

(4) by giving the widest freedom to indigenous workers to develop the work in their own countries on lines in accordance with their national character.

Resolution 35

The territorial episcopate has been the normal development in the Catholic Church, but we recognise that difference of race and language sometimes requires that provision should be made in a province for freedom of development of races side by side; the solution in each case must be left with the province, but we are clear that the ideal of the one Church should never be obscured.

Resolution 36

While maintaining the authority of the Book of Common Prayer as the Anglican standard of doctrine and practice, we consider that liturgical uniformity should not be regarded as a necessity throughout the Churches of the Anglican Communion. The conditions of the Church in many parts of the mission field render inapplicable the retention of that Book as the one fixed liturgical model.

Resolution 37

Although the inherent right of a diocesan bishop to put forth or sanction liturgical forms is subject to such limitations as may be imposed by higher synodical authority, it is desirable that such authority should not be too rigidly exercised so long as those features are retained which are essential to the safeguarding of the unity of the Anglican Communion.

Resolution 38
The Conference recommends the appointment of a committee of students of liturgical questions which would be ready to advise any diocese or province on the form and matter of services proposed for adoption, and requests the Archbishop of Canterbury to take such steps as he deems best to give early effect to this Resolution.

Resolution 39
It is of very real importance that the marriage law of the Church should be understood and administered as far as possible consistently, in all parts of the Anglican Communion, and the Conference commends to the consideration of the Church the suggestions of the Committee on Missionary Problems dealing with this subject which have been made after consultation with experts, and are contained in their Report.

Resolution 40
Whereas from time to time restrictions on missionary freedom have been imposed by governments, we desire to reaffirm the duty which rests on every Christian man and woman of propagating the faith of Christ, and to claim that any restrictions should be of a strictly temporary nature only, so that freedom of opportunity to fulfil this spiritual obligation may be afforded to Christians of all nationalities.

Resolution 41
On the subject of the relation of governments and government officials to Christianity and other faiths, the Conference gives its approval to the words used in paragraphs 2 and 3 on page 92 in the Report on Missionary Problems*, and commends them to the careful consideration of all concerned.

* ['In dealing with the large number of persons in their colonies and dependencies who profess different faiths, the policy of the British and American governments has always been that of strict religious neutrality. We heartily endorse this policy, having no desire to see any kind of political influence brought to bear upon people to induce them to change their religion. But we cannot fail to notice that in certain instances the ferment produced among primitive races who have received the Gospel of Christ has led to hindrances being placed in the way of missionaries in the prosecution of their work, and to a preference being shown for other faiths. The Church would be failing in her work if the acceptance of the truths did not awaken in her converts a higher sense of their dignity as human beings, of their rights as well as

their duties, and any government which has the real interest of subject races at heart will be glad of such awakening even though, in civil life, it raises new problems to be solved.

'We hold it to be the duty of missionaries to look at their work from the government point of view, as well as from their own, and to adapt their methods, as far as is consistent with Christian morality and justice and with the faith and order of the Church, to the policy which the government is following in dealing with such peoples. On the other hand, we claim that no discrimination should be shown against the Christian faith, and that the greatest care should be taken by public officials, lest they be betrayed into doing or saying anything which is bound to be interpreted by the people in a sense which does dishonour to our Lord. Further, we feel it is necessary to urge that the religious sentiments of Christians are entitled to be treated with the same consideration that is so markedly, and rightly, shown to those of men professing other faiths.']

Resolution 42

We gratefully acknowledge the valuable work done by British and American missionary conferences in safeguarding missionary interests, and believe that such conferences, both national and international, while claiming no coercive power, have a great part to play in fostering international understanding and goodwill, co-ordinating work, formulating common policies, and serving as a practical medium of communication between missions and governments in matters of general missionary concern.

DEVELOPMENT OF PROVINCES

Resolution 43

Whereas it is undesirable that dioceses should remain indefinitely in isolation or attached only to a distant province, the gradual creation of new provinces should be encouraged, and each newly founded diocese should as soon as possible find its place as a constituent member in some neighbouring province. The fact that dioceses proposing to form a province owe their origin to missions of different branches of the Anglican Communion need be no bar to such action.

(a)   In the opinion of the Conference four is the minimum number of dioceses suitable to form a province. No number should be considered too great to form a province, so long as the bishops and other representatives of the diocese are able conveniently to meet for mutual consultation and for the transaction of provincial business.

(b)   In the initiation of any province in the future, the organisation which the Conference deems essential to provincial life is a house or college of bishops to which the metropolitans or the presiding bishops concerned have conveyed their authority for the consecration of bishops. It is desirable that when a new province is formed the bishops of the constituent dioceses should transfer their allegiance to the metropolitan of the province or other authority constitutionally appointed to receive it, and thereafter all bishops consecrated for the service of the province should take the oath of canonical obedience to the metropolitan or make a declaration of conformity to other authority before mentioned.

(c)   In newly established provinces arrangements should be made whereby the province should have some distinct voice in the election of its metropolitan.

(d)   As to the *sedes* of the metropolitan, customs vary and the decision must depend on local circumstances.

(e)   Until a missionary diocese becomes largely self-supporting and is self-governed by a synod the appointment of its bishop should rest with the province to which it is attached, after consultation with the diocese and in such a way as the province may decide.

(f)   A newly constituted synod of bishops shall proceed as soon as possible to associate with itself in some official way the clergy and laity of the province, provided that in the case of provinces including missionary dioceses this procedure shall be subordinate to local circumstances. It is understood that each national and regional Church will determine its own constitutional and canonical enactments.

CONSULTATIVE BODY

Resolution 44

In order to prevent misapprehension the Conference declares that the Consultative Body, created by the Lambeth Conference of 1897 and consolidated by the Conference of 1908, is a purely advisory body. It is of the nature of a continuation committee of the whole Conference and neither possesses nor claims any executive or administrative power. It is framed so as to represent all branches of the Anglican Communion and it offers advice only when advice is asked for.

(a)   The existing Consultative Body shall be reconstructed on the following plan of representation: It shall consist of the Archbishop of Canterbury (ex officio) and of representative bishops appointed as follows: Province of Canterbury 1, Province of York 1, Province of Wales 1, the Church of Ireland 1, the Episcopal Church in Scotland 1, the Protestant Episcopal Church in the United States of America 4, the Church of England in Canada 1, the Church of England in the Dioceses of Australia and Tasmania 1, the Church of the Province of New Zealand 1, the Church of the Province of the West Indies 1, the Church of the Province of South Africa 1, the Church of the Province of India and Ceylon 1, the Churches in China and Japan and the Diocese of Corea 1, the missionary and other extra-provincial bishops under the jurisdiction of the Archbishop of Canterbury 1. Total 18.

(b)   The Churches that appoint representatives shall be free to fix the method of appointment, whether by the House of Bishops or by synod or convention. A representative bishop shall be appointed for a definite term not exceeding six years, and need not be a member of the body which appoints him. Any vacancy by death, resignation, or other cause, during the term of office shall be filled by the Church in the representation of which the vacancy occurs.

(c)   For the purpose of appointing the bishop who is to represent the body of missionary and other extra-provincial bishops under the jurisdiction of the Archbishop of Canterbury, each of those bishops shall be requested by the Archbishop of Canterbury to nominate a bishop to him. The list of bishops so nominated shall be then sent to all the bishops entitled to vote, and each of them shall, if he thinks fit to vote, send to the Archbishop the name of the one in that list for whom he votes. The largest number of votes shall carry the election.

(d)   The Central Consultative Body shall be prepared to consider questions referred to it by any bishop, but shall, before considering as well as in considering them, have careful regard to any limitations upon such references as may be imposed by the regulations of provinces or of national or regional Churches.

(e)   The Consultative Body shall not at any meeting come to a decision on any subject not named in the notice summoning the meeting.

Resolution 45

The Consultative Body is asked to take into its consideration the provisions of the Colonial Clergy Act with a view to their modification.

THE POSITION OF WOMEN IN THE COUNCILS AND MINISTRATIONS OF THE CHURCH

Resolution 46

Women should be admitted to those councils of the Church to which laymen are admitted, and on equal terms. Diocesan, provincial, or national synods may decide when or how this principle is to be brought into effect.

Resolution 47

The time has come when, in the interests of the Church at large, and in particular of the development of the ministry of women, the diaconate of women should be restored formally and canonically, and should be recognised throughout the Anglican Communion.

Resolution 48
The order of deaconesses is for women the one and only order of the ministry which has the stamp of apostolic approval, and is for women the only order of the ministry which we can recommend that our branch of the Catholic Church should recognise and use.

Resolution 49
The office of a deaconess is primarily a ministry of succour, bodily and spiritual, especially to women, and should follow the lines of the primitive rather than of the modern diaconate of men. It should be understood that the deaconess dedicates herself to a life-long service, but that no vow or implied promise of celibacy should be required as necessary for admission to the order. Nevertheless, deaconesses who desire to do so may legitimately pledge themselves either as members of a community, or as individuals, to a celibate life.

Resolution 50
In every branch of the Anglican Communion there should be adopted a Form and Manner of Making of Deaconesses such as might fitly find a place in the Book of Common Prayer, containing in all cases provision for:
    (a) prayer by the bishop and the laying-on of his hands;
    (b) a formula giving authority to execute the office of a deaconess in the Church of God;
    (c) the delivery of the New Testament by the bishop to each candidate.

Resolution 51
The Forms for the Making and Ordering of Deaconesses should be of the same general character, and as far as possible similar in their most significant parts, though varying in less important details in accordance with local needs.

Resolution 52
The following functions may be entrusted to the deaconess, in addition to the ordinary duties which would naturally fall to her:
    (a) to prepare candidates for baptism and confirmation;
    (b) to assist at the administration of Holy Baptism; and to be the administrant in cases of necessity in virtue of her office;
    (c) to pray with and give counsel to such women as desire help in difficulties and perplexities;

(d) with the approval of the bishop and of the parish priest, and under such conditions as shall from time to time be laid down by the bishop: (i) in church to read Morning and Evening Prayer and the Litany, except such portions as are assigned to the priest only; (ii) in church also to lead in prayer and, under licence of the bishop, to instruct and exhort the congregation.

Voting on Clause d(ii): For 117; Against 81.

Resolution 53

Opportunity should be given to women as to men (duly qualified and approved by the bishop) to speak in consecrated or unconsecrated buildings, and to lead in prayer, at other than the regular and appointed services of the Church. Such diocesan arrangements, both for men and for women, should wherever possible be subject to provincial control and co-ordination.

Resolution 54

The Conference recommends that careful inquiry should be made in the several branches of the Anglican Communion as to the position and recognition of women workers in the Church, the conditions of their employment, and the remuneration of those who receive salaries.

SPIRITUALISM, CHRISTIAN SCIENCE, THEOSOPHY

Resolution 55

We reaffirm our conviction that the revelation of God in Christ Jesus is the supreme and sufficient message given to all mankind, whereby we may attain to eternal life. We recognise that modern movements of thought connected with spiritualism, Christian Science, and theosophy join with the Christian Church in protesting against a materialistic view of the universe and at some points emphasise partially neglected aspects of truth. At the same time, we feel bound to call attention to the fact that both in the underlying philosophy and in cults and practices which have arisen out of these movements, the teaching given or implied either ignores or explains away or contradicts the unique and central fact of human history, namely, the incarnation of our Lord and Saviour Jesus Christ.

Resolution 56

We recognise that new phenomena of consciousness have been presented to us, which claim, and at the hands of competent psychologists have received, careful investigation, and, as far as possible, the application of scientific method. But such scientific researches have confessedly not reached an advanced stage, and we are supported by the best psychologists in warning our people against accepting as final theories which further knowledge may disprove, and still more against the indiscriminate and undisciplined exercise of psychic powers, and the habit of recourse to *séances*, 'seers', and mediums.

Spiritualism

Resolution 57

The Conference, while prepared to expect and welcome new light from psychical research upon the powers and processes of the spirit of man, urges strongly that a larger place should be given in the teaching of the Church to the explanation of the true grounds of Christian belief in eternal life, and in immortality, and of the true content of belief in the communion of saints as involving real fellowship with the departed through the love of God in Christ Jesus.

Resolution 58

The Conference, while recognising that the results of investigation have encouraged many people to find a spiritual meaning and purpose in human life and led them to believe in survival after death, sees grave dangers in the tendency to make a religion of spiritualism. The practice of spiritualism as a cult involves the subordination of the intelligence and the will to unknown forces or personalities and, to that extent, an abdication of the self-control to which God has called us. It tends to divert attention from the approach to God through the one Mediator, Jesus Christ, under the guidance of the Holy Spirit; to ignore the discipline of faith as the path of spiritual training; and to depreciate the divinely ordained channels of grace and truth revealed and given through Jesus Christ our Lord.

Christian Science

Resolution 59

The Conference finds that while Christian Science fixes attention on the supremacy of spirit, yet in the teaching given there is a direct tendency (a) to pantheistic doctrine, and at the same time (b) to a false antithesis between spirit and matter, and (c) to the denial of the reality of sin, and (d) to the denial of the reality of disease and suffering. Such teaching, therefore, cannot be reconciled with the fundamental truths of the Christian faith and the teaching of Scripture on atonement, penitence, forgiveness, and fellowship in the sufferings of Christ.

Resolution 60
The Conference reminds the Church that intimate communion with God has been the privilege and joy of the saints in every age. This communion, realised in union with Christ through the Holy Spirit, influences the whole personality of man, physical and spiritual, enabling him to share his Lord's triumph over sin, disease and death.

Resolution 61
We therefore urge upon the clergy of the Anglican Communion the duty of a more thorough study of the many-sided enterprise of prayer in order that they may become more efficient teachers and trainers of their people in this work, so that through the daily practice of prayer and meditation the corporate faith of the Church may be renewed, and the fruit of the Spirit may be more manifest in the daily lives of professing Christians, and the power of Christ to heal may be released.

Resolution 62
We declare our thankfulness for the devoted labours of those engaged in scientific research and for the progress made in medicine, surgery, nursing, hygiene and sanitation. Believing that all these means of healing and preventing disease and relieving suffering are gifts that come from God, we acknowledge our duty to use them faithfully for the welfare of mankind.

Resolution 63
For the general guidance of the Church the Conference requests the Archbishop of Canterbury to appoint a committee to consider and report as early as possible upon the use with prayer of the laying-on of hands, of the unction of the sick and other spiritual means of healing, the findings of such a committee to be reported forthwith to the authorities of the national, provincial, and regional Churches of the Anglican Communion.

Theosophy

Resolution 64
The Conference, while recognising that the three publicly stated objectives of the Theosophical Society* do not in themselves appear to be inconsistent with loyal membership of the Church, desires to express its conviction that there are cardinal elements in the positive teaching current in theosophical circles and literature which are irreconcilable with the Christian faith as to the person and mission of Christ and with the missionary claim and duty of the Christian religion as the message of God to all mankind. The Conference warns Christian

people, who may be induced to make a study of theosophy by the seemingly Christian elements contained in it, to be on their guard against the ultimate bearing of theosophical teaching, and urges them to examine strictly the character and credentials of the teachers upon whose authority they are encouraged or compelled to rely.

* [Quoted in the Report of the Committee as: (i) 'to form a nucleus of the Universal Brotherhood of Humanity without distinction of race, creed, sex, caste or colour', (ii) 'to encourage the study of comparative religion, philosophy and science', (iii) 'to investigate the unexplained laws of nature and the powers latent in man'.]

Resolution 65
The Conference, believing that the attraction of theosophy for some Christian people lies largely in its presentation of Christian faith as a quest for knowledge, recommends that in the current teaching of the Church due regard should be given to the mystical elements of faith and life which underlie the historic belief of Christendom, and on the other hand urges all thinking people to safeguard their Christian position by a fuller study of the Bible, Creed, and sacraments in the light of sound Christian scholarship and philosophy.

PROBLEMS OF MARRIAGE AND SEXUAL MORALITY

Resolution 66
Recognising that to live a pure and chaste life before and after marriage is, for both sexes, the unchangeable Christian standard, attainable and attained through the help of the Holy Spirit by men and women in every age, the Conference desires to proclaim the universal obligation of this standard, and its vital importance as an essential condition of human happiness.

Resolution 67
The Conference affirms as our Lord's principle and standard of marriage a life-long and indissoluble union, for better or worse, of one man with one woman, to the exclusion of all others on either side, and calls on all Christian people to maintain and bear witness to this standard.

Nevertheless, the Conference admits the right of a national or regional Church within our Communion to deal with cases which fall within the exception mentioned in the record of our Lord's words in St Matthew's Gospel, under provisions which such Church may lay down.

The Conference, while fully recognising the extreme difficulty of governments in framing marriage laws for citizens many of whom do not accept the Christian standard, expresses its firm belief that in every country the Church should be free to bear witness to that standard through its powers of administration and discipline exercised in relation to its own members.

Resolution 68

The Conference, while declining to lay down rules which will meet the needs of every abnormal case, regards with grave concern the spread in modern society of theories and practices hostile to the family. We utter an emphatic warning against the use of unnatural means for the avoidance of conception, together with the grave dangers—physical, moral, and religious—thereby incurred, and against the evils with which the extension of such use threatens the race. In opposition to the teaching which, under the name of science and religion, encourages married people in the deliberate cultivation of sexual union as an end in itself, we steadfastly uphold what must always be regarded as the governing considerations of Christian marriage. One is the primary purpose for which marriage exists, namely the continuation of the race through the gift and heritage of children; the other is the paramount importance in married life of deliberate and thoughtful self-control.

We desire solemnly to commend what we have said to Christian people and to all who will hear.

Resolution 69

The Conference, moved by responsible statements from many nations as to the prevalence of venereal diseases, bringing suffering, paralysis, insanity, or death to many thousands of the innocent as well as the guilty, supports all efforts which are consistent with high moral standards to check the causes of the diseases and to treat and, if possible, cure the victims. We impress upon the clergy and members of the Church the duty of joining with physicians and public authorities in meeting this scourge, and urge the clergy to guide those who turn to them for advice with knowledge, sympathy, and directness. The Conference must condemn the distribution or use, before exposure to infection, of so-called prophylactics, since these cannot but be regarded as an invitation to vice.

Resolution 70

The Conference urges the importance of enlisting the help of all high-principled men and women, whatever be their religious beliefs, in co-operation with or, if necessary, in bringing pressure to bear upon, authorities both national and local, for removing such incentives to vice as indecent literature, suggestive plays and films, the open or secret sale of contraceptives, and the continued existence of brothels.

Resolution 71
With regard to the education of the young in matters of sex, the Conference presses upon parents that the duty of giving right teaching on these subjects rests primarily with them, and that it is the duty of all persons giving such instruction to prepare themselves for this responsible task. Boys and girls should be guarded against the danger of acquiring knowledge of sexual subjects from wrong persons and in wrong ways.

Resolution 72
Bearing in remembrance the example of our Lord, and the prominent place that he gave in his ministry to protecting the weak and raising the fallen, the Conference deplores the common apathy of Church people in regard to preventive and rescue work*, and urges on bishops, clergy, and all Christian people the duty of taking a more active share in this essential part of the Church's life.

* [That is, in relation to sexual delinquency.]

SOCIAL AND INDUSTRIAL QUESTIONS

Resolution 73
We desire to emphasise our conviction that the pursuit of mere self-interest, whether individual or corporate, will never bring healing to the wounds of society. This conviction is at once exemplified and reinforced by what has happened in and since the war. Nor is this less true when that self-interest is equipped with every advantage of science and education. Our only hope lies in reverent allegiance to the person of Christ, whose law is the law of love, in acceptance of his principles, and reliance on his power.

Resolution 74
An outstanding and pressing duty of the Church is to convince its members of the necessity of nothing less than a fundamental change in the spirit and working of our economic life. This change can only be effected by accepting as the basis of industrial relations the principle of co-operation in service for the common good in place of unrestricted competition for private or sectional advantage. All Christian people ought to take an active part in bringing about this change, by which alone we can hope to remove class dissensions and resolve industrial discords.

Resolution 75
The Church cannot in its corporate capacity be an advocate or partisan, 'a judge or a divider', in political or class disputes where moral

issues are not at stake; nevertheless even in matters of economic and political controversy the Church is bound to give its positive and active corporate witness to the Christian principles of justice, brotherhood, and the equal and infinite value of every human personality.

Resolution 76
In obedience to Christ's teaching as to covetousness and self-seeking, the Conference calls upon all members of his Church to be foremost both by personal action and sacrifice in maintaining the superiority of the claims of human life to those of property. To this end it would emphasise the duty which is laid upon all Christians of setting human values above dividends and profits in their conduct of business, of avoiding extravagance and waste, and of upholding a high standard of honour and thoroughness in work. In a word, they must set an example in subordinating the claim for rights to the call of duty.

Resolution 77
Members of the Church are bound to take an active part, by public action and by personal service, in removing those abuses which depress and impoverish human life. In company with other citizens and organisations they should work for reform, and particularly for such measures as will secure the better care of children, including real opportunity for an adequate education; protection of the workers against unemployment; and the provision of healthy homes.

Resolution 78
The Church is bound to use its influence to remove inhuman or oppressive conditions of labour in all parts of the world, especially among the weaker races, and to give its full support to those clauses in the League of Nations Covenant which aim at raising by international agreement the status of industrial workers in all countries.

Resolution 79
The Conference notes with deep interest the prohibition by the will of the people of the sale and manufacture of intoxicating drinks in the Republic of the United States of America, and of their sale in most of the provinces of Canada, and commends this action to the earnest and sympathetic attention of the Christian Church throughout the world. The Conference urges members of the Church in other countries:
(1) to support such legislation as will lead to a speedy reduction in the use of intoxicants;
(2) to recognise the duty of combating the evil of intemperance by personal example and willing self-sacrifice.

Resolution 80
If the Church is to witness without reproach for justice and brotherhood in the world, it must show itself serious and insistent in reform-
ing abuses within its own organisation, and in promoting brotherhood
among its own members. Further, if Christian witness is to be fully
effective it must be borne by nothing short of the whole body of Christian people.

1930

THE CHRISTIAN DOCTRINE OF GOD

Resolution 1
We believe that the Christian Church is the repository and trustee of
a revelation of God, given by himself, which all members of the Church
are bound to transmit to others, and that every member of the Church,
both clerical and lay, is called to be a channel through which the divine
life flows for the quickening of all mankind.

Resolution 2
We believe that, in view of the enlarged knowledge gained in modern
times of God's ordering of the world and the clearer apprehension
of the creative process by which he prepared the way for the coming
of Jesus Christ, there is urgent need in the face of many erroneous
conceptions for a fresh presentation of the Christian doctrine of God;
and we commend the Report of our Committee to the study of all
thoughtful people in the hope that it may help towards meeting this
need.

Resolution 3
We affirm the supreme and unshaken authority of the Holy Scriptures as presenting the truth concerning God and the spiritual life in
its historical setting and in its progressive revelation, both throughout the Old Testament and in the New. It is no part of the purpose
of the Scriptures to give information on those themes which are the
proper subject matter of scientific enquiry, nor is the Bible a collec-
tion of separate oracles, each containing a final declaration of truth.
The doctrine of God is the centre of its teaching, set forth in its books
'by divers portions and in divers manners'. As Jesus Christ is the crown,
so also is he the criterion of all revelation. We would impress upon

Christian people the necessity of banishing from their minds ideas concerning the character of God which are inconsistent with the character of Jesus Christ. We believe that the work of our Lord Jesus Christ is continued by the Holy Spirit, who not only interpreted him to the Apostles, but has in every generation inspired and guided those who seek truth.

Resolution 4

The revelation of Christ was presented to the world under the forms of Jewish life and thought. It has found fuller expression, not without some admixture of misunderstanding, through the thought of Greece and Rome, and the sentiment of the Teutonic and Slavonic races. We anticipate that when this same revelation possesses their minds, the nations of Asia and Africa will still further enrich the Church of Christ by characteristic statements of the permanent Gospel, and by characteristic examples of Christian virtue and types of Christian worship.

We welcome such unfolding of the truth of the Gospel as one of the ways by which the nations may bring their riches into the service of Christ and his Church.

Resolution 5

We recognise in the modern discoveries of science—whereby the boundaries of knowledge are extended, the needs of men are satisfied and their sufferings alleviated—veritable gifts of God, to be used with thankfulness to him, and with that sense of responsibility which such thankfulness must create.

Resolution 6

For the reasons set forth in Resolutions 2 and 3, there is need for the Church to renew and redirect its teaching office:

(a) by a fresh insistence upon the duty of thinking and learning as essential elements in the Christian life;

(b) by recalling the clergy to a fuller sense of their duty in the exercise of the teaching office. Of all their functions this is one of the most important. It demands, especially in these days, prayer and study, both individual and corporate, on the self-revelation of God in Jesus Christ and the manifestations of his presence in the modern world;

(c) by the provision of similar opportunities for the laity;

(d) by a new emphasis upon the appeal to the mind as well as to the heart in the preaching of the word as an element in Christian worship; and

(e) by providing both for clergy and laity opportunities of retreats and other well-tried methods for the deepening of the spiritual life through the growth of fellowship with God and man.

We especially desire to impress upon the younger clergy that the Church requires the service of men who will devote themselves to the study of theology in all its branches. The Church needs learning, as well as spiritual power and practical ability, in its clergy.

Resolution 7

We welcome an increased readiness in many educational authorities to accept the influence and assistance of the Church in its teaching capacity, and we urge that every effort should be made throughout the Church to seek such opportunities and to use them with sympathy and discretion.

As the intellectual meaning and content of the Christian doctrine of God cannot be fully apprehended without the aid of the highest human knowledge, it is essential that Christian theology should be studied and taught in universities in contact with philosophy, science and criticism, and to that end that faculties of theology should be established in universities wherever possible.

Resolution 8

Believing as we do that men should offer their worship to God because of his great glory, and because of his supreme revelation of love in Jesus Christ, apart from any thought of benefits that may accrue to them, we urge upon the Church the absolute obligation of corporate worship. We believe that a fuller study of the Christian doctrine of God will both strengthen the sense of this obligation in the Church, and also help the Church to commend it to the world. Moreover we believe that it is through the development of their capacity for worship that men advance in their knowledge of God's nature, and may hope to penetrate further into his mysteries.

THE LIFE AND WITNESS OF THE CHRISTIAN COMMUNITY

Marriage and Sex

Resolution 9

The Conference believes that the conditions of modern life call for a fresh statement from the Christian Church on the subject of sex. It declares that the functions of sex as a God-given factor in human life are essentially noble and creative. Responsibility in regard to their right use needs the greater emphasis in view of widespread laxity of thought and conduct in all these matters.

Resolution 10

The Conference believes that in the exalted view of marriage taught by our Lord is to be found the solution of the problems with which we are faced. His teaching is reinforced by certain elements which have found a new emphasis in modern life, particularly the sacredness of personality, the more equal partnership of men and women, and the biological importance of monogamy.

Resolution 11

The Conference believes that it is with this ideal in view that the Church must deal with questions of divorce and with whatever threatens the security of woman and the stability of the home. Mindful of our Lord's words, 'What therefore God hath joined together, let not man put asunder', it reaffirms 'as our Lord's principle and standard of marriage a life-long and indissoluble union, for better or worse, of one man with one woman, to the exclusion of all others on either side, and calls on all Christian people to maintain and bear witness to this standard.'*

In cases of divorce:

(a) The Conference, while passing no judgement on the practice of regional or national Churches within our Communion, recommends that the marriage of one, whose former partner is still living, should not be celebrated according to the rites of the Church.

(b) Where an innocent person has remarried under civil sanction and desires to receive the Holy Communion, it recommends that the case should be referred for consideration to the bishop, subject to provincial regulations.

(c) Finally, it would call attention to the Church's unceasing responsibility for the spiritual welfare of all her members who have come short of her standard in this as in any other respect, and to the fact that the Church's aim, individually and socially, is reconciliation to God and redemption from sin. It therefore urges all bishops and clergy to keep this aim before them.

* Lambeth Conference 1920: Resolution 67.

Resolution 12

In all questions of marriage and sex the Conference emphasises the need of education. It is important that before the child's emotional reaction to sex is awakened, definite information should be given in an atmosphere of simplicity and beauty. The persons directly responsible for this are the parents, who in the exercise of this responsibility will themselves need the best guidance that the Church can supply.

During childhood and youth the boy or the girl should thus be prepared for the responsibilities of adult life; but the Conference urges the need of some further preparation for those members of the Church who are about to marry.

To this end the Conference is convinced that steps ought to be taken (a) to secure a better education for the clergy in moral theology; (b) to establish, where they do not exist, in the various branches of the Anglican Communion central councils which would study the problems of sex from the Christian standpoint and give advice to the responsible authorities in diocese or parish or theological college as to methods of approach and lines of instruction; (c) to review the available literature and to take steps for its improvement and its circulation.

Resolution 13

The Conference emphasises the truth that the sexual instinct is a holy thing implanted by God in human nature. It acknowledges that intercourse between husband and wife as the consummation of marriage has a value of its own within that sacrament, and that thereby married love is enhanced and its character strengthened. Further, seeing that the primary purpose for which marriage exists is the procreation of children, it believes that this purpose as well as the paramount importance in married life of deliberate and thoughtful self-control should be the governing considerations in that intercourse.

Resolution 14

The Conference affirms (a) the duty of parenthood as the glory of married life; (b) the benefit of a family as a joy in itself, as a vital contribution to the nation's welfare, and as a means of character-building for both parents and children; (c) the privilege of discipline and sacrifice to this end.

Resolution 15

Where there is a clearly felt moral obligation to limit or avoid parenthood, the method must be decided on Christian principles. The primary and obvious method is complete abstinence from intercourse (as far as may be necessary) in a life of discipline and self-control lived in the power of the Holy Spirit. Nevertheless in those cases where there is such a clearly felt moral obligation to limit or avoid parenthood, and where there is a morally sound reason for avoiding complete abstinence, the Conference agrees that other methods may be used, provided that this is done in the light of the same Christian principles. The Conference records its strong condemnation of the use of any methods of conception control from motives of selfishness, luxury, or mere convenience.

Voting: For 193; Against 67.

Resolution 16

The Conference further records its abhorrence of the sinful practice of abortion.

Resolution 17

While the Conference admits that economic conditions are a serious factor in the situation, it condemns the propaganda which treats conception control as a way of meeting those unsatisfactory social and economic conditions which ought to be changed by the influence of Christian public opinion.

Resolution 18

Sexual intercourse between persons who are not legally married is a grievous sin. The use of contraceptives does not remove the sin. In view of the widespread and increasing use of contraceptives among the unmarried and the extension of irregular unions owing to the diminution of any fear of consequences, the Conference presses for legislation forbidding the exposure for sale and the unrestricted advertisement of contraceptives, and placing definite restrictions upon their purchase.

Resolution 19

Fear of consequences can never, for the Christian, be the ultimately effective motive for the maintenance of chastity before marriage. This can only be found in the love of God and reverence for his laws. The Conference emphasises the need of strong and wise teaching to make clear the Christian standpoint in this matter. That standpoint is that all illicit and irregular unions are wrong in that they offend against the true nature of love, they compromise the future happiness of married life, they are antagonistic to the welfare of the community, and, above all, they are contrary to the revealed will of God.

Resolution 20

The Conference desires to express the debt which the Church owes to the devotion of those who in constantly changing conditions and in the face of increasing difficulties have maintained and carried forward the preventive and rescue work of the Church. Such devotion calls for greatly increased interest and support from all the members of the Church.

The removal of the causes which lead to the necessity for such work must first and foremost be sought in the creation of that healthier atmosphere and in the more thorough giving of sex instruction which are recommended in preceding Resolutions. And this is recognised to the full by the leaders in the work. There is, however, at the present time urgent need for (a) much greater financial support, so that the workers may be adequately trained and adequately paid, (b) more regular interest on the part of churchpeople generally in them and in their work, (c) the help which the men of the Church can give in technical and legal matters, as also in personal service.

The Conference further desires in this connection to place on record its appreciation of the work done by women police in Great Britain, in the British dominions and in the United States of America, and by those many social workers, in different parts of the world, who give themselves to the same difficult task.

Race

Resolution 21

The Conference affirms that the principle of trusteeship as laid down by Article XXII of the League of Nations Covenant cannot be duly applied in practice without full recognition of the fact that partnership must eventually follow as soon as two races can show an equal standard of civilisation. Accordingly, the Conference affirms that the ruling of one race by another can only be justified from the Christian standpoint when the highest welfare of the subject race is the constant aim of government, and when admission to an increasing share in the government of the country is an objective steadfastly pursued. To this end equal opportunity and impartial justice must be assured. Equal opportunity of development will result where the nation faithfully discharges its responsibility for the education of all its citizens, in which the co-operation of both the Church and the family with the state is essential; and Christian principles demand that equal justice be assured to every member of every community both from the government and in the courts of law.

Resolution 22

The Conference affirms its conviction that all communicants without distinction of race or colour should have access in any church to the Holy Table of the Lord, and that no one should be excluded from worship in any church on account of colour or race. Further, it urges that where, owing to diversity of language or custom, Christians of different races normally worship apart, special occasions should be sought for united services and corporate communion in order to witness to the unity of the Body of Christ.

The Conference would remind all Christian people that the ministrations of the clergy should never be rejected on grounds of colour or race, and in this connection it would state its opinion that in the interests of true unity it is undesirable that in any given area there should be two or more bishops of the same Communion exercising independent jurisdiction.

Resolution 23

The Conference affirms that the guiding principle of racial relations should be interdependence and not competition, though this interdependence does not of itself involve intermarriage; that the realisation in practice of human brotherhood postulates courtesy on the part of all races towards one another, co-operation in the study of racial relations and values, and a complete avoidance of any exploitation of the weaker races, such as is exemplified in the liquor traffic among the natives of Africa and enforced labour for private profit.

The Conference urges that the presence of Asiatic and African students at western universities affords an opportunity for promoting friendliness between different races, and asks that Christians should try to create such a public sentiment that these students may be received with sympathetic understanding and enabled to share in all that is best in western social life.

Resolution 24

The Conference would insist that the maintenance of the Christian obligation on the part of men to respect and honour womanhood, involving the equally chivalrous treatment of the women of all races, is fundamental; and conversely, the Christian obligation on the part of women to maintain a high standard of morals and conduct, especially in their relations with men of a different colour, is equally fundamental.

Peace and War

Resolution 25

The Conference affirms that war as a method of settling international disputes is incompatible with the teaching and example of our Lord Jesus Christ.

Resolution 26

The Conference believes that peace will never be achieved till international relations are controlled by religious and ethical standards, and that the moral judgement of humanity needs to be enlisted on the side of peace. It therefore appeals to the religious leaders of all nations to give their support to the effort to promote those ideals of peace, brotherhood and justice for which the League of Nations stands.

The Conference welcomes the agreement made by leading statesmen of the world in the names of their respective peoples, in which they condemn recourse to war for the solution of international controversies, renounce it as an instrument of national policy in their relations with one another, and agree that the settlement of all disputes which may arise among them shall never be sought except by pacific means; and appeals to all Christian people to support this agreement to the utmost of their power and to help actively, by prayer and effort, agencies (such as the League of Nations Union and the World Alliance for Promoting International Friendship through the Churches) which are working to promote goodwill among the nations.

Resolution 27
When nations have solemnly bound themselves by treaty, covenant or pact for the pacific settlement of international disputes, the Conference holds that the Christian Church in every nation should refuse to countenance any war in regard to which the government of its own country has not declared its willingness to submit the matter in dispute to arbitration or conciliation.

Resolution 28
The Conference believes that the existence of armaments on the present scale amongst the nations of the world endangers the maintenance of peace, and appeals for a determined effort to secure further reduction by international agreement.

Resolution 29
Believing that peace within the nation and among the nations is bound up with the acceptance of Christian principles in the ordering of social and industrial life, the Conference reaffirms the Resolutions (73-80) of the Lambeth Conference of 1920, which deal with that subject. While there is in many countries an increasing desire for justice and therefore a growing will to peace, the world is still faced with grave social and economic evils which are an offence to the Christian conscience, and a menace to peace. All these evils call for the best scientific treatment on international lines, and also for a practical application of the principle of united service and self-sacrifice on the part of all Christian people.

Resolution 30
The Conference recognises with thankfulness the efforts made by the League of Nations to control the drug traffic, and calls upon all Christian people to pray and to labour, as they have opportunity, that measures may soon be devised, both by national and international action, which will effectively limit the production, manufacture and sale of

dangerous drugs, particularly opium, cocaine and their derivatives, to the amounts required for scientific and medical purposes.

THE UNITY OF THE CHURCH

Resolution 31
The Conference records, with deep thanks to Almighty God, the signs of a growing movement towards Christian unity in all parts of the world since the issue of the 'Appeal to All Christian People' by the Lambeth Conference in 1920.

The Conference heartily endorses that Appeal and reaffirms the principles contained in it and in the Resolutions dealing with reunion adopted by that Conference.

The Malines Conversations

Resolution 32
Believing that our Lord's purpose for his Church will only be fulfilled when all the separated parts of his Body are united, and that only by full discussion between the Churches can error and misunderstanding be removed and full spiritual unity attained, the Conference expresses its appreciation of the courage and Christian charity of Cardinal Mercier in arranging the Malines Conversations, unofficial and not fully representative of the Churches though they were, and its regret that by the encyclical *Mortalium animos* members of the Roman Catholic Church are forbidden to take part in the World Conference on Faith and Order and other similar conferences.

The Eastern Orthodox Church

Resolution 33
(a)   The Conference heartily thanks the Oecumenical Patriarch for arranging in co-operation with the other patriarchs and the autocephalous Churches for the sending of an important delegation of the Eastern Orthodox Church under the leadership of the Patriarch of Alexandria, and expresses its grateful appreciation of the help given to its Committee by the delegation, as well as its sense of the value of the advance made through the joint meetings in the relations of the Orthodox Church with the Anglican Communion.
(b)   The Conference requests the Archbishop of Canterbury to appoint representatives of the Anglican Communion and to invite the Oecumenical Patriarch to appoint representatives of the patriarchates and autocephalous Churches of the East to be a doctrinal commission, which may, in correspondence and in consultation, prepare a

joint statement on the theological points about which there is difference and agreement between the Anglican and the Eastern Churches.
(c)   The Conference, not having been summoned as a synod to issue any statement professing to define doctrine, is therefore unable to issue such a formal statement on the subjects referred to in the *Résumé**
of the discussions between the Patriarch of Alexandria with the other Orthodox representatives and bishops of the Anglican Communion, but records its acceptance of the statements of the Anglican bishops contained therein as a sufficient account of the teaching and practice of the Church of England and of the Churches in communion with it, in relation to those subjects.

* See Report of the Lambeth Conference 1930, p 138.

Resolution 34
The Conference expresses its sympathy with the Church of Russia in its persecution and sufferings, and prays that God, in his mercy, may give liberty and prosperity once more to that Church, that it may again take its place with greater freedom and power of self-expression among the other great Churches of Christendom.

The Old Catholic Church

Resolution 35
(a)   The Conference heartily thanks the Archbishop of Utrecht and the bishops of the Old Catholic Church associated with him for coming to consult with its members on the development of closer relations between their Churches and the Anglican Communion, and expresses its sense of the importance of the step taken.
(b)   The Conference requests the Archbishop of Canterbury to appoint representatives of the Anglican Communion, and to invite the Archbishop of Utrecht to appoint representatives of the Old Catholic Churches to be a doctrinal commission to discuss points of agreement and difference between them.
(c)   The Conference agrees that there is nothing in the Declaration of Utrecht* inconsistent with the teaching of the Church of England.

* See Report of the Lambeth Conference 1930, p 142.

The Separated Eastern Churches

Resolution 36
(a)   The Conference thanks Bishop Tourian for taking counsel with one of its committees on the relations between the Church* and the Anglican Communion, and assures him of its deep sympathy with the sufferings of his nation.

(b)   The Conference expresses its deep sympathy with the Armenian, East Syrian (Assyrian) and West Syrian Christians in the hardship and suffering which they have endured since the war, and earnestly prays that they may be given strength and courage in their efforts for self-preservation, as well as that their rights may be fully secured as religious or racial minorities in the territories in which they live.

(c)   The Conference welcomes the development of closer relations between the Anglican Communion and the Separated Churches of the East which is recorded in its Committee's Report, and earnestly desires that these relations may be steadily strengthened, in consultation with the Orthodox Church, in the hope that in due course full intercommunion may be reached.

* [That is, the Armenian Church.]

The Church of Sweden

Resolution 37
The Conference thanks the Church of Sweden for the visit of the Bishop of Lund and expresses its hope that the existing fraternal relations with that Church will be maintained, and that relations may also be strengthened with the other Scandinavian Churches with a view to promoting greater unity in the future.

The Church of Finland

Resolution 38
The Conference requests the Archbishop of Canterbury, as soon as seems advisable, to appoint a committee to investigate the position of the Church of Finland and its relations to the Church of England.

The Moravians (Unitas Fratrum)

Resolution 39
The Conference is grateful to the Moravian Church for sending so important a body of representatives to confer with their Committee, and respectfully requests the Archbishop of Canterbury to appoint a new committee to confer with a committee of the Moravian Church.

South India

Resolution 40
(a)   The Conference has heard with the deepest interest of the proposals for Church union in South India now under consideration between the Church of India, Burma and Ceylon, the South India

United Church and the Wesleyan Methodist Church of South India, and expresses its high appreciation of the spirit in which the representatives of these Churches have pursued the long and careful negotiations.

(b)   The Conference notes with warm sympathy that the project embodied in the Proposed Scheme for Church Union in South India is not the formation of any fresh Church or province of the Anglican Communion under new conditions, but seeks to bring together the distinctive elements of different Christian Communions, on a basis of sound doctrine and episcopal order, in a distinct province of the Universal Church, in such a way as to give the Indian expression of the spirit, the thought and the life of the Church Universal.

(c)   We observe further, as a novel feature in the South Indian scheme, that a complete agreement between the uniting Churches on certain points of doctrine and practice is not expected to be reached before the inauguration of the union; but the promoters of the scheme believe that unity will be reached gradually and more securely by the interaction of the different elements of the united Church upon one another. It is only when the unification resulting from that interaction is complete that a final judgement can be pronounced on the effect of the present proposals. Without attempting, therefore, to pronounce such judgement now, we express to our brethren in India our strong desire that, as soon as the negotiations are successfully completed, the venture should be made and the union inaugurated. We hope that it will lead to the emergence of a part of the Body of Christ which will possess a new combination of the riches that are his. In this hope we ask the Churches of our Communion to stand by our brethren in India, while they make this experiment, with generous goodwill.

(d)   The Conference thinks it wise to point out that, after the union in South India has been inaugurated, both ministers and lay people of the united Church, when they are outside the jurisdiction of that Church, will be amenable to the regulations of the province and diocese in which they desire to officiate or to worship, and it must be assumed that those regulations will be applied to individuals in the same manner as they would now be applied to similarly circumstanced individuals, unless any province takes formal action to change its regulations.

(e)   The Conference, fully assured in the light of the Resolutions of the General Council of the Church of India, Burma and Ceylon adopted in February 1930 that nothing will be done to break the fellowship of the Churches of the Anglican Communion, confidently leaves in the hands of the bishops of that Church the task of working out in detail the principles which are embodied in the Proposed Scheme.

(f)   The Conference gives its general approval to the suggestions contained in the Report of its Committee with regard to the Proposed Scheme for Church Union in South India, and commends the Report to the attention of the Episcopal Synod and General Council of the Church of India, Burma and Ceylon.

The Church in Persia

Resolution 41

The Conference has heard with deep sympathy of the steps towards union which have been proposed in Persia; it desires to express its sincere appreciation of the missionary zeal of the Church in Persia, and it generally approves the sections in the Report of its Committee dealing with this subject.

Special Areas

Resolution 42

The Conference, maintaining as a general principle that intercommunion should be the goal of, rather than a means to, the restoration of union, and bearing in mind the general rule of the Anglican Churches that 'members of the Anglican Churches should receive the Holy Communion only from ministers of their own Church', holds, nevertheless, that the administration of such a rule falls under the discretion of the bishop, who should exercise his dispensing power in accordance with any principles that may be set forth by the national, regional or provincial authority of the Church in the area concerned. The bishops of the Anglican Communion will not question the action of any bishop who may, in his discretion so exercised, sanction an exception to the general rule in special areas, where the ministrations of an Anglican Church are not available for long periods of time or without travelling great distances, or may give permission that baptized communicant members of Churches not in communion with our own should be encouraged to communicate in Anglican churches, when the ministrations of their own Church are not available, or in other special or temporary circumstances.

EXPLANATORY NOTE

In view of the dangers of misconception, we think it desirable to say that in recognising that a bishop of the Anglican Communion may under very strict regulations and in very special circumstances permit individual communicants to join with members of other Christian bodies in their services of the administration of the Lord's Supper, we felt bound to consider the difficulties created by present conditions, especially in some parts of the mission field. But we would point out that the very special circumstances and the very strict regulations specified in this Resolution of themselves show that we are not departing from the rule of our Church that the minister of the sacrament of Holy Communion should be a priest episcopally ordained.

The Church of Scotland

Resolution 43
The Conference expresses its gratitude to the distinguished members of the Church of Scotland* who accepted the invitation to confer with its Committee. It hopes that an invitation may soon be issued to the now happily united Church of Scotland to enter into free and unrestricted conference with representatives of the Anglican Communion on the basis of the 'Appeal to All Christian People' issued in 1920.

* The Very Revd John White, DD, and the Hon. Lord Sands, Senator of the College of Justice.

Evangelical Free Churches of England

Resolution 44
The Conference cordially thanks the influential delegation from the Federal Council of the Evangelical Free Churches of England* for attending one of the sessions of its Committee, and for the help of that delegation in defining the issues which have still to be resolved before further advance towards organic union is possible. The Conference notes with satisfaction and gratitude the great measure of agreement on matters of faith reached at the Conferences held from 1921 till 1925 between representatives of the Church of England and representatives of the Federal Council of Evangelical Free Churches, and hopes that at an early date such conferences may be resumed with a view to ascertaining whether the Proposed Scheme of Union prepared for the Churches in South India, or other proposals which have been put forward, suggest lines on which further advance towards agreement on questions of order can be made, and that similar conferences may be held elsewhere.

* The Revd A.E. Garvie, DD, the Revd M.E. Aubrey, MA, the Revd J.T. Barkby, the Revd S.M. Berry, DD, the Revd D. Brook, DCL, the Revd Charles Brown, DD, the Revd J. Scott Lidgett, DD, the Revd W.L. Robertson, DD, the Revd P. Carnegie Simpson, DD, the Revd H.J. Taylor and Bishop Arthur Ward.

Schemes of Reunion

Resolution 45
In view of the various schemes of reunion and other projects and advances towards union and intercommunion which have been the subject of discussion or negotiation, the Conference reminds the Church that it is a paramount duty to seek unity among Christians in every direction, and assures all who are working for this end of its cordial support in their endeavours; it also reminds the Church that until full

and final schemes are set out and terms of intercommunion are definitely arranged, the expression of final judgements on individual schemes is premature.

Co-operation in Evangelism

Resolution 46
Meanwhile the Conference urges the desirability of organising and participating in efforts of evangelism in co-operation with Christians of other Communions, both as a means of bearing effective witness to the multitudes who are detached from all forms of organised Christianity, and as a means of expressing and strengthening that sense of unity in the Gospel which binds together in spiritual fellowship those who own allegiance to different Churches.

Unity among Anglicans

Resolution 47
The Conference calls upon all members of the Anglican Communion to promote the cause of union by fostering and deepening in all possible ways the fellowship of the Anglican Communion itself, so that by mutual understanding and appreciation all may come to a fuller apprehension of the truth as it is in Jesus, and more perfectly make manifest to the world the unity of the Spirit in and through the diversity of his gifts.

THE ANGLICAN COMMUNION

Resolution 48
The Conference affirms that the true constitution of the Catholic Church involves the principle of the autonomy of particular Churches based upon a common faith and order, and commends to the faithful those sections of the Report of Committee IV which deal with the ideal and future of the Anglican Communion.

Resolution 49
The Conference approves the following statement of the nature and status of the Anglican Communion, as that term is used in its Resolutions:

The Anglican Communion is a fellowship, within the one Holy Catholic and Apostolic Church, of those duly constituted dioceses, provinces or regional Churches in communion with the See of Canterbury, which have the following characteristics in common:

(a) they uphold and propagate the Catholic and Apostolic faith and order as they are generally set forth in the Book of Common Prayer as authorised in their several Churches;

(b) they are particular or national Churches, and, as such, promote within each of their territories a national expression of Christian faith, life and worship; and

(c) they are bound together not by a central legislative and executive authority, but by mutual loyalty sustained through the common counsel of the bishops in conference.

The Conference makes this statement praying for and eagerly awaiting the time when the Churches of the present Anglican Communion will enter into communion with other parts of the Catholic Church not definable as Anglican in the above sense, as a step towards the ultimate reunion of all Christendom in one visibly united fellowship.*

* Compare Encyclical Letter of the Lambeth Conference 1878 with [its] 'Report of Committee on the best mode of maintaining union among the various Churches of the Anglican Communion'. *The Six Lambeth Conferences 1867-1920*, pp 82-83.

The Consultative Body

Resolution 50

(a)   The Conference reaffirms the opinion expressed in Resolution 44 of the Lambeth Conference of 1920, 'that the Consultative Body is of the nature of a continuation committee of the Lambeth Conference, and neither possesses nor claims any executive or administrative power.'

The Conference recommends that:

(b)   The Consultative Body should be prepared to advise on questions of faith, order, policy or administration, referred to it by any bishop or group of bishops, calling in expert advisers at its discretion, and reserving the right to decline to entertain any particular question.

Consequently, the Committee of Students of Liturgical Questions appointed in accordance with Resolution 38 of the Lambeth Conference of 1920 need not be reappointed.

(c)   The usual duties of the Consultative Body of the Lambeth Conference should be:

(i) To carry on the work left to it by the preceding Conference.

(ii) To assist the Archbishop of Canterbury in the preparation of the business of the ensuing Conference.

(iii) To deal with matters referred to the Archbishop of Canterbury on which he requests its aid.

(iv) To deal with matters referred to it by any bishop or group of bishops, subject to any limitations upon such references which may be imposed by the regulations of local and regional Churches.

(d)   Hereafter the members of the Consultative Body should consist of not less than 18 members, appointed to represent the Lambeth Conference by the Archbishop of Canterbury, with due regard to regional requirements, after consultation with the metropolitans and presiding bishops: vacancies being filled in the same way. Further, the first appointment should be made within 18 months of this meeting of the Conference, the present Consultative Body continuing to function in the meantime, and those then appointed should hold office until the next meeting of the Conference.

Appellate Tribunal

Resolution 51
The Conference, believing the formation of a central appellate tribunal to be inconsistent with the spirit of the Anglican Communion, holds that the establishment of final courts of appeal should be left to the decision of local and regional Churches.

Provincial Organisation

Resolution 52
Saving always the moral and spiritual independence of the divine society, the Conference approves the association of dioceses or provinces in the larger unity of a 'national Church', with or without the formal recognition of the civil government, as serving to give spiritual expression to the distinctive genius of races and peoples, and thus to bring more effectually under the influence of Christ's religion both the process of government and the habit of society.

Resolution 53
(a)   In view of the many advantages of the organisation of dioceses into provinces and the difficulties and dangers of isolation, the formation of provinces should everywhere be encouraged.
(b)   The minimum organisation essential to provincial life is a college or synod of bishops which will act corporately in dealing with questions concerning the faith, order and discipline of the Church.
(c)   The minimum number of dioceses suitable to form a province is four.
(d)   The balance between provincial authority and diocesan autonomy may vary from province to province according to the constitutions agreed upon in each case.

Resolution 54
Without prejudice to the provisions of any constitution already adopted by any province or regional Church, the Conference advises that when

the bishops of a group of dioceses under the oversight of the Archbishop of Canterbury or attached to some other province have prepared and accepted a tentative constitution for a province, they should notify this to the authorities under which they have hitherto worked, and request that the new province be recognised as such and that they be released from obedience to other authority, as far as is necessary to enable them to subscribe to the constitution of the new province, and (if so required) take the oath of canonical obedience to its metropolitan. If this request be granted, the new province may then be formally constituted. The proper procedure would be that the bishops and clergy should subscribe to its constitution and that the bishops (if so required) should take the oath of canonical obedience to its metropolitan. The metropolitan or presiding bishop should thereupon notify all metropolitans and presiding bishops in the Anglican Communion of the formation of the province.

Resolution 55
Where the office of metropolitan is attached to a particular see, the other dioceses of the province should have some effective voice in the election of a bishop to that see.

Resolution 56
(a)   The successive stages at which a newly founded diocese can be entrusted with greater responsibility, whether for legislation and general government, or for the election of its bishop, should be determined by the provincial authorities or the Archbishop of Canterbury (as the case may be) in consultation with the bishop.
(b)   Where the appointment of a bishop still remains with the provincial authorities or the Archbishop of Canterbury, it is generally desirable that the diocese should in some way be consulted before such appointment is made.

Resolution 57
The Conference recognises with thankfulness the provincial organisation attained in Japan and China, whereby the Nippon Sei Kokwai and the Chung Hua Sheng Kung Hui have become constituent Churches of the Anglican Communion, and welcomes the Japanese and Chinese bishops now present for the first time in the history of the Lambeth Conference as bishops of these Churches.

Resolution 58
The Conference welcomes the measure of progress already made towards the formation of a single province in East Africa.

Resolution 59
In view of differences of standard and qualification for Holy Orders demanded in various provinces, the Conference considers the principle of discrimination involved in such regulations as the Colonial Clergy Act to be legitimate, not only in England, but in any province which so desires.

Resolution 60
The Conference requests the Archbishop of Canterbury to appoint a committee of persons representing each Church concerned to confer with the Church of England Pensions Board on the comprehensive scheme of reciprocal arrangements for clergy pensions which has been submitted by the Board, so that such representatives may report thereon to their respective Churches.

THE MINISTRY OF THE CHURCH

The supply and training of men for Holy Orders

Resolution 61
Inasmuch as the ministry is the gift of God through Christ and is essential not only to the being and wellbeing of his Church but also to the extension of his Kingdom; and inasmuch as our Lord taught us to pray for its increase, the Conference expresses the hope that regular and earnest prayer for the ministry may be offered, and teaching about vocation may be given, throughout the whole Church both at the Ember seasons and at other times.

The Conference is convinced not only that it is the duty of the Church to foster vocation to the ministry but that it behoves every clergyman, schoolmaster, parent, and indeed every Christian man and woman to seek out and encourage signs of such vocation.

Resolution 62
While recognising with gratitude the support given in recent years to funds which assist the training of candidates for the ministry, and while believing that those who have heard the call should exercise all possible self-help in responding to it, the Conference places on record its conviction that it is the privilege and duty of the Church to find, when necessary, the means for the training of those whom God has called.

Resolution 63
In view of the rise in the standard of education and of the constantly increasing opportunities of university training, the Conference deems it important that candidates for Holy Orders should in most cases be

graduates of a university as well as properly trained in the special studies which belong to their calling.

The Conference expresses the hope that the Church will take every opportunity both for seeking and for training candidates in new universities which have been established in great cities and elsewhere. With a view to promoting theological study in these and other universities, the Conference recommends that, where the conditions allow, the Church should establish theological colleges in close connection with universities, and should join with the representatives of other Churches in establishing theological faculties in them.

Resolution 64

In the matter of special preparation of candidates for the ministry, the Conference regards a competent knowledge of the Bible, of Christian worship, history, theology and morals, and pastoral work, together with training in the devotional life, as of the first importance. To this should be added instruction in reading and preaching. Beyond this we are anxious not to overload the curriculum of our theological colleges, but we believe it to be advantageous that students should be given such elementary instruction in psychology, the art of teaching, social economics and other studies bearing upon their life work as will encourage them to maintain their interest in these subjects after ordination. We express the hope that greater efforts will be made to stimulate the intellectual and spiritual life of the clergy especially in the earlier years of their service.

Resolution 65

The Conference for reasons given in the Report of its Committee on the ministry cannot recommend a widespread adoption of the proposal that men of mature age and assured position might be called by authority, and, if willing, ordained to the priesthood without being required to give up their present occupation. But while declaring that ordination to the priesthood involves full and life-long service, not to be made subservient to any other interests, it sees no insuperable objection to the ordination, with provincial sanction and under proper safeguards, where the need is great, of such *auxiliary priests*.

Further, in order to meet the present pressing need, the Conference would not question the action of any bishop who, with the sanction of the national, regional or provincial Church concerned, should authorise such licensed *readers* as he shall approve to administer the chalice at the request of the parish priest.

The Ministry of Women

Resolution 66
The Conference wishes to insist on the great importance of offering to women of ability and education, who have received adequate special training, posts which provide full scope for their powers and bring to them real partnership with those who direct the work of the Church, and genuine responsibility for their share of it, whether in parish or diocese; so that such women may find in the Church's service a sphere for the exercise of their capacity.

Resolution 67
The order of deaconess is for women the one and only order of the ministry which we can recommend our branch of the Catholic Church to recognise and use.

Resolution 68
The ordination of a deaconess should everywhere include prayer by the bishop and the laying-on of hands, the delivery of the New Testament to the candidate, and a formula giving authority to execute the office of a deaconess in the Church of God. Such ordination need not be at the Ember seasons, and should not be combined with an ordination of priests or deacons, but should always be held in the face of the Church.

Resolution 69
The Conference re-asserts the words in Resolution 49 of the Lambeth Conference of 1920, viz. 'The office of a deaconess is primarily a ministry of succour, bodily and spiritual, especially to women, and should follow the lines of the primitive rather than of the modern diaconate of men.' It should be understood that the deaconess dedicates herself to a life-long service, but no vow or implied promise of celibacy should be required as necessary for admission to the order.

Resolution 70
Under the sanction of the province, the bishop may, on the request of the parish priest, entrust the following functions to the ordained deaconess:
(a) to assist the minister in the preparation of candidates for baptism and for confirmation;
(b) to assist at the administration of Holy Baptism by virtue of her office;
(c) to baptize in church, and to officiate at the Churching of Women;

(d) in church to read Morning and Evening Prayer and the Litany, except such portions as are reserved to the priest, and to lead in prayer; with the licence of the bishop, to instruct and preach, except in the service of Holy Communion.

Resolution 71
The Conference recommends that bishops give commissions to women of special qualifications to speak at other than the regular services, or to conduct retreats, or to give spiritual counsel.

Resolution 72
Every stipendiary woman worker, whether parochial or other, should receive formal recognition from the bishop, who should satisfy himself not only of her general fitness, but also that an adequate stipend is secured to her with provision for a pension, and that she works under a definite form of agreement.

The Ministry of Healing

Resolution 73
(a) The Conference commends to the Church *The Ministry of Healing* (SPCK, 1924), being the Report of a Committee set up in accordance with Resolution 63 of the Lambeth Conference of 1920.
(b) Methods of spiritual healing, such as unction or the laying-on of hands, should be used only in close conjunction with prayer and spiritual preparation.
(c) There is urgent need for co-operation between clergy and doctors since spiritual and physical treatment are complementary and equally necessary for true wellbeing.
(d) Seeing that the ministry of the Church is a ministry for the whole man, it is of the utmost importance that the clergy should equip themselves for a fuller understanding of the intimate connection between moral and spiritual disorders and mental and physical ills.

Religious Communities

Resolution 74
The Conference recognises with thankfulness the growth of religious communities both of men and women in the Anglican Communion and the contribution which they have made to a deeper spiritual life in the Church and their notable services in the mission field, but advises the establishment, by canon or other means, of closer co-operation between the episcopate and the communities on the general lines indicated in the Report of the Committee.

YOUTH AND ITS VOCATION

Resolution 75
The Conference commends the Report of the Committee on Youth and its Vocation to the careful attention of the Church and hopes that in all parts of the Anglican Communion the bishops, with the assistance of the clergy and laity, particularly those qualified to represent youth, will face the facts of the situation and the challenge which they constitute to the whole Christian Church; believing that the great tasks before the Church today call for a new measure of devotion to Christ and his Church on the part of all, both young and old.

1948

THE CHRISTIAN DOCTRINE OF MAN

Resolution 1
The Conference, believing that man's disorders and conflicts are primarily due to ignorance or rejection of the true understanding of his nature and destiny as revealed by God in Jesus Christ, affirms that man has a spiritual as well as a material nature, and that he can attain full stature only as he recognises and yields to the love of God as revealed in Jesus Christ and to the influence of his Holy Spirit.

Resolution 2
The Conference affirms that this world, though corrupted by sin, is God's world and man's appointed training ground for eternity; and that the grace of God, offered to him through Jesus Christ, enables him to rise superior to his environment and to live in this world as the child of God.

Resolution 3
The Conference welcomes the great advance in scientific discovery characteristic of our age, and repudiates the suggestion that any check should be placed upon it. But we insist that the consequent growth of man's knowledge increases his moral responsibility for the use he makes of it.

Resolution 4
We fully share man's aspiration for fellowship in an ordered society and for freedom of individual achievement, but we assert that no view of man can be satisfactory which confines his interests and hopes to

91

this world and to this life alone; such views belittle man and blind him to the greatness of his destiny.

Resolution 5
The Conference believes that both the recognition of the responsibility of the individual to God and the development of his personality are gravely imperilled by any claim made either by the state or by any group within the state to control the whole of human life. Personality is developed in community, but the community must be one of free persons. The Christian must therefore judge every social system by its effect on human personality.

THE CHURCH AND THE MODERN WORLD

Human Rights

Resolution 6
The Conference declares that all men, irrespective of race or colour, are equally the objects of God's love and are called to love and serve him. All men are made in his image; for all Christ died; and to all there is made the offer of eternal life. Every individual is therefore bound by duties towards God and towards other men, and has certain rights without the enjoyment of which he cannot freely perform those duties. These rights should be declared by the Church, recognised by the state, and safeguarded by international law.

Resolution 7
The Conference declares that among such rights are security of life and person; the right to work, to bring up a family, and to possess personal property; the right to freedom of speech, of discussion and association, and to accurate information; and to full freedom of religious life and practice; and that these rights belong to all men irrespective of race or colour.

Resolution 8
The Conference endorses the proposed Covenant on Human Rights, now before the United Nations, and declares it necessary for full religious freedom that

(a) every person shall have the right to freedom of religion, conscience, and belief, including the right, either alone or in community with other persons of like mind, to hold and manifest any religious or other belief, to change his belief and to practise any form of religious worship and observance, and he shall not be required to do any act that is contrary to such worship and observance; and that

(b) every person of full age and sound mind shall be free, either alone or in community with other persons of like mind, to give and receive any form of religious teaching, and in the case of a minor the parent or guardian shall be free to determine what religious teaching he shall receive.

The Conference believes that the above rights should be subject only to such limitations as are internationally recognised as necessary to protect public order, morals, and the rights and freedoms of others. Any such limitations should be clearly defined by law, and there should be appeal concerning them before impartial courts of justice.

The Church and War

Resolution 9

The Conference reaffirms Resolution 25 of 1930, 'that war as a method of settling international disputes is incompatible with the teaching and example of our Lord Jesus Christ.'

Resolution 10

The Conference affirms that it is the duty of governments to work for the general reduction and control of armaments of every kind and for their final elimination, except those which may be necessary for international police protection; but until such time as this is achieved, it recognises that there are occasions when both nations and individuals are obliged to resort to war as the lesser of two evils.

Resolution 11

The Conference urges that the use of atomic energy be brought under such effective international inspection and control as to prevent its use as a weapon of war.

Resolution 12

The Conference appeals to all Christians to unite in working for the reconciliation of the nations which have been at war, and urges the allied nations to agree without delay upon treaties of peace with Germany and Japan, based on principles of justice.

Resolution 13

The Conference, moved by the tragic plight of vast numbers of men and women who, owing to political conditions, have been exiled from their home country, and believing that there is room in which they may find new and permanent homes, urges the governments of all countries represented in this Conference where such room can be found to take active steps for the admission of as many as possible of those men and women with their families as new settlers; and calls upon all Christian people within countries wherein they are permitted to settle to give them every help in their power.

Resolution 14
The Conference urges the statesmen of the world together with their people to do their utmost to frame a world policy for the fuller development and a juster distribution of the world's economic resources, to meet the needs of men and women in all nations.

Resolution 15
The Conference believes that the nations of the world must have an organ of co-operation to which each nation must be ready to yield some of its sovereignty, and trusts that the United Nations may be used, strengthened, and improved to that end.

Palestine

Resolution 16
The Conference feels deep concern for the future of Palestine: it prays that good order and peace may be restored to the land sacred to millions of Christians as well as to Muslims and Jews. It greatly appreciates the efforts made to restore peace and expresses its sympathy with all of every race, and particularly Christians of every Church, who are suffering.

The Conference appeals to the nations of the world to deal with the problem not as one of expediency—political, strategic, or economic—but as a moral and spiritual question that touches a nerve centre of the world's religious life. And for that reason it urges the United Nations to place Jerusalem and its immediate environs under permanent international control, with freedom of access to sacred places secured for the adherents of the three religions.

The Church and the Modern State

Resolution 17
The Conference affirms that the doctrine that power is its own justification is a most corrupting influence in political thought and practice today.

Resolution 18
The Conference affirms it to be the duty of the Church constantly to proclaim the sovereignty of God who is the Father of all and whose law is above all nations; it condemns the concept of the unbridled

sovereignty of the nation and such usurpation of power by the state as is opposed to the basic truths of Christianity; further, it denies that the individual exists for the state, but asserts that one of the principal ends of the state is the development of personality, the highest good of the individual.

Resolution 19
We believe that the state is under the moral law of God, and is intended by him to be an instrument for human welfare. We therefore welcome the growing concern and care of the modern state for its citizens, and call upon Church members to accept their own political responsibility and to co-operate with the state and its officers in their work.

Resolution 20
The Conference affirms that the Church must be free to order its worship and fellowship, to teach, and to evangelise. In view of a tendency of the state to encroach on the freedom of individuals and voluntary associations, it urges Christians in all lands to guard such freedoms with vigilance and to convince public opinion that their preservation is essential to the maintenance of true democracy and personal and national wellbeing.

Resolution 21
Recognising that in the quest for a just social order the differences between those who value tradition and those who feel most urgently the need for change and reform may provoke enmity, the Conference believes that, however strong these tensions are, the fellowship of the Christian community should contain them, and that in times of controversy Church members can make this significant contribution of unity in Christ to the life of neighbourhood or nation.

Resolution 22
The Conference calls the Church to think out afresh the Christian gospel of work in terms relevant to modern working conditions, and calls on all Church members to find their incentive to work, not only in security and gain, but chiefly in service and good workmanship, as an offering to the glory of God.

Resolution 23
Since the state, industry, and community services are offering an increasing number of posts which may be made spheres of Christian influence, the Conference calls upon Church members to bring to such posts not only professional training and a sense of vocation but also a sound knowledge of the Christian doctrine of God and man.

Resolution 24
Welcoming recent declarations of more humane governmental policy towards the peoples of undeveloped countries, we call upon the governments concerned to ensure to these peoples their economic rights and the best elements of the spiritual and cultural heritage of their own lands and of other civilisations, so that they may take their rightful part in the whole family of nations, and we urge all Christians, whether in government service or as private citizens, to see that these declarations of policy are put into practice.

Communism

Resolution 25
The Conference, while recognising that in many lands there are Communists who are practising Christians, nevertheless declares that Marxian Communism is contrary to Christian faith and practice, for it denies the existence of God, revelation, and a future life; it treats the individual man as a means and not an end; it encourages class warfare; it regards the moral law not as absolute but as relative to the needs of the state. The Conference holds that while a state must take the precautions it regards as necessary to protect good order and peace from all subversive movements, it is the special duty of the Church to oppose the challenge of the Marxian theory of Communism by sound teaching and the example of a better way, and that the Church, at all times and in all places, should be a fearless witness against political, social, and economic injustice.

Resolution 26
The Conference believes that Communism is presenting a challenge to Christian people to study and understand its theory and practice, so that they may be well instructed as to which elements in it are in conflict with the Christian view of man and must therefore be resisted, and which elements are a true judgement on the existing social and economic order.

Education

Resolution 27
The Conference holds that the Church should press for the best educational opportunity everywhere for all, without racial distinction and without privilege for wealth.

Resolution 28
The Conference gratefully recognises the admirable work done by

Christian teachers throughout the world and urges churchmen to bring the opportunity of this high calling to the attention of young men and women.

Resolution 29
The Conference while giving full support to state education is convinced that there is a unique value for the community in the long tradition of Church education. The Conference believes that the freedom of experiment which this tradition affords and the religious, moral, and social training which is its specific purpose are invaluable for the best interests of education and that everything possible should be done to open the benefits of such Church education to all who desire them.

Resolution 30
The Conference affirms that the Church owes a deep debt of gratitude to Sunday and day school teachers and youth leaders who, in the face of increasing difficulties, have forwarded the Church's teaching ministry to children and young people with devoted service. The Conference emphasises the responsibility of individual clergymen and parishes in the work of Christian education.

Resolution 31
The Conference welcomes the statutory provision made in England in 1944 for religious instruction and worship in schools, as well as similar developments in other countries. We urge universities and training colleges to provide adequately for the training of teachers in this field.

Resolution 32
The Conference welcomes the steps taken in some universities to make provision for courses designed to give general instruction in Christian faith and practice to those who are not students in theology. It also urges that a chapel for corporate worship should be provided in every university and university college.

Resolution 33
The Conference calls special attention to the urgent need for more effective and continuous adult education through study and discussion. It believes that adult religious education should be included in the normal work of parish and diocese.

Resolution 34
Recognising the great influence of films and broadcasting both for good and for evil, we welcome the efforts now being made to improve

their quality; sharing the anxiety of many teachers and educational authorities lest the films shown to children should undermine sound educational influences, we particularly welcome the provision of wholesome films and broadcasts for children.

Resolution 35
The Conference urges further investigation and experiment on the part of the Church in film production and radio programmes as a means of religious and missionary education, and full co-operation with experts in these fields.

The Church Militant

Resolution 36
The Conference, assured that the Gospel of Christ is the power of God unto salvation and that the conversion of mankind to him is the only way whereby evil in the world today can be overcome, and being convinced of the need for spiritual leadership and venture at this time, issues:

(a) a summons to all members of the Church to acknowledge their failure, both personal and corporate, to make Christ universally known, and humbly to rededicate themselves to the task committed to the people of God;

(b) a call to the individual members of every local church to strengthen the corporate life and worship of their church, and so to increase its influence upon the life of the community;

(c) an appeal to all bishops of the Anglican Communion to take the initiative in this time of urgency, calling both clergy and laity to survey and undertake the task set before the Church in their immediate localities. We would urge upon the clergy the importance of pastoral visitation, of making contacts in factory, field, and office, and of fuller participation in the everyday life of the people, so as to win from them a hearing which would result in a new approach to worship, and a new understanding of the universal sovereignty of God.

Resolution 37
The Conference urges all Church people to look upon their membership of Christ in the Church as the central fact in their lives. They should regard themselves as individually sharing responsibility for the corporate life and witness of the Church in the places where they live. They should discharge this responsibility and give a distinctive witness

(a) by the regularity of their attendance at public worship and especially at the Holy Communion;

(b) by the practice of private prayer, Bible reading, and self-discipline;

(c) by bringing the teaching and example of Christ into their everyday lives;

(d) by the boldness of their spoken witness to their faith in Christ;

(e) by personal service to Church and community;

(f) by the offering of money, according to their means, for the support of the work of the Church, at home and overseas.

Thus there will be in every locality a living centre of Christian faith, witness, and fellowship.

Resolution 38
While to every member of the Church there falls a share of responsibility for its life and work, yet it is impossible to over-estimate the importance of maintaining and indeed increasing the supply of men and women who are prepared to devote their whole time to some special form of ministry for Christ and his Church. The Conference therefore urges clergy, teachers, and parents to seek for and encourage among young people vocations to Holy Orders, to the teaching ministry, to religious communities, and to other forms of full-time service in the Church, at home and abroad.

The Christian Way of Life

Resolution 39
The Conference affirms that wholeness of personality can be attained only in so far as a man is consciously associated with Jesus Christ. This wholeness necessitates membership of the perfect society, the Kingdom of God proclaimed by Christ. The growth of that Kingdom is advanced by all honest and rightly directed work and service in every sphere of art and science, politics and industry. But it is the calling of the Church to act as God's special instrument in its extension everywhere. It is therefore in the society of their fellow Christians that men will find an adequate purpose in life, an assurance of their individual worth, and the power to become true men.

Resolution 40
The Conference values the witness given by those who, in response to a special vocation, keep themselves apart from the life of the world. But we believe that Christians generally are called by God to take their part in the life of the world, and through the power of God's grace to transform it.

Resolution 41
The Conference believes that the unity in Christ which exists between Church people ought to find more definite expression outside the church building, and we urge the members of every congregation to seek for opportunities of expressing their unity by the undertaking of common tasks.

Resolution 42
The Conference reminds members of the Church of the grievous fact that many among their friends and neighbours are in no vital contact with the Christian religion; and we urge them so to prepare themselves by prayer and thought that they may be able by the help of God to use every opportunity to bring others to Christ in his Church.

Resolution 43
The Conference is convinced that discrimination between men on the grounds of race alone is inconsistent with the principles of Christ's religion. We urge that in every land men of every race should be encouraged to develop in accordance with their abilities; and that this involves fairness of opportunity in trades and professions, in facilities for travelling and in the provision of housing, in education at all stages, and in schemes of social welfare. Every churchman should be assured of a cordial welcome in any church of our Communion, and no one should be ineligible for any position in the Church by reason of his race or colour.

Resolution 44
The Conference draws attention to the grave moral and social evils that have arisen in many lands through the prevalence of gambling on a vast scale. In view of these evils we urge that no Church organisation should make money by gambling. We deprecate the raising of money by the state or by any organisation through sweepstakes and similar methods, however good may be the object for which the money is raised; and we warn men and women of the danger of acquiring the habit of gambling, which has led in so many cases to the deterioration of character and the ruin of homes.

Resolution 45
The Conference stresses the urgency of providing that every family should have a home of its own which provides for fellowship and privacy.

Resolution 46
The Conference affirms that education should be more than a training

for a livelihood or even for citizenship. It should be based upon the fact that every child is a child of God created by God for citizenship in heaven as well as on earth.

Resolution 47
The Conference affirms that work ought to be a vocation. Therefore all possible guidance should be given to young people in their choice of a life work, in order to foster their sense of vocation and to ensure that they are enabled to take up work which they can rightly regard as a form of service to God and their fellow men.

Resolution 48
The Conference, recognising that marriage and motherhood remain the normal vocation of women, urges the importance of fostering in girls the sense of the dignity of this calling and the need to prepare for it. At the same time it welcomes the great contributions now being made by women in many walks of life, and urges that girls and young women be given the fullest possible opportunities for vocational training.

Resolution 49
The Conference believes that there is great need of a fresh understanding of the nature and function of universities, and the place therein of theology in its full meaning, as a part of any curriculum which claims to be complete. We welcome the growing readiness to found schools and faculties of theology in centres of higher education, and we urge, on educational as well as more strictly religious grounds, that they be set up where they do not yet exist.

THE UNITY OF THE CHURCH

Co-operation in Christian Action

Resolution 50
The Conference believes that it is the duty of the Church to bear united witness to God's redeeming grace in Jesus Christ, to do battle against the powers of evil, and to seek the glory of God in all things. It therefore appeals to Christians in all Communions, whatever the differences which may separate them in Church order and doctrine, to join in Christian action in all parts of the world irrespective of political party for the application of the principles of the Christian religion to all departments of national and international life.

Thankfulness for Growing Unity

Resolution 51
The Conference records its thankfulness to Almighty God for the revival of interest in the cause of Christian unity which has been increasingly manifested in many parts of the world. It also pays a tribute of gratitude to all those in our own and in other Communions who have displayed courage, enterprise, and vision in the service of this cause.

The Church of South India

Resolution 52
We
(a)   endorse generally the paragraphs in the Report of our Committee on Unity which refer to South India;
(b)   give thanks to God for the measure of unity locally achieved by the inauguration of the Church of South India, and we pledge ourselves to pray and work for its development into an ever more perfect fulfilment of the will of God for his Church; and we
(c)   look forward hopefully and with longing to the day when there shall be full communion between the Church of South India and the Churches of the Anglican Communion.

Suggestions Relating to the Constitution of the Church of South India

Resolution 53
The Conference expresses the hope that, so soon as it may appear to the authorities of the Church of South India to be expedient to take up the matter, such provisions of the Constitution of that Church and such statements contained therein as are known to have given rise either to uncertainty or to grave anxiety in the minds of many, may be reconsidered with a view to their amendment. The Conference would call special attention to the six points specified in the Report of its Committee on Unity.

The Anglican Communion and the Church of South India

Resolution 54
In the sphere of immediate and practical action, the Conference recommends:
(a)   That former Anglicans, clerical or lay, who are now members of the Church of South India, and also Anglicans who hereafter join

should be accepted and allowed full privileges of ministry and communion in any Church, province, or diocese of the Anglican Communion, subject to the regulations of the responsible authorities in the area concerned.

(b)   That members, whether clerical or lay, of the Churches of the Anglican Communion, who may go to South India, should not be subject to censure if they join the Church of South India or take work of any kind in it.

(c)   That clerical or lay members of the Churches of the Anglican Communion visiting the territory of the Church of South India should not be subject to censure if they accept the hospitality of that Church for the performance of priestly functions or the receiving of Holy Communion, subject to the regulations of the Churches, provinces, or dioceses to which they belong.

(d)   That ministers of the Church of South India who have not been episcopally ordained should not be regarded as having acquired any new rights or status in relation to the Anglican Communion as a whole solely by reason of the fact that they are ministers of that Church.

(e)   In regard to the bishops, presbyters, and deacons consecrated or ordained in the Church of South India at or after the inauguration of that Church, the Conference is unable to make one recommendation agreed to by all. It therefore records the two following views:

(i) one view (held by a majority) that such bishops, presbyters, and deacons should be acknowledged as true bishops, presbyters, and deacons in the Church of Christ and should be accepted as such in every part of the Anglican Communion, subject only to such regulations as are normally made in all such cases by the responsible authorities in each area;

(ii) another view (held by a substantial minority) that it is not yet possible to pass any definite judgement upon the precise status of such bishops, presbyters, and deacons in the Church of Christ or to recommend that they be accepted in the Anglican Communion as bishops, presbyters, or deacons.

The Conference records the fact that no member of the Conference desires to condemn outright or to declare invalid the episcopally consecrated and ordained ministry of the Church of South India. It recognises that there will be differences in the attitude of Churches, provinces, or dioceses regarding the status of the bishops, presbyters, and deacons of the Church of South India, but it expresses the unanimous hope that such differences may never in any part of the Anglican Communion be made a ground for condemnation of action taken by any Church, province, or diocese.

(f)   That lay communicants who in the Church of South India have received episcopal confirmation should, in Churches of the Anglican

Communion, be received as communicants, subject to the approval of responsible authority, but should not thereby acquire any new status or rights in relation to the Anglican Communion as a whole; and

(g) that other recognised communicants of the Church of South India should, in Churches of the Anglican Communion, subject to the approval of responsible authority and to any such regulations as may locally obtain, be admissible to communion by an exercise of the principle of 'economy'.

Resolution 55
The Conference expresses its concurrence with the recommendations contained in the Report of its Committee on Unity with reference to the Nandyal area in South India.

Further Approaches to Reunion

Resolution 56
The Conference calls upon all the Churches of the Anglican Communion to seek earnestly by prayer and by conference the fulfilment of the vision 'of a Church, genuinely Catholic, loyal to all truth, and gathering into its fellowship "all who profess and call themselves Christians", within whose visible unity all the treasures of faith and order, bequeathed as a heritage by the past to the present, shall be possessed in common and made serviceable to the whole Body of Christ.' It recognises that 'within this unity Christian Communions now separated from one another would retain much that has long been distinctive in their methods of worship and service.'

In the hope of setting forward the fulfilment of this vision, the Conference recalls the principles set forth in the 'Appeal to All Christian People' and the relevant Resolutions of the Lambeth Conference of 1920 on the reunion of Christendom, and records certain counsels and considerations which it believes should guide the Churches of our Communion in future approaches to reunion:

(a) The theological issues, especially those concerning the Church and the ministry, should be faced at the outset, and to this end the negotiating Churches should obtain the help of theologians in framing schemes for reunion or intercommunion.

(b) The unification of the ministry in a form satisfactory to all the bodies concerned, either at the inauguration of the union or as soon as possible thereafter, is likely to be a prerequisite to success in all future proposals for the reunion of the Churches.

(c) The integral connection between the Church and the ministry should be safeguarded in all proposals for the achievement of inter-

communion through the creation of a mutually recognised ministry.
(d) The goal in any steps towards a united Church within a given area should always be a Church with which the Anglican Churches could eventually be in full communion.
(e) Because the Anglican Communion is itself a treasured unity with a special vocation, a part of our Communion contemplating a step which would involve its withdrawal from the Anglican family of Churches should consult the Lambeth Conference or the provinces and member Churches of this family of Churches before final commitment to such a course.

Schemes for Organic Union

Resolution 57
The Conference has heard with satisfaction and hope of proposals for organic union in various areas, and, while calling the attention of those concerned in such schemes to the warnings contained in the Report of the Committee on Unity, believes that schemes of this type have undoubted advantages.

Schemes for the Provision of a Mutually Recognised Ministry

Resolution 58
The Conference has heard with interest and sympathy of proposals for the provision of a mutually recognised ministry in advance of any explicit plans for organic union. In spite of the disadvantages attaching to such schemes, which are noted in the Report of the Committee on Unity, the Conference is not prepared to discourage further explorations along this line, if they are linked with provisions for the growing together of the Churches concerned and with the definite acceptance of organic union as their final goal.

Faith and Order Statement

Resolution 59
The Conference agrees that the Statement of Faith and Order prepared by the Joint Commission on Approaches to Unity of the Protestant Episcopal Church in the United States of America is in entire harmony with the Lambeth Quadrilateral, and may be used in negotiations of the Protestant Episcopal Church with any interested Christian body.

The Church of Scotland

Resolution 60
The Conference welcomes the proposal to resume the conversations between delegates appointed by Archbishop Lang and representatives of the Church of Scotland, begun in 1932 and suspended in 1934, in view of the new situation created by the Archbishop of Canterbury's sermon at Cambridge, November 1946.

The Evangelical Free Churches of England

Resolution 61
The Conference cordially welcomes the renewed opening of negotiations, arising out of the initiative of the Archbishop of Canterbury in his Cambridge sermon, between the Evangelical Free Churches of England and delegates appointed by the Archbishop of Canterbury to act on behalf of the Church of England, and expresses the hope that the conversations thus happily begun may, by the blessing of God, lead to fruitful results.

Ceylon

Resolution 62
The Conference has learned with deep interest of the proposed scheme for Church union in Ceylon, regards it as being, in many respects, among the most promising of the various schemes of its type in different parts of the world, and expresses the hope that, subject to the assent of the Church of India, Burma, and Ceylon, the projected union may, under the blessing of God, in due course be carried into effect.

North India

Resolution 63
The Conference welcomes generally the negotiations informally begun in North India with a view to union, desires to encourage the authorities of the Church of India, Burma, and Ceylon to go forward, and expresses the hope that in the working out of the proposed scheme account may be taken both of the lessons to be derived from South India and of the proposals made in Ceylon.

Iran

Resolution 64
The Conference expresses its deep sympathy with the Bishop and

Church in Iran in the difficulties, arising largely from relative isolation and from the small scale of the Church in that country, by which they are confronted. It endorses generally the advice given in the section of the Report of its Committee on Unity which relates to Iran, believes that the negotiations directed towards the attainment of local Church unity in Iran should be continued, and concurs in the view that the assistance of theologians should be made available to the Bishop in Iran and to those taking part with him in the negotiations.

Nigeria

Resolution 65
The Conference, having heard with sincere thankfulness of the progress made towards union in Nigeria and of the recent setting-up of a Joint Union Committee for the whole of Nigeria so that proposals may cover a sufficiently wide area, recommends that the Union Committee pursue its efforts, especially bearing in mind:
    (a) such advice as may be given by theologians;
    (b) the provisions and progress of other schemes such as that of Ceylon;
    (c) the future relationship of any united Church to the proposed province of West Africa and to the whole Anglican Communion.

The Eastern Orthodox Churches

Resolution 66
(a)   The Conference has received the Report of the Joint Doctrinal Commission appointed by the Oecumenical Patriarch and the Archbishop of Canterbury, which met in 1931, dealt with some of the theological points of importance about which there is difference and agreement, and examined the measure of agreement between the Anglican and Orthodox Communions. It thanks the theologians concerned for their valuable work in elucidating the 'Suggested Terms of Intercommunion', as originally propounded by the Archbishop of Canterbury's Eastern Churches Committee, and asks the Archbishop of Canterbury, in co-operation with the Oecumenical Patriarch, to appoint a further Joint Commission with a view to the continuance of this study.
(b)   The Conference expresses its sense of deep fellowship with the Eastern Orthodox Communion in all its branches, and offers its sympathy to those members of the Eastern Orthodox Church who in different countries are exposed to special trial and difficulty at the present time, praying that God in his mercy may once again grant them liberty and peace. The Conference is convinced that the contribution of

the Orthodox tradition is essential to the full life and witness of the Universal Church, and that a deepened understanding and fellowship between our two Communions has much to give to the healing of the nations, and especially to the growth of mutual understanding between East and West in the world today.

(c)   The Conference heartily welcomes and thanks God for the re-establishment of relations with the Russian Orthodox Church and hopes that these relations may be progressively strengthened and deepened.

(d)   The Conference expresses its deep sympathy with the Church of Greece in its great difficulties, and prays that God will bless and strengthen it in its ministrations to the people of Greece in their present afflictions.

The Old Catholic Churches

Resolution 67
(a)   The Conference welcomes with particular pleasure the unanimous agreement reached between representatives of the Anglican Communion and of the Old Catholic Churches at Bonn in 1931, which has resulted in the establishment of a state of intercommunion between the Old Catholic Churches and certain Churches of the Anglican Communion. It cordially subscribes to the agreement then reached that 'intercommunion does not require from either Communion the acceptance of all doctrinal opinion, sacramental devotion, or liturgical practice characteristic of the other, but implies that each believes the other to hold all the essentials of the Christian Faith.' The Conference recommends that this agreement should be considered by those Churches of the Anglican Communion which have not yet considered it.

(b)   The Conference notes with satisfaction and approval that in line with the Bonn agreement, the Protestant Episcopal Church in the USA by action of its General Convention in 1940, and the Polish National Catholic Church by similar action of its General Synod in 1946, have thereby achieved full intercommunion with each other.

The Lesser Eastern Churches

Resolution 68
(a)   The Conference approves the section of the Report of its Committee on Unity which refers to the Lesser Eastern Churches, and is happy to note the continued good relations between the Anglican Communion and these Churches. It looks forward to the strengthening and deepening of spiritual fellowship with them, which may in God's providence lead in due time to full intercommunion.

(b)   The Conference, learning with deep satisfaction of the happy relations existing in various parts of the world between the Armenian Church and Churches of the Anglican Communion, requests the Archbishop of Canterbury as President of the Conference to seek to initiate discussions between theologians of the two Churches, to be appointed by himself and the Supreme Catholicos of the Armenians, with a view to strengthening the relations between the two Churches; such discussions to be held, if possible, in Etchmiadzin or in some other convenient centre in the Near East.

(c)   The Conference expresses its deep sympathy with the hardship and suffering endured by the Assyrian people since the last Conference and earnestly prays for their preservation in peace and safety. It hopes that the relations between the Anglican Communion and the Assyrian Church may be maintained and strengthened and that all possible help may be given to assist that Church in its many problems and difficulties.

Scandinavian Churches

Resolution 69
The Conference welcomes the steady growth in friendship between the Scandinavian Churches and the Anglican Communion. It calls attention to the Resolutions adopted by the Conference of 1920 concerning relations with the Church of Sweden and recommends that they be formally brought to the notice of such Churches and provinces of the Anglican Communion as have not yet considered them.

The Church of Finland

Resolution 70
The Conference receives with approval the Report of the committee appointed by the Archbishop of Canterbury to confer with representatives of the Church of Finland, published in 1934, notes the conclusions reached in that Report and recommends that the Report, together with the recommendations, be brought to the attention of such Churches and provinces of the Anglican Communion as have not yet considered them.

The Churches of Latvia and Estonia

Resolution 71
The Conference receives the Report of conferences between representatives appointed by the Archbishop of Canterbury on behalf of the

Church of England and representatives of the Evangelical Lutheran Churches of Latvia and Estonia in 1936 and 1938, published in 1938. It records its sympathy and offers its prayers for these Churches, many of whose clergy and laity are now scattered abroad, having no home or possessions of their own, and having suffered grievous hardship. It recommends that Anglicans should give all material and spiritual help possible to these unhappy exiles, and looks forward to the day when it will be possible, after full agreement in faith and order, to advance further the relations between the Anglican Communion and these Churches in conditions of mutual confidence and understanding.

The Churches of Norway, Denmark, and Iceland

Resolution 72
The Conference requests the Archbishop of Canterbury to appoint a committee to confer with a similar committee or committees representing the Churches of Norway, Denmark, and Iceland, for the purpose of considering the relations of these Churches with the Anglican Communion.

The Lusitanian and Spanish Reformed Churches

Resolution 73
The Conference, recalling the sympathy expressed by former Conferences with the Spanish Reformed Church and the Lusitanian Church, and noting the assistance given since 1885 by bishops of the Church of Ireland in the ordination of their clergy and in other ways, requests the Archbishop of Armagh (i) to cause an enquiry to be made into the doctrine and discipline of these Churches and (ii) to present the report of such an enquiry to the Consultative Body of the Conference with a view to advising any bishop or group of bishops that may refer to it.

A Larger Episcopal Unity

Resolution 74
The Conference, welcoming the fact that some of the Churches of the Anglican Communion are already in intercommunion with the Old Catholic Churches, looking forward to the time when they will enter into communion with other parts of the Catholic Church not definable as Anglican, and desiring that Churches thus linked together should express their common relationship in common counsel and mutual aid, recommends that bishops of the Anglican Communion and bishops

of other Churches which are, or may be, in communion with them should meet together from time to time as an episcopal conference, advisory in character, for brotherly counsel and encouragement.

Foreign Relations

Resolution 75
Believing that the increasing development of friendly relations between the Anglican Communion and Churches in foreign countries is of primary importance to the Universal Church, the Conference welcomes the establishment of the Church of England Council on Foreign Relations by the Archbishops of Canterbury and York, of the Advisory Council on Ecclesiastical Relations by the Presiding Bishop of the Protestant Episcopal Church in the United States of America, and of the Committee appointed by the Scottish Episcopal Church. Further, considering the exchange of information between Churches of the Anglican Communion about the relations of our Communion with such foreign Churches to be of great advantage to all concerned, it hopes that each Church or province of the Anglican Communion will arrange for some similar council, or other agency, for this purpose.

The Conference expresses its sense of the value of the work done by chaplains of the Anglican Communion in foreign countries, especially in the establishment of friendly relations with the Churches of the countries where they are resident. Further, it trusts that suitability for this special work will be a major consideration in the selection of chaplains for such posts, and that the Church will make the utmost possible use of such men when so appointed.

The World Council of Churches

Resolution 76
The Conference cordially welcomes the formation of the World Council of Churches and desires to place on record its deep appreciation of the valuable services already rendered to the cause of Christian unity by the officers and members of its Provisional Committee, and sends its good wishes to the Council for its first Assembly at Amsterdam and prays that God may guide and direct all its deliberations. The Conference hopes that the results of the Assembly at Amsterdam may be made widely known throughout the Anglican Communion, and that an active interest in the World Council of Churches may be encouraged in all dioceses and parishes.

Friendship between Christians

Resolution 77
The Conference recognises that work of great value for the cause of reunion has been accomplished by the cultivation of personal friendships between Christians of different denominations; it believes that such friendships assist the growth of mutual understanding and of intercession; and it encourages members of the Anglican Communion to cultivate such friendships.

THE ANGLICAN COMMUNION

The Book of Common Prayer

Resolution 78
(a)   The Conference holds that the Book of Common Prayer has been, and is, so strong a bond of unity throughout the whole Anglican Communion that great care must be taken to ensure that revisions of the Book shall be in accordance with the doctrine and accepted liturgical worship of the Anglican Communion.
(b)   The Conference urges that special services of thanksgiving be held in 1949 throughout the whole Anglican Communion to commemorate the English Books of Common Prayer, of which the first was published in 1549.

Provinces

Resolution 79
In view of the pronouncements of the Lambeth Conferences of 1920 and 1930, the Conference notes with satisfaction and encourages the continuance of the steps which are being taken in East, West and Central Africa, and the Pacific, towards the formation of provinces or other regional groupings.

An Advisory Council

Resolution 80
(a)   The Conference is of opinion that the setting up of an advisory council on missionary strategy would enable the whole Anglican Communion to deal effectively with matters of world-wide strategy which concern the task God has entrusted to it and the welfare of the whole Communion; that the organisation and work of the council should follow the lines suggested in the Committee's Report; and that such an advisory council should be established as soon as possible.

(b)   We recommend that the proposed advisory council on mission-ary strategy shall work in close conjunction with all Councils on Foreign Relations which are or may be set up by constituent Churches of the Anglican Communion.

Appointment of Officers

Resolution 81
To promote closer co-operation and a clearer understanding between the different parts of the Anglican Communion, the Conference is of opinion that a responsible officer should be appointed in each national or regional Church to keep in touch with the different Churches and to secure a regular exchange of information between them.

Recruiting

Resolution 82
The Conference gives thanks to Almighty God for the faithful wit-ness of many martyrs in recent years. It urges Christian people every-where to accept the challenge of this witness as a call to a new self-offering in prayer, sacrifice, and service, for the extension of Christ's Kingdom in all lands.

Resolution 83
The Conference urges boys and young men who are faithful mem-bers of the Church, before committing themselves to other vocations, to consider seriously whether God is calling them to be ordained to the ministry of his Church in this day of opportunity and peril.

Resolution 84
The Conference urges all bishops and clergy constantly to keep before their people world-wide evangelisation as the primary and still unful-filled duty of the Church; and calls all the younger members of the Anglican Churches, clerical and lay, to consider seriously whether mis-sionary service is God's will for them.

Training of Ordinands

Resolution 85
In the opinion of this Conference, whereas a man is ordained into the ministry of the Church of God and not into that of any one dio-cese of the Church, it is desirable that the highest possible standard of training should be aimed at throughout the whole body, and to this end we urge a systematic exchange of information relating to:

(a) methods of recruiting, selection, and testing of candidates;
(b) standards of theological and general education required for ordination;
(c) the character of the theological institutions and faculties, including methods of support by the Church;
(d) schemes of post-ordination training.

A Central College

Resolution 86
In the opinion of this Conference the establishment of a central college for the Anglican Communion is highly desirable and steps should immediately be taken to establish this college, if possible at St Augustine's College, Canterbury.

A Congress

Resolution 87
The Conference welcomes the suggestion that a congress representative of the Anglican Communion be held if possible in June 1953, and respectfully requests the President to take steps toward this end.

Reciprocal Pensions

Resolution 88
The Conference urges the pensions authorities of every area of the Anglican Communion which possesses an established scheme of pensions for the clergy working within it, to consider together the adoption of a reciprocal scheme between all such areas.

The Status of Certain Japanese Bishops

Resolution 89
The Conference approves and welcomes the expressed intention of the Nippon Sei Ko Kwai to receive back the six bishops as bishops of the Nippon Se Ko Kwai without jurisdiction.

Resolution 90
The Conference also desires to make clear that in its opinion it is open at any time to the Nippon Sei Ko Kwai in its discretion to entrust the six bishops thus recognised with episcopal functions or jurisdiction, to be exercised in accordance with the canonical and disciplinary requirements of the Nippon Sei Ko Kwai.

Resolution 91
The Conference recommends the Nippon Sei Ko Kwai formally to communicate its action with regard to these bishops to all metropolitans for information.

THE CHURCH'S DISCIPLINE IN MARRIAGE

Resolution 92
Faced with the great increase in the number of broken marriages and the tragedy of children deprived of true home life, this Conference desires again to affirm that marriage always entails a life-long union and obligation; it is convinced that upon the faithful observance of this divine law depend the stability of home life, the welfare and happiness of children, and the real health of society. It calls upon members of the Church and others to do their utmost by word and example to uphold the sanctity of the marriage bond and to counteract those influences which tend to destroy it. It is convinced that maintenance of the Church's standard of discipline can alone meet the deepest needs of men; and it earnestly implores those whose marriage, perhaps through no fault of their own, is unhappy to remain steadfastly faithful to their marriage vows.

Resolution 93
The Church has a primary duty in the pastoral care of those who are married or are about to be married, not less than in the exercise of discipline for upholding Christian standards. To this end:
(a) regular and systematic instruction of the congregation on the meaning and responsibilities of marriage, and particular preparation of engaged persons, should be regarded as a normal pastoral duty in every parish, and all parish priests should be equipped for these tasks; and
(b) Church people should be urged to co-operate in the valuable work in education, guidance, and reconciliation done by many marriage guidance councils and other similar bodies, which uphold Christian standards of marriage.

Resolution 94
The Conference affirms that the marriage of one whose former partner is still living may not be celebrated according to the rites of the Church, unless it has been established that there exists no marriage bond recognised by the Church.

Resolution 95
Mindful of the needs of those who are in deep distress and claim the

Church's sympathy, the Conference urges that provincial and regional Churches should consider how best their pastoral responsibility towards those who do not conform to our Lord's standard can be discharged.

Resolution 96

Confirmed members of the Church who marry contrary to the law of the Church, as accepted in the provincial or regional Church to which they belong, should be regarded as subject to the discipline of the Church in respect of admission to Holy Communion. Their admission to Holy Communion lies within the discretion of the bishop, due regard being had to their own spiritual good and the avoidance of scandal to others. It is important that the practice within each province or regional Church in this matter should be uniform. We restate Resolution 11(b) of the Lambeth Conference 1930, as follows:

> That in every case where a person with a former partner still living is remarried and desires to be admitted to Holy Communion the case should be referred to the bishop, subject to provincial or regional regulations.

Resolution 97

Inasmuch as easy divorce in Great Britain, the United States, and elsewhere, has gravely weakened the idea of the life-long nature of marriage, and has also brought untold suffering to children, this Conference urges that there is a strong case for the reconsideration by certain states of their divorce laws.

Resolution 98

The Conference earnestly warns members of our Communion against contracting marriages with Roman Catholics under the conditions imposed by modern Roman canon law, especially as these conditions involve, among other things, a promise to have their children brought up in a religious system which they cannot themselves accept.

Resolution 99

The Conference stresses the importance of building up a sound Christian tradition of family life in the younger Churches of the Anglican Communion, and therefore urges their members to observe loyally the marriage canons and rules of their provinces or dioceses.

BAPTISM AND CONFIRMATION

Resolution 100

This Conference, acknowledging that the Christian Church derives all its life from God, the Holy and Eternal Trinity, and is dependent upon his creative, redeeming, and sanctifying activity, calls upon the members of the Anglican Communion to pray for spiritual renewal throughout the world.

Resolution 101
Believing that one and the same Spirit sustains and orders the life of the Church, the Conference emphasises the essential unity and interdependence of the ministry of the word and the ministry of the sacraments.

Resolution 102
The Conference emphasises the importance of thinking of divine grace in terms of personal relations between God and man, and of faith as personal surrender and adherence to Christ.

Resolution 103
Recognising that in its ministration of the sacramental rites of initiation the Anglican Communion preserves the essential factors of Christian tradition with a proper emphasis upon their moral and rational requirements, the Conference considers that it is not desirable to change the present sequence of Baptism, Confirmation, and admission to Holy Communion.

Resolution 104
While deprecating the hasty adoption of any policy which would lead to the widespread exclusion of infants from baptism, the Conference affirms that the service of Infant Baptism presupposes that the infant will be brought up in the faith and practice of the Church, and reminds parents and guardians that they cannot be exempted from a major share in the responsibility for the Christian nurture and education of their children, and it therefore urges the clergy to put them in mind of this duty before their children are baptized and at other times as opportunity may be made.

Resolution 105
The Conference calls attention to the rubric of the Prayer Book of 1662 that Baptism should normally be administered 'when the most number of people come together' and after due notice, and recommends that the sacrament should be administered more frequently in the regular services of the Church and that notice should be required.

Resolution 106
Seeing that the local congregation shares in the responsibility for bringing a new member, whether infant or adult, into the full fellowship of the Church, the Conference regards it as desirable:

(a) that no unbaptized person should act as godparent;

(b) that at least one godparent should be a practising communicant of the Anglican Communion;

(c) that, seeing that parents or guardians are sometimes unable or unwilling to invite active Church people to act as godparents, Church people should be encouraged to offer themselves, whether as members of a sponsors' guild or in some other way, for definite service as godparent in suitable cases;

(d) that one or both of the parents of an infant should be permitted to act as godparent if otherwise eligible.

Resolution 107
The Conference calls the attention of all who undertake the responsibilities of godparent to the seriousness of the promises which they make on behalf of the child, both in the sight of God and of his Church. It counsels them to continue diligently in prayer for their godchildren throughout their lives.

Resolution 108
The Conference recommends that a minister, baptizing the child of persons not resident in his parish or on his Membership Roll, should consult the minister of the parish in which the parents of the child reside, in order that the child and the family concerned may be the more surely linked up with the life of that congregation.

Resolution 109
The Conference recommends to the clergy the system of the 'Baptismal Roll'.

Resolution 110
The Conference recommends that care should be taken to see that before confirmation all candidates are given definite instruction about repentance and about the means provided by God in his Church by which troubled consciences can obtain the assurance of his mercy and forgiveness, as set forth in the Exhortation in the Order of Holy Communion.

Resolution 111
The Conference recommends that those who have been confirmed should from time to time be given opportunity, after due preparation, for the reaffirmation of vows and rededication.

Resolution 112
The Conference acknowledges the faithful work which is done by the

clergy generally in the preparation of candidates for confirmation and recommends that the preparation of candidates for confirmation should include, from their early years:

(a) participation, with their family, in regular worship in church and at home;

(b) group instruction in the Church's faith and practice;

(c) training in fellowship and service through membership of a parochial society or group.

They should be led on to accept a rule of life comprising daily prayer and Bible reading, regular worship, and self-discipline, including almsgiving and personal service.

PROPOSED CHINESE CANON

Resolution 113

The General Synod of the Church in China having brought before the Lambeth Conference a proposal received from the Diocese of South China that for an experimental period of twenty years a deaconess might (subject to certain conditions) be ordained to the priesthood, and the General Synod having referred to the Conference the question 'whether or not such liberty to experiment within the framework of the Anglican Communion would be in accordance with Anglican tradition and order', the Conference feels bound to reply that in its opinion such an experiment would be against that tradition and order and would gravely affect the internal and external relations of the Anglican Communion.

Resolution 114

The Conference reaffirms Resolution 67 of the Conference of 1930 that 'the order of deaconess is for women the one and only order of the ministry which we can recommend our branch of the Catholic Church to recognise and use'. It also approves the resolution adopted in 1939–1941 in both Houses of the Convocations of Canterbury and York 'that the order of deaconesses is the one existing ordained ministry for women in the sense of being the only order of ministry in the Anglican Communion to which women are admitted by episcopal imposition of hands'.

Resolution 115

The Conference is aware that in some quarters there is a desire that the question of ordination of women to the priesthood should be reconsidered. The Conference, recalling that the question was examined in England by the Archbishops' Commission on the Ministry of Women whose Report was published in 1935, is of opinion that the time has not come for its further formal consideration.

Resolution 116
The Conference desires to draw attention again to the wide and important range of work which may be entrusted to deaconesses by the constituted authorities of any province of the Anglican Communion; and recommends that in all parts of the Anglican Communion the work of deaconesses should be encouraged and their status and function defined.

ADMINISTRATION OF HOLY COMMUNION

Resolution 117
The Conference affirms that the giving of Communion in both kinds is according to the example and precept of our Lord, was the practice of the whole Catholic Church for twelve centuries, has remained the practice of the Orthodox Churches, and has been universally upheld by the teaching and practice of the Anglican Communion since the Reformation.

Resolution 118
The Conference holds that administration from a common chalice, being scriptural and having a symbolic meaning of great value, should continue to be the normal method of administration in the Anglican Communion; but is of opinion that there is no objection to administration of both kinds by the method of intinction where conditions require it, and that any part of the Anglican Communion by provincial regulation according to its own constitutional procedure has liberty to sanction administration by intinction as an optional alternative to the traditional method, and that the methods of intinction to be adopted or permitted should not be left to the discretion of individual priests.

1958

THE BIBLE

Resolution 1

The Conference affirms its belief that the Bible discloses the truths about the relation of God and man which are the key to the world's predicament and is therefore deeply relevant to the modern world.

Resolution 2

The Conference affirms that our Lord Jesus Christ is God's final Word to man, and that in his light all Holy Scripture must be seen and interpreted, the Old Testament in terms of promise and the New Testament in terms of fulfilment.

Resolution 3

The Conference affirms that Jesus Christ lives in his Church through the Holy Spirit according to his promise, and that the Church is therefore both guardian and interpreter of Holy Scripture; nevertheless the Church may teach nothing as 'necessary for eternal salvation but what may be concluded and proved by the Scripture'.

Resolution 4

The Conference gratefully acknowledges our debt to the host of devoted scholars who, worshipping the God of Truth, have enriched and deepened our understanding of the Bible, not least by facing with intellectual integrity the questions raised by modern knowledge and modern criticism. It also acknowledges the Church's debt to the men and women in our universities, colleges, and schools who by their teaching and example inspire new generations to love the Scriptures.

Resolution 5

The Conference welcomes every sign of the revival of Bible study within the common life of the Church. It calls on all Church people to re-establish the habit of Bible reading at home, and commends the growing practice of group Bible study.

Resolution 6

The Conference recognises with gratitude the dominant place which the Anglican Communion has always given to the Holy Scriptures in all its public worship. It welcomes in the contemporary liturgical revival the growing realisation of the close relation of word and sacrament.

Resolution 7
The Conference affirms the importance of preaching, both evangelistic and expository, ministered as a means of grace, by men who have experienced the power of the Gospel in their own lives.

Resolution 8
The Conference acknowledges gratefully the work of scientists in increasing man's knowledge of the universe, wherein is seen the majesty of God in his creative activity. It therefore calls upon Christian people both to learn reverently from every new disclosure of truth, and at the same time to bear witness to the biblical message of a God and Saviour apart from whom no gift can be rightly used.

Resolution 9
In view of the lack of understanding which can develop in consequence of the different thought and language of the Bible and the modern world, the Conference urges Christian scholars and leaders to co-operate with men of science and other kinds of modern learning in the study of their respective modes of thought and speech.

Resolution 10
The Conference believes that the presentation of the message of the Bible to the world requires great sensitiveness to the outlook of the people of today, and urges that imaginative use be made of all the resources of literature, art, music, and drama, and of new techniques appealing to eye as well as to ear.

Resolution 11
The Conference welcomes the new translations of the Scriptures in many languages, and would encourage our people to give all possible support to those societies whose concern is the distribution of the Scriptures to all lands. Much still remains to be done in this field and the need is urgent.

Resolution 12
In the light of the previous eleven Resolutions the Conference invites the Churches of the Anglican Communion to engage in a special effort during the next ten years to extend the scope and deepen the quality of personal and corporate study of the Bible.

CHURCH UNITY AND THE CHURCH UNIVERSAL

Christian Unity

Resolution 13
The Conference welcomes and endorses the 'Statement on Christian Unity' contained in the Report of the Committee on Church Unity and the Church Universal.

Full Communion and Intercommunion

Resolution 14
The Conference endorses the paragraph in the Report of the Committee on Church Unity and the Church Universal which refers to the use of the terms 'full communion' and 'intercommunion', and recommends accordingly that where between two Churches, not of the same denominational or confessional family, there is unrestricted *communio in sacris* including mutual recognition and acceptance of ministries, the appropriate term to use is 'full communion', and that where varying degrees of relation other than 'full communion' are established by agreement between two such Churches the appropriate term is 'intercommunion'.

Resolution 15
The Conference therefore requests the Archbishop of Canterbury to communicate this Resolution to the Faith and Order Commission of the World Council of Churches for its information.

Wider Episcopal Fellowship

Resolution 16
The Conference reaffirms Resolution 74, passed by the Lambeth Conference 1948, regarding 'A Larger Episcopal Unity', and strongly recommends that within the next five years the Archbishop of Canterbury should invite to a conference representative bishops from each province of the Anglican Communion, together with representative bishops from each Church possessing the historic episcopate with which Churches and provinces of the Anglican Communion are in full communion or in a relation of intercommunion.

Resolution 17
The Conference notes the recommendation of the Committee on Church Unity and the Church Universal concerning future Lambeth Conferences, and commends it to the attention of the President and

the Consultative Body for consideration before the next Lambeth Conference.

The Church of South India

Resolution 18
The Conference welcomes and endorses the Report of the Committee on Church Unity and the Church Universal concerning the Church of South India.

Nandyal

Resolution 19
The Conference is agreed that, notwithstanding the recommendations of the Lambeth Conferences of 1930 and 1948 that no province of the Anglican Communion should set up dioceses or congregations in the area of the Church of South India, the Church of India, Pakistan, Burma, and Ceylon should be left free to make the arrangements which seem best to that Church for the spiritual oversight of Christians in the Nandyal area, after consulting the Church of South India and with the goodwill of that Church, bearing in mind that the union of Christians in that area is the ultimate aim.

The Scheme of Church Union in Ceylon and The Plan of Church Union in North India and Pakistan

Resolution 20
The Conference endorses generally the paragraphs of the Committee on Church Unity and the Church Universal which refer to the Scheme of Church Union in Ceylon and the Plan of Church Union in North India and Pakistan, and gives thanks to God for manifest signs of the work of the Holy Spirit in the negotiations which have brought the Scheme and Plan to this stage.

Resolution 21
The Conference advises that when Churches have united in such a way that the whole ministry of the United Church has been episcopally united, permission to visiting ministers, not episcopally ordained, of Churches in communion with the United Churches at the time of the union, to celebrate the Holy Communion occasionally when visiting a United Church, be not regarded as a bar to relations of full communion between the United Church and the Churches and provinces of the Anglican Communion; provided that due constitutional provisions are made to safeguard the conscience of worshippers.

Ceylon

Resolution 22
The Conference calls attention to the recommendation of the Committee on Church Unity and the Church Universal concerning the unification of the ministry in the Scheme of Church Union in Ceylon, and advises the Church of India, Pakistan, Burma, and Ceylon to recommend to the Negotiating Committee the suggested amendments to the Scheme.

Resolution 23
The Conference advises the Churches and provinces of the Anglican Communion that they should be willing to enter into full communion with the resulting Church of Lanka on its inauguration.

The Church of North India and the Church of Pakistan

Resolution 24
(a)   The Conference wholeheartedly desires that the Plan for reunion in North India and Pakistan may go forward, and that the intention of the Plan may be secured, that the ministry of the United Church shall be 'fully accredited in the eyes of all its members, and so far as may be of the Church throughout the world'.
(b)   The Conference wholly shares the desire of the Church of India, Pakistan, Burma, and Ceylon that the Anglican Communion should be able to enter into full communion with the United Church; it believes that the Churches and provinces of the Anglican Communion could enter into full communion if the recommendations concerning the service for the unification of the ministry could be accepted.
(c)   Should further explanation and discussion concerning the recommendations be desired, the Conference requests the President to appoint a small commission of bishops to be immediately available for consultation with the Church of India, Pakistan, Burma, and Ceylon.

Relations between Anglican and Presbyterian Churches

Resolution 25
The Conference welcomes the taking up in a new spirit of the problem of the relations between the Episcopalian and Presbyterian systems of Church order, of which the Report on *Relations between Anglican and Presbyterian Churches* (published in 1957) is a signal illustration.

Resolution 26
The Conference, having noted the careful study which has been given to this Report by the Inter-Church Relations Committee of the Church of Scotland and the six questions addressed to Anglicans by that Committee, commends for further discussion the comments made on these questions by the Committee on Church Unity and the Church Universal.

Resolution 27
The Conference commends this Report for wider study by clergy and laity throughout the Anglican Churches, especially in those parts of the world in which Churches of the Anglican and Presbyterian traditions are in contact with one another.

Resolution 28
The Conference notes with satisfaction and thankfulness the remarkable measure of constructive theological agreement which the theologians on both sides were able to reach and record, and expresses the hope that serious consideration may be given to the possibility of drawing the Anglican and Presbyterian traditions more closely together by a process of mutual assimilation of their respective Church orders such as is suggested in the Report.

The Methodist Church

Resolution 29
The Conference has heard with interest and sympathy of the conversations now proceeding between representatives of the Church of England and representatives of the Methodist Church in England, and between representatives of the Protestant Episcopal Church and representatives of the Methodist Church in the USA.

Resolution 30
The Conference calls attention to the Report of the Committee on Unity; and encourages continuance of the conversations with a view to the making of concrete proposals, as offering a possible first step on the way to reunion in the particular historic situations in which the Churches concerned are placed; but on the understanding that organic union is definitely accepted as the final goal, and that any plans for the interim stage of intercommunion are definitely linked with provisions for the steady growing together of the Churches concerned.

West Africa

Resolution 31
The Conference expresses its sincere thankfulness at the growing interest within the Province of West Africa in conversations on reunion, having had before it the proposed Scheme of Union for Nigeria and the Cameroons which is at present receiving the prayerful consideration of the dioceses of the Province of West Africa and of the Methodist and Presbyterian Churches in Nigeria and the Cameroons.

Resolution 32
The Conference, while recognising the weight to be attached to arguments in favour of retaining the model of the Church of South India and the policy of gradualness therein expressed, but aware also of the desire within the Province that from the outset full communion should be maintained between Churches of the Anglican Communion and any united Church which might be formed, strongly recommends to the Province of West Africa further consideration of the Ceylon scheme as a model, since only so does it seem likely that the desired result will be achieved.

Resolution 33
The Conference recommends that in any reunion scheme the Ceylon or North India/Pakistan statement as to the faith of the Church should be followed.

Resolution 34
The Conference further recommends that should any far-reaching decision be reached by the dioceses of the Province, the advice of the Lambeth Consultative Body should be sought.

The Jerusalem Archbishopric

Resolution 35
The Conference welcomes such action towards Church unity as has been taken by the bishoprics in the Middle East and recognises the peculiar importance there of our relationship with the Orthodox and other Eastern Churches.

Resolution 36
The Conference commends to the bishoprics concerned the Ceylon scheme for Church union as a model for any further discussions which it is hoped will take place.

Resolution 37
The Conference urges that at every stage reference be made to the Lambeth Consultative Body.

The Roman Catholic Church

Resolution 38
The Conference welcomes the permission given by Roman Catholic authority for contacts, discussions, and co-operation between Roman Catholics and other Christians, as contained in the document *Instruction to Local Ordinaries on the Oecumenical Movement* issued by the Supreme Sacred Congregation of the Holy Office in December 1949; and expresses the hope, first, that these permissions may be more widely and generously used, secondly, that they may be further extended in the interests of Christian understanding and fellowship, and thirdly, that Anglicans will make full use of these and all other available opportunities for promoting charitable understanding.

The Eastern Orthodox Church

Resolution 39
The Conference deeply appreciates the presence of a distinguished group of Eastern Orthodox leaders at the opening of its proceedings, and is grateful for the opportunity thus given of having informal talks with them. It sincerely hopes that the relations between Orthodox and Anglicans may grow ever closer, and that advantages will be taken of every opportunity to further that aim, both in the interests of Christian unity and as an important contribution to understanding and confidence between peoples.

Resolution 40
The Conference has learned with satisfaction of the correspondence between the Archbishop of Canterbury and the Oecumenical Patriarch, and warmly endorses the desire of the Patriarch for a continuation of joint Anglican–Orthodox doctrinal discussion on the pattern of the Joint Doctrinal Commission of 1931.

Resolution 41
The Conference has heard with keen interest and approval of the conversations between representatives of the Russian Orthodox Church and those of the Church of England held in Moscow in 1956, and draws attention to the Report of the proceedings since published.

Other Eastern Churches

Resolution 42
The Conference welcomes the prospect of discussion with representatives of the Armenian Church with the object of promoting closer fellowship between the Anglican and the Armenian Churches. It views with sorrow the present internal difficulties experienced by members of this ancient Church, and prays that they may soon be overcome. The Conference asks the Archbishop of Canterbury to take steps to arrange discussions with representatives of the Armenian Church when the time seems to him to be propitious.

Resolution 43
The Conference encourages the Metropolitan of the Church of India, Pakistan, Burma, and Ceylon to continue the plan to have further discussions with the Malankara Jacobite Syrian Church. It recommends that as the next step other Churches, provinces, and dioceses of the Anglican Communion which have a direct interest in these questions should be consulted, and that they should be represented in any further discussions with the Syrian Orthodox Church.

Resolution 44
The Conference notes with interest the discussions now in progress between the Church of India, Pakistan, Burma, and Ceylon and the Mar Thoma Church. It recommends that, before these discussions are brought to a conclusion, other Churches, provinces, and dioceses of the Anglican Communion which are concerned with relations with Mar Thoma Christians should be taken into consultation so that if possible a common agreement may be reached by all the authorities concerned.

Resolution 45
The Conference hopes that in all such negotiations any steps taken should be such as to encourage the recovery of unity among Syrian Christians.

Old Catholic Churches

Resolution 46
The Conference notes with satisfaction that the Bonn agreement has now been adopted by nearly all the provinces of the Anglican Communion.

Resolution 47
The Conference welcomes the suggestions made by a meeting between some Anglicans and Old Catholics in Holland, that the two Churches should co-operate in practical action to meet the spiritual needs of Dutch-speaking Christians who wish to resort to Anglican Churches in that country. It is of the opinion that such practical action would not only be a valuable demonstration of the intercommunion which exists between the Anglican and Old Catholic Churches, but also a means of deepening the fellowship that exists between the members of those Churches.

Scandinavian Churches

Resolution 48
The Conference welcomes the action taken by several Churches and provinces in accordance with Resolutions 69, 70, and 71 of the Lambeth Conference of 1948.

Resolution 49
The Conference welcomes the report of the discussions with the Churches of Norway, Denmark, and Iceland in accordance with Resolution 72 of the Lambeth Conference of 1948, and encourages their continuance.

Netherlands Reformed Church

Resolution 50
The Conference, having heard with interest of discussions held between Anglican and Dutch theologians at the official request of the Netherlands Reformed Church—the first official discussion of the kind held with a Reformed Church on the continent of Europe in recent years—requests the Archbishop of Canterbury to encourage the continuation of such discussions when opportunity offers.

Spanish Reformed Episcopal Church
and Lusitanian Church

Resolution 51
The Conference, being entirely satisfied with reports received on the present doctrine and discipline of the Spanish Reformed Episcopal Church and the Lusitanian Church, welcomes the news of the consecration of Bishop Molina in Spain and of Bishop Fiandor in Portugal by bishops of the Episcopal Church of the United States and of the Church of Ireland, and prays that these Churches may be blessed

by God in the service of his Kingdom. The Conference hopes that the desire of these Churches for the same relationship with Churches of the Anglican Communion as have the Old Catholic Churches will soon be fulfilled.

Resolution 52
The Conference suggests that the bishops of these two Churches be invited to any conference arranged in accordance with the recommendation of Resolution 74—'A Larger Episcopal Unity'—of the Lambeth Conference of 1948.

Philippine Independent Church (Aglipayan)

Resolution 53
The Conference records its pleasure at the vigorous growth of the Philippine Independent Church and welcomes the progress being made in the relations between this Church and the Protestant Episcopal Church in the United States of America since the consecration of three bishops of the Philippine Independent Church by bishops of the Protestant Episcopal Church in the United States of America in 1948. The Conference is gratified to learn that priests of the Philippine Independent Church are receiving their theological training at St Andrew's Theological Seminary in Manila.

Episcopi Vagantes

Resolution 54
The Conference draws attention to the fact that there are *episcopi vagantes* who call themselves either 'Old Catholic' or 'Orthodox', in combination with other names. It warns its members of the danger of accepting such persons at their own valuation without making further inquiries. The Conference reiterates the principle contained in Resolution 27 of the 1920 Lambeth Conference, that it cannot recognise the Churches of such *episcopi vagantes* as properly constituted Churches, or recognise the orders of their ministers, and recommends that any such ministers desiring to join an Anglican Church, who are in other respects duly qualified, should be ordained *sub conditione* in accordance with the provisions suggested in the Report of the relevant Committee of the 1920 Lambeth Conference.

The World Council of Churches

Resolution 55
The Conference records its thankfulness to Almighty God for the

formation, growth, and achievements of the World Council of Churches, and urges all the Churches and provinces of the Anglican Communion to ensure that they are adequately represented in its counsels, take a full share in its work, and assume a just part of its financial responsibility.

Inter-Church Aid

Resolution 56
The Conference commends to all members of the Anglican Communion the outstanding work of relief and reconciliation carried out by the World Council of Churches Department of Inter-Church Aid and Service to Refugees, in which they have gladly participated. It urges them to support it wholeheartedly and, when possible, themselves to offer sanctuary and the deepest charity to those who, for whatever cause, have lost their home and citizenship.

Prayer for Christian Unity

Resolution 57
The Conference wishes to emphasise the importance of widespread prayer for the unity of all Christian people, and commends to all Anglicans the observance of the Week of Prayer for Christian Unity in the spirit of the late Abbé Paul Couturier, who taught many to pray for the unity of Christ's people in the way he wills and by the means he chooses. It welcomes the remarkable growth of such prayer and commends the formation of local groups of Christians of different traditions for the purpose of promoting prayer for Christian unity.

PROGRESS IN THE ANGLICAN COMMUNION
MISSIONARY APPEAL AND STRATEGY

The Mission of the Church

Resolution 58
The Conference calls on every Church member, clergy and laity alike, to take an active part in the mission of the Church. It is a mission to the whole world, not only in area but in all the concerns of mankind. It has no frontiers between 'home' and 'foreign' but is concerned to present Christ to people everywhere.

Each generation needs to be evangelised and to this all-important task we summon the people of God in every land.

Resolution 59
The Conference affirms that while the Church of Jesus Christ transcends all national or racial limitations, every Church should endeavour to share fully in the life of the people in the country in which it exists. The Conference rejoices that, in all parts of the world, a strong ministry is growing up from among the people. It notes with satisfaction that, under the guidance of the Holy Spirit, and in accordance with Catholic practice, bishops are being appointed and elected without reference to race or nationality.

Advisory Council on Missionary Strategy

Resolution 60
The Conference accepts the recommendations of the Committee on Progress in the Anglican Communion concerning the Advisory Council on Missionary Strategy, and respectfully requests that action be taken by His Grace the President as soon as possible.

The Consultative Body

Resolution 61
The Conference, while reaffirming the opinion expressed in Resolution 44 of the Lambeth Conference of 1920 that the Consultative Body is of the nature of a continuation committee of the Lambeth Conference, recommends that its duties and composition should be redefined as follows:
(a)   The duties of the Consultative Body shall be:
(i) to carry on work left to it by the preceding Conference;
(ii) to assist the Archbishop of Canterbury in the preparation of business of the ensuing Conference;
(iii) to consider matters referred to the Archbishop of Canterbury on which he requests its aid and to advise him;
(iv) to advise on questions of faith, order, policy, or administration referred to it by any bishop or group of bishops, calling in expert advisers at its discretion, and reserving the right to decline to entertain any particular question;
(v) to deal with matters referred to it by the Archbishop of Canterbury or by any bishop or group of bishops, subject to any limitations upon such references which may be imposed by the regulations of local and regional Churches;
(vi) to take such action in the discharge of the above duties as may be appropriate, subject to the condition that with regard to Churches, provinces and dioceses of the Anglican Communion its functions are advisory only and without executive or administrative power.

(b)   The Consultative Body shall consist of:
(i) The Archbishop of Canterbury as ex officio Chairman, and the Archbishop of York.
(ii) The primates or presiding bishops of national or provincial Churches in the following countries or areas:
  Wales; Ireland; Scotland; USA; Canada; India, Pakistan, Burma, and Ceylon; Australia; New Zealand; South Africa; West Indies; Japan; China; West Africa; Central Africa; Middle East.
(iii) Such members to represent other dioceses under the jurisdiction of the Archbishop of Canterbury as he may appoint.
Each member shall have the right to nominate a bishop to take his place at any meeting which he is unable to attend.
(c)   The Archbishop of Canterbury with the approval of the Consultative Body shall appoint a secretary, to serve under the directions of the Archbishop, who may, if the Advisory Council so agrees, be also the Secretary of that Council.
(d)   The Consultative Body shall meet when summoned by the Archbishop of Canterbury or on his behalf; and in between meetings may conduct business by correspondence. All minutes and papers shall be sent to every member and if so desired to alternates also.
(e)   Expenses incurred on behalf of the Consultative Body shall be borne by the fund provided for the Advisory Council on Missionary Strategy, if that Council so agrees.

Communication

Resolution 62
The Conference urges that every opportunity be taken, at the local and provincial level, to make effective use of such channels of communication as television, radio, films, religious drama, and the secular and religious press.

Resolution 63
The Conference suggests that through the Advisory Council on Missionary Strategy there could be an exchange of material, talent, skill, and technical knowledge between regional Churches of the Anglican Communion.

Christian Stewardship

Resolution 64
The Conference recalls Church people to the duty and privilege of stewardship, of which sacrificial, planned, and systematic giving is a part, to the end that the souls of the people may be enriched, and

the needs of the Church met, including the adequate support of its ministry and provision for the extension of its work. The Conference urges that the Church in every field be encouraged to become self-supporting.

Movement of Peoples

Resolution 65
The Conference emphasises the importance of the witness for Christ which can be borne when Christians go from one country to another, especially to countries where Christians are a small minority, and urges that ways and means be developed to assist both clergy and members of the laity to do so effectively. It also urges that every effort be made, especially on the parochial level, to practise Christian fellowship with people of other nations and races who come to live permanently in a new land.

Regional Councils

Resolution 66
The Conference welcomes the fact that regional councils have been formed in the South-east Pacific and the South-west Pacific to assist common counsel and co-operation.

Religious Freedom

Resolution 67
The Conference is deeply concerned by restrictions upon religious freedom in many areas, imposed in some cases by the state alone and in others by the state influenced by a dominant religious group. To those who suffer under these conditions the Conference extends the assurance of its sympathy and support. It affirms its conviction that freedom of religion includes not only freedom to worship but also freedom to propagate and to teach, as essential parts of the Christian faith.

Anglican Congress

Resolution 68
The Conference, holding the Anglican Congress to be of great value to the life of the Anglican Communion,
    (a) reaffirms the desire expressed at the Anglican Congress of 1954 that another such Congress be held;
    (b) respectfully requests the Archbishop of Canterbury and the Presiding Bishop of the Protestant Episcopal Church in the United

States of America to appoint a committee of bishops, priests, and lay persons to make arrangements, in accordance with the resolution of the Anglican Congress 1954;

(c) asks that special consideration be given by this committee to the question of holding this Congress outside the English-speaking countries;

(d) suggests that the date of the Congress be 1963; and

(e) recommends that the major topic should be 'The World-wide Mission of the Church'.

The Anglican Cycle of Prayer

Resolution 69
The Conference calls attention to the Anglican Communion Cycle of Prayer prepared by the Overseas Council of the National Assembly of the Church of England, issued in response to the request of the Lambeth Conference 1948, and commends it for the widest possible use in all our Churches by circulation in the dioceses.

The Pan-Anglican Review

Resolution 70
The Conference appreciates the value of the *Pan-Anglican* review, and commends it to the attention of the Churches and provinces of the Anglican Communion, as a means of disseminating information about the Anglican Communion.

Christian Literature

Resolution 71
The Conference recommends that literature should be recognised as an important instrument of the Church in fulfilling its mission; and that steps should be taken to secure that in every language area suitable literature is made available for the training of ordinands, the use of the clergy, the instruction and equipment of the laity, and not least for the commending of Christianity to those outside the Church.

Resolution 72
The Conference urges that men and women ready to devote themselves to Christian literary work, including journalism, should be enlisted and trained to regard such work as a true vocation in the service of the Church.

THE BOOK OF COMMON PRAYER

Prayer Book Revision

Resolution 73

The Conference welcomes the contemporary movement towards unanimity in doctrinal and liturgical matters by those of differing traditions in the Anglican Communion as a result of new knowledge gained from biblical and liturgical studies, and is happy to know of parallel progress in this sphere by some Roman Catholic and Reformed theologians. It commends the Report of the Sub-committee on the Book of Common Prayer on this subject to the careful study of all sections of the Anglican Communion.

Resolution 74

The Conference, recognising the work of Prayer Book revision being done in different parts of the Anglican Communion,

(a) calls attention to those features in the Books of Common Prayer which are essential to the safeguarding of our unity: i.e. the use of the canonical Scriptures and the Creeds, Holy Baptism, Confirmation, Holy Communion, and the Ordinal;

(b) notes that there are other features in these books which are effective in maintaining the traditional doctrinal emphasis and ecclesiastical culture of Anglicanism and therefore should be preserved;

(c) and urges that a chief aim of Prayer Book revision should be to further that recovery of the worship of the primitive Church which was the aim of the compilers of the first Prayer Books of the Church of England.

Resolution 75

The Conference commends to the study of the whole Anglican Communion the counsel on Prayer Book revision given in the Report of the Sub-committee on the Book of Common Prayer.

The Holy Communion Service

Resolution 76

The Conference requests the Archbishop of Canterbury, in cooperation with the Consultative Body, to appoint an advisory committee to prepare recommendations for the structure of the Holy Communion service which could be taken into consideration by any Church or province revising its eucharistic rite, and which would both conserve the doctrinal balance of the Anglican tradition and take account of present liturgical knowledge.

The Commemoration of Saints and Heroes of the Christian Church in the Anglican Communion

Resolution 77
The Conference holds that the purpose of a Kalendar is to increase our thankfulness to God and to strengthen our faith by recalling regularly the great truths of the Gospel, the principal events in the life of our Lord, and the lives and examples of men and women who have borne pre-eminent witness to the power of the Holy Spirit, and are with us in the communion of saints.

Resolution 78
The Conference considers that the power to revise or amend Kalendars should be exercised by the same authority as is required for the revision of the Book of Common Prayer within each several Church or province, which authority may allow supplementary commemorations for local use in addition to the Kalendar at the request of a diocese.

Resolution 79
The Conference is of opinion that the following principles should guide the selection of saints and heroes for commemoration:
(a) In the case of scriptural saints, care should be taken to commemorate men or women in terms which are in strict accord with the facts made known in Holy Scripture.
(b) In the case of other names, the Kalendar should be limited to those whose historical character and devotion are beyond doubt.
(c) In the choice of new names economy should be observed and controversial names should not be inserted until they can be seen in the perspective of history.
(d) The addition of a new name should normally result from a widespread desire expressed in the region concerned over a reasonable period of time.

Resolution 80
The Conference recommends that the Church should continue to commemorate the saints in three ways: by Red Letter days, Black Letter days, or a memorial collect alone.

MINISTRIES AND MANPOWER

The Needs of the Ministry

Resolution 81
The Conference, while feeling deep concern about the numerical inadequacy of the ministry available to consolidate the Church's present work, and to serve its expanding mission, nevertheless recognises that there is no short cut to the solution of problems of manpower, and that nothing less than a wide response in terms of vocational dedication to the ministry will meet present needs and provide for expansion.

It therefore urges upon every diocese and upon every priest the need for presenting the vocation to the ministry in terms which will challenge the laymen of the Church to consider a call to this life of sacrifice and devotion.

Areas of Special Need

Resolution 82
The Conference desires to emphasise that there is a continuing need in 'missionary' provinces and dioceses for a supply of men for the ordinary ministerial needs of the Church from outside their own area.

It recognises that from time to time there is need also for men of mature experience, sound learning, and pastoral gifts, to undertake work of special responsibility. It therefore recommends that the missionary agencies of the Church throughout the Anglican Communion should keep this in mind, and seek to have available priests and lay workers for this purpose.

The Staffing of Theological Colleges

Resolution 83
The Conference desires to emphasise the need for first-class theological teachers for colleges in the developing areas of the Church, and calls upon the missionary agencies of the Anglican Communion to take such steps as are practicable to meet this pressing need. Financial aid is also needed for the improvement of buildings and for the provision of adequate library facilities.

United Colleges

Resolution 84
The Conference, recognising that there is much common ground in theological training which can be covered in united colleges, and that

139

such colleges can exert a considerable influence in creating better understanding between the several Churches which they serve and in fostering the growth towards greater unity, welcomes the development of united colleges. Nevertheless it considers it essential to secure for Anglican students adequate arrangements for the worship and discipline customary in the Church and to ensure that the Anglican theological contribution is fully and worthily made in the united college.

Theological Faculties or Departments

Resolution 85
The Conference urges that every endeavour should be made to provide resources whereby theological faculties or departments may be established and supported at the newer universities which are coming into being throughout the area covered by the Anglican Communion. The Conference welcomes the progress which has already been made towards this end, and urges the Church to make the fullest use of these faculties when they are created, both as training centres for the ministry, and as providing opportunities for a real integration of Christian faith and scholarship with the intellectual life of other academic disciplines.

Standards of Training

Resolution 86
The Conference urges each province of the Anglican Communion to keep under continuous review its standards for training for ordination, both with regard to the period required and the content of the course, having regard to the demands made upon the clergy in modern conditions.

Post-ordination Training

Resolution 87
The Conference draws attention to the importance of post-ordination training, and recommends that adequate opportunity and financial provision may be available for such training.

The Office of Deacon

Resolution 88
The Conference recommends that each province of the Anglican Communion shall consider whether the office of deacon shall be restored to its primitive place as a distinctive order in the Church, instead of being regarded as a probationary period for the priesthood.

The Supplementary Ministry

Resolution 89
The Conference considers that, while the fully trained and full-time priesthood is essential to the continuing life of the Church, there is no theological principle which forbids a suitable man from being ordained priest while continuing in his lay occupation. While calling attention to Resolution 65 of the Lambeth Conference of 1930, the Conference now wishes to go further and to encourage provinces to make provision on these lines in cases where conditions make it desirable. Such provision is not to be regarded as a substitute for the full-time ministry of the Church, but as an addition to it.

The Office of Reader

Resolution 90
The Conference, gratefully recognising the value of the lay ministry (i.e. sub-deacon, reader, and catechist), whether stipendiary or voluntary, is of opinion that it should be controlled and directed (a) by admission to office by the bishop or his deputy, and (b) by the bishop's formal licence. The Conference is of opinion that the work of these ministries should be described as an office, not an order, nor should the office be deemed to possess the character of indelibility. The Conference urges the importance of adequate training and examination before admission to office.

Resolution 91
The Conference emphasises the necessity for due care in the exercise of the facility recommended in the latter part of Resolution 65 of the Lambeth Conference of 1930, for the authorising by a bishop of certain readers to assist in the administration of the Holy Communion. It recommends that this should be done only to meet pressing need, and that this authority should be given explicitly in writing from time to time.

Religious Orders and Communities

Resolution 92
The Conference, greatly valuing the special form of vocation evident in religious orders and communities, hopes that this form of vocation may find its expression in a wide range of ecclesiastical tradition within the Anglican Communion.

The Contribution of Women

Resolution 93
The Conference thankfully recognises the particular contribution of women to the mission of the Church; and urges that fuller use should be made of trained and qualified women, and that spheres of progressive responsibility and greater security in service should be planned for them.

The Task of the Laity

Resolution 94
The Conference, believing that the laity, as baptized members of the Body of Christ, share in the priestly ministry of the Church and in responsibility for its work, calls upon Anglican men and women throughout the world to realise their Christian vocation both by taking their full part in the Church's life and by Christian witness and dedication in seeking to serve God's purpose in the world.

St Augustine's College, Canterbury

Resolution 95
The Conference expresses its satisfaction at the establishment and progress of St Augustine's College, Canterbury, as a central college for the Anglican Communion. It approves of the way in which its work is developing and would encourage its continuance on the present lines.

Resolution 96
The Conference requests the College Consultative Council to continue its work as a necessary link between the College and the Anglican Communion as a whole.

Resolution 97
The Conference recommends that, in view of the financial needs of the College, the provinces of the Anglican Communion should be asked to increase their contributions for the upkeep of the College from £11,000 to £14,000 per annum.

Resolution 98
The Conference endorses the policy whereby St Augustine's College awards a diploma to students who have satisfactorily completed a prescribed course.

Resolution 99

The Conference requests provinces of the Anglican Communion to seek to ensure that suitable men are set free for a course of study at St Augustine's.

THE RECONCILING OF CONFLICTS BETWEEN AND WITHIN NATIONS

The Church's Work of Reconciliation

Resolution 100

The Conference is convinced that the Church's work of reconciliation must be powerfully expressed within the parish or local congregation. Consequently here it would lay emphasis upon the following points:

(a)   There is a need for Christians to understand more deeply the meaning of God's providence in history and the ground of Christian hope, as distinct from a belief in automatic social progress. This needs to be emphasised in preaching and teaching.

(b)   There is need for persistent intercessory prayer, not only in general terms but specifically and by name for those in positions of great responsibility. Such prayers should be offered for those in nations which oppose us as well as those friendly to us.

(c)   There is need to emphasise the disastrous effect on the common life of those who come to the Lord's Table unreconciled to their neighbours and with bitterness towards them in their hearts. We would recall that the Invitation to the Holy Communion is addressed to those who are 'in love and charity with their neighbours'.

(d)   Where there are divisions in the local community, the Christian congregation in that place should face them fearlessly and, by the action of its members, should serve as an agent of reconciliation.

(e)   While there are many elements in the reconciling of conflicts, none are more important than the character and conduct of individual people. Success or failure in any particular instance may in the end depend on the individual: not only on his knowledge, his judgement, and his zeal, but also on the spirit of Christ mirrored in a life which bears the marks of the cross and the fruits of the Spirit.

Resolution 101

The Conference urges all members of the Anglican Communion to further the ministry of reconciliation by:

(a) developing deeper understanding and fellowship with churchmen of every land;

(b) extending the use of clergy and lay workers in lands other than

their own, the exchange of teachers and seminarians, and the participation by lay visitors in the Church life of the countries they visit;
(c) the general use of the Anglican Cycle of Prayer to undergird this wider sense of community;
(d) participation everywhere in the wider community of all Christian people in the ecumenical opportunities open to them.

Christian Citizenship

Resolution 102
The Conference calls upon all Christian people to recognise their duty of exercising to the full their responsibility as citizens in the national and international policies of their governments.

Resolution 103
The Conference calls upon all Christian people to strive by the exercise of mutual understanding, calm reason, and constant prayer, to reconcile all those who are involved in racial, political, economic, or other conflicts.

The Rights of Men and Nations

Resolution 104
The Conference declares that the Church is not to be identified with any particular political or social system, and calls upon all Christians to encourage their governments to respect the dignity and freedom of people within their own nations and the right of people of other nations to govern themselves.

Sharing Material Resources

Resolution 105
The Conference draws attention to the widespread poverty in many parts of the world; it notes with thankfulness the measures taken to help under-developed countries to become self-supporting, and calls upon Christians in more favoured lands to use their influence to encourage their governments in the task of relieving poverty by a generous sharing of their material and technical resources with those in need.

Modern Warfare and Christian Responsibility

Resolution 106
The Conference reaffirms that war as a method of settling international disputes is incompatible with the teaching and example of our

Lord Jesus Christ, and declares that nothing less than the abolition of war itself should be the goal of the nations, their leaders, and all citizens. As an essential step towards achieving this goal the Conference calls upon Christians to press through their governments, as a matter of the utmost urgency, for the abolition by international agreement of nuclear bombs and other weapons of similar indiscriminate destructive power, the use of which is repugnant to the Christian conscience. To this end governments should accept such limitations of their own sovereignty as effective control demands.

The Conference further urges the governments of the leading nations of the world to devote their utmost efforts at once to framing a comprehensive international disarmament treaty, which shall also provide for the progressive reduction of armed forces and conventional armaments to the minimum necessary for the maintenance of internal security and the fulfilment of the obligations of states to maintain peace and security in accordance with the United Nations Charter.

Resolution 107
The Conference calls Christians to subject to intense prayer and study their attitudes to the issues involved in modern warfare, and urges the Church to continue to consult regularly with scientists and political leaders about the many problems of ethics and conscience which arise from advances in nuclear research.

The United Nations

Resolution 108
The Conference affirms the need for strengthening the United Nations and to this end:
(a) urges that serious consideration be given to the revision of its Charter, the more effective use of, and respect for, the existing processes of international justice, and to the creation of adequate means for enforcing its decisions;
(b) commends wholeheartedly the work done under the aegis of the United Nations, whereby the skills and resources of member nations are made available for the benefit of the whole of humanity;
(c) recommends that all Church people be asked to pray for God's blessing upon the officers and declared purposes of the United Nations;
(d) urges that all Church people be asked to encourage community study regarding the constitution, the plans, and the needs of the United Nations.

Resolution 109
The Conference draws attention to the work of the Committee of the Churches on International Affairs (within the World Council of Churches) and urges Anglicans to support its efforts to bring an informed Christian opinion to bear on international issues.

Condemnation of Racial Discrimination

Resolution 110
The Conference affirms its belief in the natural dignity and value of every man, of whatever colour or race, as created in the image of God. In the light of this belief the Conference affirms that neither race nor colour is in itself a barrier to any aspect of that life in family and community for which God created all men. It therefore condemns discrimination of any kind on the grounds of race or colour alone.

The Conference would urge that in multi-racial societies members of all races shall be allowed:
(a) a fair and just share in the government of their country;
(b) a fair and just share in the control, development, and rewards of the natural resources of their country, including advancement to the highest level of attainment;
(c) the right to associate freely in worship, in education, in industry, in recreation, and in all other departments of the common life.

The Church in an Industrial Age

Resolution 111
The Conference urges the provinces of the Anglican Communion to give special study to the task, strategy, and ministry of the Church within industrial society, and by the use of bold and imaginative experiments to strengthen the impact of the Christian faith upon the whole life and pattern of industry.

THE FAMILY IN CONTEMPORARY SOCIETY

Marriage

Resolution 112
The Conference records its profound conviction that the idea of the human family is rooted in the Godhead and that consequently all problems of sex relations, the procreation of children, and the organisation of family life must be related, consciously and directly, to the creative, redemptive, and sanctifying power of God.

Resolution 113
The Conference affirms that marriage is a vocation to holiness, through which men and women may share in the love and creative purpose of God. The sins of self-indulgence and sensuality, born of selfishness and a refusal to accept marriage as a divine vocation, destroy its true nature and depth, and the right fullness and balance of the relationship between men and women. Christians need always to remember that sexual love is not an end in itself nor a means to self-gratification, and that self-discipline and restraint are essential conditions of the responsible freedom of marriage and family planning.

Resolution 114
The Conference welcomes, with thankfulness, the increasing care given by the clergy to preparation for marriage both in instructing youth, through confirmation classes and other means, and also immediately before marriage. It urges that the importance of this ministry should continue to be emphasised and that special attention should be given to our Lord's principle of life-long union as the basis of all true marriage.

Resolution 115
The Conference believes that the responsibility for deciding upon the number and frequency of children has been laid by God upon the consciences of parents everywhere: that this planning, in such ways as are mutually acceptable to husband and wife in Christian conscience, is a right and important factor in Christian family life and should be the result of positive choice before God. Such responsible parenthood, built on obedience to all the duties of marriage, requires a wise stewardship of the resources and abilities of the family as well as a thoughtful consideration of the varying population needs and problems of society and the claims of future generations.

Resolution 116
The Conference calls upon all Church people to have in mind that, since our Lord's ministry gave a new depth and significance to forgiveness, his Church and the families within it must be a forgiving society, and that there are no wrongs done by its members, one to another, that are unforgivable, or in which a costly forgiveness may not lead to repentance and, through repentance, to reconciliation and a new beginning in living together.

The Conference believes that many tensions in marriage and family life are allowed to reach a breaking point because self-righteousness or a sense of injury takes priority of forgiveness, and that marital relations also break down because those involved do not in time take counsel with a wise adviser. It affirms that no husband or wife has the right to contemplate even legal separation until every opportunity of reconciliation and forgiveness has been exhausted.

Resolution 117
The Conference welcomes the growth of marriage guidance councils, which prepare people for marriage and assist in maintaining stable married life. It recommends that the clergy and Church people of mature faith and with the right qualifications should be encouraged to offer themselves for training as counsellors. It believes that such counsel, given as a Christian vocation by well-trained Christian husbands and wives, is a volunteer service of great value, makes an important contribution to the community, and deserves government support.

Resolution 118
The Conference recognises that divorce is granted by the secular authority in many lands on grounds which the Church cannot acknowledge, and recognises also that in certain cases, where a decree of divorce has been sought and may even have been granted, there may in fact have been no marital bond in the eyes of the Church. It therefore commends for further consideration by the Churches and provinces of the Anglican Communion a procedure for defining marital status, such as already exists in some of its provinces.

Resolution 119
The Conference believes that the Resolutions of the 1948 Lambeth Conference concerning marriage discipline have been of great value as witnessing to Christ's teaching about the life-long nature of marriage, and urges that these Resolutions, and their implications, should continue to be studied in every province.

Polygamy

Resolution 120
(a)   The Conference bears witness to the truth that monogamy is the divine will, testified by the teaching of Christ himself, and therefore true for every race of men.
(b)   It acknowledges that the introduction of monogamy into societies that practise polygamy involves a social and economic revolution and raises problems which the Christian Church has as yet not solved.
(c)   The Conference urges upon Church members the continuance of thorough study and earnest prayer that God may lead his Church to know the manner of its witness and discipline in this issue.

(d)   The Conference, recognising that the problem of polygamy is bound up with the limitation of opportunities for women in society, urges that the Church should make every effort to advance the status of women in every possible way, especially in the sphere of education.
(e)   The Conference further requests His Grace the President to refer this problem to the Advisory Council on Missionary Strategy.

The Christian Family

Resolution 121
The Conference commends, as an aid to better teaching about marriage and home life, the following summary of the marks of a Christian family. Such a family:
   (a) seeks to live by the teaching and example of Jesus Christ;
   (b) joins in the worship of Almighty God on Sundays in church;
   (c) joins in common prayer and Bible reading, and grace at meals;
   (d) is forgiving one to another, and accepts responsibility for one another;
   (e) shares together in common tasks and recreation;
   (f) uses abilities, time, and possessions responsibly in society;
   (g) is a good neighbour, hospitable to friend and stranger.

Resolution 122
The Conference believes that a most important answer to the crushing impact of secularism on family life lies in a return to the discipline of family prayer and in a faithful common Christian life in the household. It urges that the clergy work towards this end by teaching both the privilege and the means of such worship, and of Bible reading, in which fathers should take their due place with mothers and children as members and ministers of a worshipping community.

Resolution 123
The Conference, recognising that there is a world-wide need for decent and suitable housing, records its belief that every married couple should have adequate privacy and shelter, for the better bringing up of the family as well as for the benefit of its own married life; and that national and local government share fully with private enterprise the community's obligation to meet this end.

Resolution 124
The Conference, noting the increasing proportion of older people in many parts of the world, calls attention to the fact that, although some are entirely dependent upon the care of others, many of them, by reason of experience or special skills, still have much to give. It expresses

149

its warm appreciation of the studies and projects bearing on this problem which have already been made, and records its belief that the Church, in all its provinces, should initiate and assist such studies, and should also seek practical means of meeting the needs they reveal. It further emphasises the responsibility of sons and daughters for the needs of elderly parents and, where possible, for making such provision as will keep them closely within the life and activity of their family circle.

The Duties of the Laity

Resolution 125
The Conference rejoices that, more and more, lay men and women are finding their true Christian ministry in their daily work in the world, as well as in the organised life of the Church. All of us need to remember that the field of Christian service for the laity lies mainly in the secular sphere, where their integrity and competence can best serve the needs of the world and the glory of God. The clergy need to understand this, and to help, by their teaching and by sharing in the thoughts and problems of the laity in their daily work, to deepen this ministry. The laity need equally to understand it, to help one another by Christian discussion and loyal comradeship to bear a better witness, and to offer in their work both their responsible, skilled gifts, and a deeper understanding of the Christian faith about God and man.

Gambling, Drunkenness, and the Use of Drugs

Resolution 126
The Conference draws attention to the widespread and growing reliance on undesirable and artificial means of responding to the restlessness of our present age, and to the resulting weakening of family life. It utters a warning against the dangers implicit in gambling, drunkenness, and the use of drugs, and calls for renewed teaching of responsible and disciplined standards of behaviour.

Migratory Labour

Resolution 127
The Conference, recognising the family as the God-given unit of human life and society, condemns those systems of migratory labour that break up family life by enforcing the unjustified residential separation of man and wife, or of parents and children.

Refugees and Stateless Persons

Resolution 128
The Conference calls the attention of churchmen to the tragic plight
of refugees and stateless persons, as a continuing feature of the world
today. It believes their plight is a cause both of intense personal suffering and of political unrest; and that neither this, nor the size of the
problem, is sufficiently appreciated. It therefore calls:
(a) for continuing support, in the form of both gifts and personal
service, for the Inter-Church Aid and Refugee Service Department
of the World Council of Churches, so that such people may be
assisted;
(b) for more sustained action through the United Nations and
through the governments concerned, to finance migrants and place
them in new countries; and
(c) for special care in keeping together the members of families in
such distress.

The Religious Duties of Churchmen

Resolution 129
The Conference urges that the sections of the Report on the Family
in Contemporary Society dealing with industrial pressures on the
family, and, by implication, upon the religious duties of churchmen,
should be carefully studied by Christians in industry and should be
made a basis for discussions between representatives of the Churches
and industrial managers and trade unionists.

Co-operation with Secular Agencies

Resolution 130
The Conference believes it to be most desirable that the clergy and
Church workers should take every opportunity of meeting health and
social workers, as well as teachers, in a locality, and discussing with
them the welfare of the community and its family life.

The Mutual Exchange of Information

Resolution 131
The Conference, believing that a need exists within the Anglican Communion for a far greater sharing of study, and that, especially in areas
where research is advancing rapidly, and where social and political
changes are pressing, the usefulness of the Anglican Communion,
under God, depends upon the maintenance of the closest possible

relations between the provinces and their various activities of exploration and investigation, and recommends that His Grace the President and the Consultative Body consider and adopt appropriate means of establishing and maintaining such common conversations and mutual exchange.

1968

Section Reports

Resolution 1
The Conference, without committing itself to the endorsement of the Section Reports, commends them to the continuing study of the Church as statements of the views of the bishops concerned.

Faith in the Living God

Resolution 2
The Conference, having considered and welcomed
   (a) the increasing extent of human knowledge,
   (b) the prospect of human control of the natural environment,
   (c) the searching enquiries of the theologians,
calls the Church to a faith in the living God which is adventurous, expectant, calm, and confident, and to faith in the standards of Christ, who was, and is, and is to come, as the criterion of what is to be welcomed and what is to be resisted in contemporary society.

Resolution 3
The Conference recommends that theologians be encouraged to continue to explore fresh ways of understanding God's revelation of himself in Christ, expressed in language that makes sense in our time. It believes that this requires of the theologian respect for tradition and, of the Church, respect for freedom of inquiry.

The Contemporary Life of Prayer

Resolution 4
The Conference affirms that the primary task of the Church is to glorify God by leading all mankind into life in Christ, and that this always involves a continuous advance in the practice of prayer in the Spirit; and therefore calls upon the clergy and laity of the whole Anglican

Communion to join with the bishops in their determination, in humble and penitent dependence upon God, to deepen and strengthen their life of prayer, remembering always that our Lord's periods of withdrawal for prayer were a prelude and preparation for his further service in the world that the Father might be glorified.

To this end the Church should search to discover those forms of spirituality and methods of prayer, both corporate and personal, which meet the needs of men and women today, such as those expressed by Abbé Michel Quoist in his book *Prayers of Life*. The Church should pay more attention to the development of that capacity for silent prayer which exists in all her members, and should encourage corporate and personal waiting upon God.

Religious Communities

Resolution 5
The Conference recognises with gratitude the contribution of the religious communities, both of men and of women, to the life of the Church, and values their witness to the absolute character of the claims of God on the life of man, to the fruitfulness of a life given to prayer and service, and to the unity of the Church across the divisions which at present exist. It calls upon the communities to take their part in the present renewal of the Church, in particular by seeking to renew themselves according to the priorities of the Gospel and the original intention of their foundation. It recommends that, in all provinces where communities exist, close co-operation between the bishops and the communities should be maintained and developed.

Man's Stewardship of Nature

Resolution 6
The Conference urges all Christians, in obedience to the doctrine of creation, to take all possible action to ensure man's responsible stewardship over nature; in particular in his relationship with animals, and with regard to the conservation of the soil, and the prevention of the pollution of air, soil, and ocean.

Conservation of the Seabed

Resolution 7
The Conference endorses the initiative of Dr Pardo, leader of the Maltese delegation at the United Nations, urging that steps be taken to draft a treaty embodying the following principles:

That the seabed beyond the limits of present national jurisdiction

(a) be conserved against appropriation by nations or their nationals, so that the deep ocean floor should not be allowed to become a stage for competing claims of national sovereignty;

(b) be explored in a manner consistent with the principles and purposes of the charter of the United Nations;

(c) be exploited economically or made use of with the aim of safeguarding the interests of mankind;

(d) be conserved exclusively for peaceful purposes in perpetuity.

War

Resolution 8

This Conference

(a)   reaffirms the words of the Conference of 1930 that 'war as a method of settling international disputes is incompatible with the teaching and example of our Lord Jesus Christ';

(b)   states emphatically that it condemns the use of nuclear and bacteriological weapons;

(c)   holds that it is the concern of the Church

   (i) to uphold and extend the right of conscientious objection;

   (ii) to oppose persistently the claim that total war or the use of weapons however ruthless or indiscriminate can be justified by results;

(d)   urges upon Christians the duty to support international action either through the United Nations or otherwise to settle disputes justly without recourse to war; to work towards the abolition of the competitive supply of armaments; and to develop adequate machinery for the keeping of a just and permanent peace.

Human Unity

Resolution 9

The Conference affirms that human unity can only be achieved if all governments are willing to work towards a form of world government designed to serve the interests of all mankind.

Consultation Regarding World Peace

Resolution 10

The Conference invites the Archbishop of Canterbury on its behalf to consult with the Pope and the Oecumenical Patriarch and the Praesidium of the World Council of Churches on the possibility of approaching leaders of the other world religions with a view to convening a conference at which in concert they would speak in the interests of humanity on behalf of world peace.

Christianity and Other Faiths

Resolution 11
It is the conviction of the Conference that, in their obedience to Christ's mission and command and in their obligation towards the contemporary world, the Christian Churches must endeavour such positive relationship to the different religions of men, and to the doubt and denial of faith, as will
(a) set forward the common unity of mankind and a common participation in its present history;
(b) encourage Christians to increasing co-operation with men of other faiths in the fields of economic, social, and moral action;
(c) call Christians not only to study other faiths in their own seriousness but also to study unbelief in its real quality.

Religious Dialogue

Resolution 12
The Conference recommends a renewed and vigorous implementation of the task of inter-religious dialogue already set in hand in the study centres organised by the World Council of Churches and other bodies, and urges increased Anglican support both in the seconding of personnel and in the provision of money. It also commends similar assistance for dialogue with Marxists and those who profess no religious faith.

The Christians of the Southern Sudan

Resolution 13
The Conference wishes to place on record its gratitude to God for the faith and courage of the Christians of the Southern Sudan during the past years of testing of the Church.

The Conference sends to them and to the many thousands of their fellow Sudanese the assurance that in their suffering and the loss of homes and schools, hospitals and churches, they are not forgotten in our prayers.

The Conference rejoices to know of the tireless efforts of the Sudanese clergy, evangelists, teachers, and other church workers in their task of proclaiming the gospel of reconciliation, both in the refugee areas and in the heart of the countryside.

The Conference prays Almighty God to lead the responsible authorities speedily to find a just and lasting solution to the existing problem.

West Africa

Resolution 14

The Conference receives the Statement* from the Bishops of the Province of West Africa with deep thankfulness for the Christian spirit of compassion and reconciliation that informs it. It has been deeply distressed by the prolonged conflict which has divided the peoples of Nigeria and of the former Eastern Region, and which has brought, even in the days in which the Conference has been meeting, death through starvation and disease to so many innocent men, women, and children.

With the West African bishops, we call, in the words of the Fourth Assembly of the World Council of Churches held recently at Uppsala, for 'all governments to work effectively towards peace and reconciliation, and to refrain from any action which would prolong the conflict in the area'.

The Conference welcomes any agreement between the belligerent parties to provide channels for the supply of food, medicine, and clothing to those in need. It calls on governments to engage in a massive inter-governmental relief operation on both sides of the conflict, and commends the work of the Division of Inter-Church Aid, Refugee and World Service of the World Council of Churches and of other voluntary agencies in meeting immediate and longer-term needs.

The Conference assures its fellow Christians on both sides of the conflict of continuing fellowship with them in the Gospel. They may be sure of the prayers of the bishops and Churches of the Anglican Communion and of all possible support, as in Christ's name they minister to the suffering and work for reconciliation and peace among all their people.

* STATEMENT FROM THE BISHOPS OF THE PROVINCE OF WEST AFRICA
The Bishops of the Province of West Africa desire to give thanks to Almighty God for the prayers, the sympathy, and the work for reconciliation which have supported us and enabled us to endure these fourteen months of civil war. We are especially grateful to His Grace the Archbishop of Canterbury for his message sent to us when war broke out, for his initiative in the visits of fraternal delegations to the churches on both sides, and for his persistent work for peace. We were heartened by the joint appeal for peace made in March by the Roman Catholic Church and the World Council of Churches, calling for 'an immediate cessation of armed hostilities and for the establishment of a lasting peace by honourable negotiation in the highest African tradition'. We are grateful to the Commonwealth Secretariat and to the Organization of African Unity for the efforts they have made and are continuing to make to bring the two sides together. We also desire to record our deep gratitude to the voluntary agencies and to our fellow Christians in all parts of the world who have contributed by their generous gifts, their prayers, and their concern to alleviate the sufferings of our war-saddened peoples.

Yet the war still goes on. We are deeply grieved and feel bound to acknowledge in penitence our ineffective witness to the compassion and mercy and reconciling love of Christ. In our failure we seek the sympathetic aid of the Lambeth Conference as follows:

(1) To call, in the words of the Resolution of the Uppsala World Council meeting, for 'all governments to work effectively towards peace and reconciliation, and to refrain from any action which would prolong the conflict in the area'.

(2) To call on the government of both sides in the war to look with pity on those who are sick and starving and to give every facility to the organisations which are endeavouring to bring them food and medical supplies.

(3) To consider offering, in co-operation with other Churches, a further delegation to visit the leaders on both sides to promote the work of reconciliation so powerfully put before us in the Archbishop of East Africa's sermon.

Finally, we state our belief that the conflict can be resolved positively in a creative way only when each side is prepared to abandon exclusive positions and to seek to reach agreement on how to secure the vital interests of the peoples of both sides.

The Middle East

Resolution 15
The Conference views with concern the continuing tensions in the Middle East; the tragic plight of hundreds of thousands of Arab refugees who have lost homes and means of livelihood; and the absence, in spite of United Nations resolutions, of any sign of progress towards the establishment of peace. The Conference endorses the resolutions of the World Council of Churches at Uppsala and urges men of good will to use their influence in each nation and in the United Nations towards the finding of a just solution.

Racism

Resolution 16
The Conference commends the following statement of the World Council of Churches meeting at Uppsala:

Racism is a blatant denial of the Christian faith. (i) It denies the effectiveness of the reconciling work of Jesus Christ, through whose love all human diversities lose their divisive significance; (ii) it denies our common humanity in creation and our belief that all men are made in God's image; (iii) it falsely asserts that we find our significance in terms of racial identity rather than in Jesus Christ.

The Conference acknowledges in penitence that the Churches of the Anglican Communion have failed to accept the cost of corporate witness to their unity in Christ, and calls upon them to re-examine their life and structures in order to give expression to the demands of the Gospel (a) by the inclusiveness of their worship, (b) by the creation of a climate of acceptance in their common life, and (c) by their justice in placing and appointment.

Further, the Conference calls upon the Churches to press upon governments and communities their duty to promote fundamental human rights and freedoms among all their peoples.

The Conference welcomes especially the contribution of Human Rights Year towards the solution of the problem of racism.

The Use of Power

Resolution 17
The Conference, profoundly aware of the effect on human life of the responsible and irresponsible use of power at all levels of human society, considers that the Church should address itself energetically to the range of problems arising in this area.

The Study of Social and Political Change

Resolution 18
The Conference recommends that the provinces should set up study groups, Anglican and ecumenical, to study the documents on all aspects of violent and non-violent social and political change.

In view of the urgent nature of this matter, it further recommends that these groups promptly report their findings and recommendations to the Anglican Consultative Council or Lambeth Consultative Body, which will make them generally available to the Anglican Communion.

Resolution 19
The Conference recommends:
(a)   That, recognising that for the foreseeable future the greater part of the earth will retain agrarian forms of society, the provinces of the Anglican Communion co-operate with the World Council of Churches and other agencies to carry out the regional surveys necessary to determine specific technological and other development needs in both agrarian and industrial areas; and further, that the local Church in agrarian communities be urged to promote or co-operate in appropriate political, economic, and social development projects as its witness to the Gospel of the incarnate Lord; and that in both agrarian and industrial areas the structures of the Church, devised for static and pre-industrial societies, be renewed for more effective impact on rapidly changing societies.
(b)   That the normal pattern for the missionary structure of the Church be that of ecumenical action and that every use be made of consultants from the social sciences and related fields.
(c)   That the Church increasingly call on the skills of full-time professionals in such fields as social work, community organisation, education, recreational activities, and the mass media, and that they be regarded as members of the integral staff of the Church.

(d)   That the Church increasingly work for social goals which really benefit human beings, e.g. in housing, education, health, and adequate wages, using both secular agencies and, where appropriate, its own social agencies.

(e)   That the Church increasingly give itself seriously to the redeployment of resources of men and money so as to take the initiatives that effective mission requires both at home and abroad.

(f)   That, in consequence of the last recommendation, a serious study be made of existing buildings and the planning of new ones.

Resolution 20
The Conference, conscious of the many and complex social, political, economic, and cultural problems of our time, on which Christians need guidance, urges upon the Anglican Communion the close study of the World Council of Churches Report *World Conference on Church and Society, 1966.*

Developing Countries

Resolution 21
The Conference welcomes the deep concern about the economic and social frustration of developing countries expressed by the World Council of Churches at its recent Assembly in Uppsala. To produce decisive and wise action in this serious situation it recommends to the provinces of the Anglican Communion:

(a)   The careful study of the issues of development including the new economic and political structures which it demands; and effective dissemination of knowledge about the issues to the Churches and to the public.

(b)   That the efforts of the United Nations agencies to bring about world economic justice receive the active support and prayers of all the Churches.

(c)   That they endorse the appeal of the World Council of Churches at Uppsala that the Churches should do their utmost to influence the governments of industrialised countries:

(i) to increase annually the percentage of Gross National Product officially transferred as financial resources, exclusive of private investment, to developing countries, with the minimum net amount of one per cent to be reached by 1971;

(ii) to conclude agreements stabilising and supporting at an acceptable level the prices of vulnerable primary products and providing preferential access to developed markets for the manufactured products of developing countries.

(d)   That they should urge their members to support more actively existing funds, and particularly the Division of Inter-Church Aid, Refugee and World Service, to help meet some of the present emergencies in world poverty and hunger.

Responsible Parenthood

Resolution 22

This Conference has taken note of the papal encyclical letter *Humanae vitae* recently issued by His Holiness Pope Paul VI. The Conference records its appreciation of the Pope's deep concern for the institution of marriage and the integrity of married life.

Nevertheless, the Conference finds itself unable to agree with the Pope's conclusion that all methods of conception control other than abstinence from sexual intercourse or its confinement to the periods of infecundity are contrary to the 'order established by God'. It reaffirms the findings of the Lambeth Conference of 1958 contained in Resolutions 112, 113, and 115 which are as follows:

112. The Conference records its profound conviction that the idea of the human family is rooted in the Godhead and that consequently all problems of sex relations, the procreation of children, and the organisation of family life must be related, consciously and directly, to the creative, redemptive, and sanctifying power of God.

113. The Conference affirms that marriage is a vocation to holiness, through which men and women may share in the love and creative purpose of God. The sins of self-indulgence and sensuality, born of selfishness and a refusal to accept marriage as a divine vocation, destroy its true nature and depth, and the right fullness and balance of the relationship between men and women. Christians need always to remember that sexual love is not an end in itself nor a means to self-gratification, and that self-discipline and restraint are essential conditions of the responsible freedom of marriage and family planning.

115. The Conference believes that the responsibility for deciding upon the number and frequency of children has been laid by God upon the consciences of parents everywhere: that this planning, in such ways as are mutually acceptable to husband and wife in Christian conscience, is a right and important factor in Christian family life and should be the result of positive choice before God. Such responsible parenthood, built on obedience to all the duties of marriage, requires a wise stewardship of the resources and abilities of the family as well as a thoughtful consideration of the varying population needs and problems of society and the claims of future generations.

The Conference commends the Report of Committee 5 of the Lambeth Conference 1958, together with the study entitled *The Family in Contemporary Society* which formed the basis of the work of that Committee, to the attention of all men of good will for further study in the light of the continuing sociological and scientific developments of the past decade.

Marriage Discipline

Resolution 23
The Conference recognises that polygamy poses one of the sharpest conflicts between the faith and particular cultures.

The Church seeks to proclaim the will of God in setting out the clear implications of our Lord's teaching about marriage. Hence it bears witness to monogamous life-long marriage as God's will for mankind.

The Conference believes that such marriage alone bears adequate witness to the equal sanctity of all human beings which lies at the heart of the Christian revelation; yet recognises that in every place many problems concerning marriage confront the Church.

The Conference therefore asks each province to re-examine its discipline in such problems in full consultation with other provinces in a similar situation.

THE MINISTRY

The Laity

Resolution 24
The Conference recommends that no major issue in the life of the Church should be decided without the full participation of the laity in discussion and in decision.

Resolution 25
The Conference recommends that each province or regional Church be asked to explore the theology of baptism and confirmation in relation to the need to commission the laity for their task in the world, and to experiment in this regard.

Resolution 26
The Conference requests that information about experiments in lay training be made available to the whole of the Anglican Communion.

Resolution 27
The Conference believes that there is an urgent need for increase in

the quantity and quality of training for laypeople for their task in the world.

Youth and Human Welfare

Resolution 28
The Conference values the initiative shown by young people in witnessing to their faith in Christ; and urges that they should be encouraged to do this in their own way and through their own media, and that the Church should have regard to their concern for the renewal of society and of the Church.

Resolution 29
The Conference, thankful for the intensified interest of young people in human welfare, conscious of the value of their informed insights, and recognising the need to involve them more directly in decision-making, in both secular and ecclesiastical society, requests provinces, dioceses, and parishes to promote this involvement in every way possible.

Fellowships for Church Women

Resolution 30
The Conference welcomes the appearance of fellowships for Church women in various parts of the Anglican Communion and commends the development and extension of these associations for an increase of devotion and neighbourliness and for witness to the faith of Jesus Christ.

Priesthood

Resolution 31
The Conference commends the study of the paragraphs on 'Priesthood' in the Report of Section II as an Anglican contribution towards an understanding of the nature of priesthood in the present ecumenical situation.

The Diaconate

Resolution 32
The Conference recommends:
(a)   That the diaconate, combining service of others with liturgical functions, be open to
  (i) men and women remaining in secular occupations,

(ii) full-time church workers,
(iii) those selected for the priesthood.
(b)   That Ordinals should, where necessary, be revised:
(i) to take account of the new role envisaged for the diaconate;
(ii) by the removal of reference to the diaconate as 'an inferior office';
(iii) by emphasis upon the continuing element of *diakonia* in the ministry of bishops and priests.
(c)   That those made deaconesses by laying-on of hands with appropriate prayers be declared to be within the diaconate.
(d)   That appropriate canonical legislation be enacted by provinces and regional Churches to provide for those already ordained deaconesses.

Voting on (c) above: For 221; Against 183.

A Wider Ordained Ministry

Resolution 33
This Conference affirms Resolution 89 of the Lambeth Conference 1958 on the supplementary ministry and recommends a wider and more confident use of this ministry. The Resolution reads as follows:
89. The Conference considers that, while the fully trained and full-time priesthood is essential to the continuing life of the Church, there is no theological principle which forbids a suitable man from being ordained priest while continuing in his lay occupation. While calling attention to Resolution 65 of the Lambeth Conference of 1930, the Conference now wishes to go further and to encourage provinces to make provision on these lines in cases where conditions make it desirable. Such provision is not to be regarded as a substitute for the full-time ministry of the Church, but as an addition to it.

Ordination of Women to the Priesthood

Resolution 34
The Conference affirms its opinion that the theological arguments as at present presented for and against the ordination of women to the priesthood are inconclusive.

Resolution 35
The Conference requests every national and regional Church or province to give careful study to the question of the ordination of women to the priesthood and to report its findings to the Anglican Consulta-

tive Council (or Lambeth Consultative Body) which will make them generally available to the Anglican Communion.

Resolution 36

The Conference requests the Anglican Consultative Council (or Lambeth Consultative Body)

(a) to initiate consultations with other Churches which have women in their ordained ministry and with those which have not;

(b) to distribute the information thus secured throughout the Anglican Communion.

Resolution 37

The Conference recommends that, before any national or regional Church or province makes a final decision to ordain women to the priesthood, the advice of the Anglican Consultative Council (or Lambeth Consultative Body) be sought and carefully considered.

Resolution 38

The Conference recommends that, in the meantime, national or regional Churches or provinces should be encouraged to make canonical provision, where this does not exist, for duly qualified women to share in the conduct of liturgical worship, to preach, to baptize, to read the Epistle and Gospel at the Holy Communion, and to help in the distribution of the elements.

The Episcopate

Resolution 39

The Conference recommends that bishops should have opportunities of training for their office and requests the Anglican Consultative Council to make provision for such training where regional Churches are unable to do so.

Resolution 40

The Conference affirms its opinion that all coadjutor, suffragan and full-time assistant bishops should exercise every kind of episcopal function and have their place as bishops in the councils of the Church.

Resolution 41

The Conference recommends that the bishops, as leaders and representatives of a servant Church, should radically examine the honours paid to them in the course of divine worship, in titles and customary address, and in style of living, while having the necessary facilities for the efficient carrying on of their work.

Post-ordination Training

Resolution 42
The Conference urges dioceses to provide continuing training for the clergy after ordination, and to relate the programmes of study to the new situations and developments presented by a rapidly changing world.

The Thirty-nine Articles

Resolution 43
The Conference accepts the main conclusion of the Report of the Archbishops' Commission on Christian Doctrine entitled *Subscription and Assent to the Thirty-nine Articles* (1968) and in furtherance of its recommendation:
   (a) suggests that each Church of our Communion consider whether the Articles need be bound up with its Prayer Book;
   (b) suggests to the Churches of the Anglican Communion that assent to the Thirty-nine Articles be no longer required of ordinands;
   (c) suggests that, when subscription is required to the Articles or other elements in the Anglican tradition, it should be required, and given, only in the context of a statement which gives the full range of our inheritance of faith and sets the Articles in their historical context.

Voting: Adopted, with 37 dissentients.

RELATIONS WITH OTHER CHURCHES

Renewal in Unity

Resolution 44
The Conference recommends that the following affirmations be referred to each province for consideration, as means of furthering renewal in unity.
(a)   We believe that each bishop of the Anglican Communion should ask himself how seriously he takes the suggestion of the Lund Conference on Faith and Order that we should do together everything which conscience does not compel us to do separately. To do so immediately raises the need to review Church structures (conduct of synods, budgets, areas of jurisdiction, etc.) to see where they can be altered to foster rather than hinder co-operation. It involves giving encouragement in this direction to all whom we can influence. It involves also the exploration of *responsible experiment* so that ecumenical work

beyond the present limits of constitutional provision is encouraged to keep in touch with the common mind of the Church and not tempted to break away.

(b) We believe that prior attention in ecumenical life and action should be given to the local level, and point to local ecumenical action as the most direct way of bringing together the whole Christian community in any area.

(c) We believe that as ecumenical work develops in local, national, and regional areas the need becomes more apparent for an ecumenical forum on the widest possible scale. We therefore endorse the hope expressed at the Uppsala Assembly that 'the members of the World Council of Churches, committed to each other, should work for the time when a genuinely universal council may once more speak for all Christians'. Our interim confessional and ecumenical organisations should be tested by their capacity to lead in this direction.

(d) We believe that areas in which little ecumenical activity is at present possible have a claim upon the encouragement and support of the more strongly established areas, which should make provision of time and money to maintain fellowship with them.

Admission of Non-Anglicans to Holy Communion

Resolution 45
The Conference recommends that, in order to meet special pastoral needs of God's people, under the direction of the bishop Christians duly baptized in the name of the Holy Trinity and qualified to receive Holy Communion in their own Churches may be welcomed at the Lord's Table in the Anglican Communion.

Anglicans Communicating in other than Anglican Churches

Resolution 46
The Conference recommends that, while it is the general practice of the Church that Anglican communicants receive the Holy Communion at the hands of ordained ministers of their own Church or of Churches in communion therewith, nevertheless under the general direction of the bishop, to meet special pastoral need, such communicants be free to attend the Eucharist in other Churches holding the apostolic faith as contained in the Scriptures and summarised in the Apostles' and Nicene Creeds, and as conscience dictates to receive the sacrament, when they know they are welcome to do so.

Voting: For 351; Against 75.

Reciprocal Acts of Intercommunion

Resolution 47
The Conference recommends that, where there is agreement between an Anglican Church and some other Church or Churches to seek unity in a way which includes agreement on apostolic faith and order, and where that agreement to seek unity has found expression, whether in a covenant to unite or in some other appropriate form, a Church of the Anglican Communion should be free to allow reciprocal acts of intercommunion under the general direction of the bishop; each province concerned to determine when the negotiations for union in which it is engaged have reached the stage which allows this intercommunion.
Voting: For 341; Against 87.

The Church of South India

Resolution 48
The Conference recommends:
(a)   That when a bishop or episcopally ordained minister of the Church of South India visits a diocese of the Anglican Communion and exercises his ministry in Anglican churches there should now be no restriction on the exercise of his ministry in other Churches with which the Church of South India is in communion.
(b)   That Churches and provinces of the Anglican Communion re-examine their relation to the Church of South India with a view to entering into full communion with that Church.

The Churches of North India and Pakistan

Resolution 49
The Conference recommends that Churches and provinces of the Anglican Communion should enter into full communion with the Churches of North India and Pakistan upon their inauguration and should foster the relations of fellowship which this involves.

The Church of Lanka

Resolution 50
The Conference recommends that Churches and provinces of the Anglican Communion should enter into full communion with the Church of Lanka upon its inauguration and should foster the relations of fellowship which this involves.

167

Anglican–Methodist Unity in Great Britain

Resolution 51
The Conference welcomes the proposals for Anglican–Methodist unity in Great Britain and notes with satisfaction the view expressed in the Report of Section III that the proposed Service of Reconciliation is theologically adequate to achieve its declared intentions of reconciling the two Churches and integrating their ministries.

The Roman Catholic Church

Resolution 52
The Conference welcomes the proposals made in the Report of Section III which concern Anglican relations with the Roman Catholic Church.

Resolution 53
The Conference recommends the setting up of a Permanent Joint Commission, for which the Anglican delegation should be chosen by the Lambeth Consultative Body (or its successor) and be representative of the Anglican Communion as a whole.

Resolution 54
In view of the urgent pastoral questions raised by mixed marriages the Conference welcomes the work of the Joint Commission on the Theology of Marriage and its Application to Mixed Marriages, and urges its speedy continuance.

Collegiality

Resolution 55
The Conference recommends that the principle of collegiality should be a guiding principle in the growth of the relationships between the provinces of the Anglican Communion and those Churches with which we are, or shall be, in full communion, and draws particular attention to that part of the Section III Report which underlines this principle.

The Orthodox Churches

Resolution 56
The Conference warmly welcomes the proposed resumption of the pan-Orthodox and pan-Anglican discussions which began in 1931.

Resolution 57
The Conference welcomes the proposals concerning Anglican relations with the Orthodox and Oriental (Orthodox) Churches, urging joint biblical study with Orthodox theologians and dialogue at the local level.

Resolution 58
The Conference recommends the circulation to all Anglican provinces of the report of the delegation to Bucharest in 1935 and of the terms in which this report was accepted and endorsed by the Convocations of Canterbury and York 'as consonant with the Anglican formularies and a legitimate interpretation of the faith of the Church as held by the Anglican Communion'.

The Lutheran Churches

Resolution 59
The Conference recommends the initiation of Anglican–Lutheran conversations on a world-wide basis as soon as possible.

THE ROLE OF THE ANGLICAN COMMUNION

The Anglican Presence in Europe

Resolution 60
The Conference welcomes the proposals in the Report of Section III concerning the Anglican presence in Europe.

The Anglican Centre in Rome

Resolution 61
The Conference expresses its willingness to support the Anglican Centre in Rome, which with its library and its facilities for lectures, discussions, and personal advice, will help Roman Catholics and others to learn more about the life and thought of the Anglican Communion in all its aspects.

The Anglican Presence in Geneva

Resolution 62
The Conference recommends that the Anglican presence in Geneva should be strengthened, and that the Lambeth Consultative Body (or its successor) should take appropriate steps to effect this.

Parallel Jurisdictions

Resolution 63
The Conference deplores the existence of parallel Anglican jurisdictions in Europe and in other areas, and recommends that the Lambeth Consultative Body (or its successor) should give early attention to the problems involved. The Conference recommends that, in any such area where there exists a Church with which we are in full communion, that Church should participate in the consultations.

The Anglican Presence in Latin America

Resolution 64
The Conference records its conviction that, in the light of the growing importance of Latin America and the rapid social, economic, political, and religious changes there taking place, there is an urgent need for an increasing Christian witness and involvement in which the Anglican Churches must make their unique and full contribution.

The Conference rejoices in the growth and indigenisation of Anglican witness in Latin America since Lambeth 1958 and in the increased participation and awareness of some parts of the Anglican Communion, and hopes that this participation and interest will extend to the whole Anglican Communion.

The Conference recommends that the member Churches of the Anglican Communion should place prominent emphasis upon Latin America in their missionary education, their prayers, and their commitment to the world mission, as outlined in the document entitled *The Anglican Communion and Latin America.*

General Episcopal Consultation

Resolution 65
The Conference recommends:
(a) That a General Episcopal Consultation (drawn from many countries) be held in the near future, and expresses the hope that the Archbishop of Canterbury will take the initiative in sending invitations primarily to those Churches which are in full or partial communion with the See of Canterbury or with other provinces of the Anglican Communion.
(b) That Regional Episcopal Consultations should be held on a wider basis of representation than that suggested for the General Episcopal Consultation, under such local auspices and arrangements as seem appropriate and helpful in each region.

Inter-Anglican Structures

Resolution 66
The Conference approves the recommendations listed under the general heading 'Inter-Anglican Structures' in the Report of Section III.

Mutual Responsibility and Interdependence

Resolution 67
(a)   The Conference records its gratitude for the concept of mutual responsibility and interdependence in the Body of Christ, and for the renewed sense of responsibility for each other which it has created within our Communion.
(b)   The Conference believes that a developing MRI has a vital contribution to make to our relationships within the whole Church of God. It therefore summons our Churches to a deeper commitment to Christ's mission through a wide partnership of prayer, by sharing sacrificially and effectively their manpower and money, and by a readiness to learn from each other.
(c)   The Conference urges that serious attention be paid to the need for co-operation, at every level of Anglican and ecumenical life, in the planning, implementing, and review of all work undertaken, along the lines set out in the Report of Section III.
(d)   The Conference believes that the time has come for a reappraisal of the policies, methods, and areas of responsibility of the Anglican Communion in discharging its share of the mission of Christ and that there is a need for a renewed sense of urgency.

Budgets

Resolution 68
The Conference approves the approximate budgets for 1969, 1970, and 1971 submitted by the ad hoc finance committee and asks the member Churches to support this Central Budget according to the present tables of apportionment.

Anglican Consultative Council

Resolution 69
The Conference accepts and endorses the appended proposals concerning the Anglican Consultative Council and its Constitution and submits them to the member Churches of the Anglican Communion for approval. Approval shall be by a two-thirds majority of the member Churches and shall be signified to the Secretary of the Lambeth Consultative Body not later than 31 October 1969.

ANGLICAN CONSULTATIVE COUNCIL

FUNCTIONS

1   To share information about developments in one or more provinces with the other parts of the Communion and to serve as needed as an instrument of common action.
2   To advise on inter-Anglican, provincial, and diocesan relationships, including the division of provinces, the formation of new provinces and of regional councils, and the problems of extra-provincial dioceses.
3   To develop as far as possible agreed Anglican policies in the world mission of the Church and to encourage national and regional Churches to engage together in developing and implementing such policies by sharing their resources of manpower, money, and experience to the best advantage of all.
4   To keep before national and regional Churches the importance of the fullest possible Anglican collaboration with other Christian Churches.
5   To encourage and guide Anglican participation in the ecumenical movement and the ecumenical organisations; to co-operate with the World Council of Churches and the world confessional bodies on behalf of the Anglican Communion; and to make arrangements for the conduct of pan-Anglican conversations with the Roman Catholic Church, the Orthodox Churches, and other Churches.
6   To advise on matters arising out of national or regional Church union negotiations or conversations and on subsequent relations with united Churches.
7   To advise on problems of inter-Anglican communication and to help in the dissemination of Anglican and ecumenical information.
8   To keep in review the needs that may arise for further study and, where necessary, to promote inquiry and research.

CONSTITUTION

Membership
1   The Council shall be constituted initially with a membership according to the Schedule below. With the assent of two-thirds of the metropolitans, it shall have power to make alterations in the Schedule as changing circumstances may require.
2   Members shall be chosen as provincial, national, or regional machinery provides. Alternates shall be named by each Church and shall be invited to attend if a Church would otherwise be unrepresented for a whole session of the Council.
3   The Council shall have power to co-opt as set out in the Schedule of Membership.
4   The term of office for members appointed according to the Schedule, and for co-opted members, shall be six years. Except as provided in the recommendation below for the initial period, members shall be ineligible for immediate re-election. Bishops and other clerical members shall cease to be members on retirement from ecclesiastical office, and all members shall similarly cease to be members on moving to another regional Church or province of the Anglican Communion. Casual vacancies shall be filled by the appointing bodies, and persons thus appointed shall serve for the unexpired term.
5   The Council shall have the right to call in advisers, Anglicans or others, at its discretion.
6   *Officers*
    (a) The Archbishop of Canterbury shall be President of the Council and, when present, shall preside at the inaugural session of each meeting of the Council. He shall be ex officio a member of its committees.

(b) The Council shall elect a Chairman and Vice-Chairman from its own number, who shall hold office for six years.

(c) The Council shall appoint for a specified term a Secretary, who shall be known as the Secretary General of the Council, and shall determine his duties.

7   *Frequency of Meetings*

The Council shall meet every two years at the call of the Chairman in consultation with the President and the Secretary General.

8   *Standing Committee*

The Council shall appoint a Standing Committee of nine members, which shall include the Chairman and Vice-Chairman of the Council. The Secretary General shall be its Secretary. The Standing Committee shall meet annually. It shall have the right to call advisers.

9   *Locality of Meetings*

As far as possible, the Council and its Standing Committee shall meet in various parts of the world.

10   *Budget*

The Council shall produce an annual budget, including the stipend and expenses of the Secretary General, his staff, and office, and this shall be apportioned among the member Churches of the Anglican Communion.

11   *Amendment of the Constitution*

Amendments to this Constitution shall be submitted by the Council to the constitutional bodies of the member Churches and must be ratified by two-thirds of such bodies.

NB. It is recommended that, in order to provide for continuity in Council membership, at the beginning one-third of the delegates shall be appointed as elected for a two-year period, one-third for a four-year period, and the remaining third for a single period of six years. Those elected for a two-year or four-year period shall be eligible for appointment for one further period of six years. Thereafter all appointments or elections shall be for six years.

Schedule of Membership

The membership of the Council shall be as follows:

(a) The Archbishop of Canterbury

(b) Three from each of the following, consisting of a bishop, a priest or deacon, and a lay person:

The Church of England

The Episcopal Church in the United States of America

The Church of India, Pakistan, Burma, and Ceylon

The Anglican Church of Canada

The Church of England in Australia.

(c) Two from each of the following, consisting of a bishop, and a priest, deacon, or lay person:

The Church in Wales

The Church of Ireland

The Episcopal Church in Scotland

The Church of the Province of South Africa

The Church of the Province of West Africa

The Church of the Province of Central Africa

The Church of the Province of East Africa

The Church of the Province of Uganda, Rwanda, and Burundi

The Church of the Province of New Zealand

The Church of the Province of the West Indies
Nippon Sei Ko Kai
The Archbishopric in Jerusalem
The Council of the Church of South-East Asia
The South Pacific Anglican Council
Latin America
any province of the Anglican Communion not at present represented.
(d) Co-opted members: The Council shall have power to co-opt up to six additional members, of whom at least two shall be women and two lay persons not over 28 years of age at the time of appointment.

1978

Resolution 1: Today's world

The Conference approves the following statement as expressing some of the concerns of the bishops about today's world in which today's Church must proclaim a total Gospel. It is printed here for study, and action wherever possible, by the member Churches.

We, the bishops of the Anglican Communion gathered from many parts of the world, having experienced a deep unity in the conviction of our faith and in our calling as bishops, wish to share with all people some matters of universal concern.

On earlier occasions we have appealed not only to Anglicans but to all Christian people. Today because we have discovered a new dimension of unity in our intense concern for the future wellbeing of all mankind in the new era of history which we are now entering we dare to appeal also to governments, world leaders, and people, without distinction, because all countries, however nationalistic in sentiment, are now interdependent. No nation is an island unto itself.

The choices before us are real, and so are the consequences of them. On the one hand there are great potentialities for advance in human wellbeing but there are also real possibilities of catastrophic disaster if present attitudes and the expectations of individuals do not swiftly change and if vital problems of society are not confronted and resolved by governments and through international co-operation.

We draw attention to the following areas where there is need for a change in attitude and practice:
1   We need to see the necessary exchange of commodities in the market place as an area where human values can be affirmed and not ignored; to seek to ensure that those involved are not treated merely as functional units but as being worthy of and able to enter into relations of friendship.

2   We need to challenge the assumptions that 'more is better' and 'having is being' which add fuel to the fire of human greed.

3   We need to stress that the wellbeing of the whole human family is more important than egoistic self-interest.

4   We need to change the focus on technology and see it not as the master with an insidious fascination of its own but as the servant of the world and its people, beginning with those in need. We must face the threat of science and technology as well as their promise.

5   We need to be diverting our planning and action to the development of a new kind of society. Much time is still spent in overtaking problems. We must direct our efforts to the achievement of a kind of society where the economy is not based on waste, but on stewardship, not on consumerism but on conservation, one concerned not only with work but with the right use of leisure. We may need to contemplate a paradox: an increasing use of appropriate technology, while returning, where possible, to many of the values of pre-industrial society. In some places this can include home industries, the local market, the fishing village, and the small farm.

6   We need to recognise that at present all over the world there tends to be a growing urbanisation. Many cities are in crisis due to the growing number of people with little hope of freedom of choice. The gap between the rich and the poor, between the powerful and the powerless, continues to grow.

7   We need to recognise that some earlier evaluations of the place of work in human life are becoming dangerously obsolete. In many societies more goods are produced, but there is less employment. We need to orientate education so as to help people develop new attitudes both to work and leisure.

8   We need to help people in the parts of the world classed as economically underdeveloped not to mirror industrialised societies, but to retain or shape a style of life which affirms both the dignity of the person and the value of close human community.

9   We need to help the developed industrial nations and the people who live in them to face the necessity of a redistribution of wealth and trading opportunities. Such a redistribution could place the major burden on those groups within such societies which are already most vulnerable. We need, therefore, to urge such nations to face the challenge to work for much greater internal justice.

10   We need to recognise that expenditure on armaments is disproportionate to sums spent on such essentials as health and education and constitutes a vast misdirection of limited resources that are badly needed for human welfare, especially for the eradication of poverty. The escalation of weapons systems with their ever-increasing technological complexity diverts attention from the real needs of mankind.

We call all people to protest, in whatever ways possible, at the escalation of the commerce in armaments of war and to support with every effort all international proposals and conferences designed to achieve progressive world disarmament in a way that recognises the need for power balances. New initiatives are urgently required for mutual co-existence and toleration which are essential if real justice and peace are to be established.

11   The resources of our planet are limited; delicate ecological balances can be disturbed by modern technology, or threatened by the toxic effects of human ingenuity. Ways must be found to stop waste, to recycle resources and to monitor and control the manufacture of substances dangerous to life and health. The use of nuclear fuel must be subject to the safe and permanent disposal of its toxic by-products. Alternative sources of energy must be harnessed for use.

Such changes will not be easy to make and will require wise leadership from both secular and religious sources. Creative solutions will require both technical knowledge and moral insights. Decisions will be not only difficult but unpopular.

We recognise and acknowledge with gratitude the many people and agencies who have pioneered in thinking and acting towards the future wellbeing of the human family. We confess that the Churches to which we belong have shared in attitudes and acquiesced in structures which have been hurtful to the true welfare of the peoples of the world.

We do not pretend to a knowledge of the practical solutions for these problems. But we do affirm that God intends all of us to enjoy this planet and not ruin it; he intends all of us, as his children, to live together peaceably and creatively; to use our skills and knowledge not to destroy but to fulfil human potentialities.

We believe that time is running out. Beneath all the choices lies the ultimate choice of life or death. We join with all men of goodwill in appealing that we shall choose life. We know that tasks and situations which to human view seem hopeless can, with the boundless resources of God's grace, be transformed.

Resolution 2: A response
The Conference believes that a response to the foregoing statement needs to be made at three levels.

First, we appeal to leaders and governments of the world:
1   to participate actively in the establishment of a new economic order aimed at securing fair prices for raw materials, maintaining fair prices for manufactured goods, and reversing the process by which the rich become richer and the poor poorer;

2   to consider seriously all efforts towards a peaceful settlement of international disputes;

3   to persist in the search for ways leading to progressive world disarmament, in particular limiting and reducing the production of, and commerce in, arms;

4   so to limit the development of nuclear energy that they guard against the proliferation of nuclear weapons, at the same time applying every effort to the development of alternative sources of energy;

5   aware that the world is one indivisible system in its operation, to provide that those whose lives are affected by global decisions should be heard in the formulation of policies;

6   to pay attention to human needs in the planning of cities, especially in those places where growing industrialisation brings people together in such numbers that human dignity is at risk;

7   to make provision for a new understanding of the place of work in the life of individuals. If the human race as a whole is to reassess its philosophy of economic growth in order to conserve our environment, we will have to find new ways of human fulfilment, paying as much attention to leisure as to paid employment. This needs re-education and a redistribution of resources at national and international levels.

Second, we call on the Churches and in particular the Anglican Communion:

1   to make provision locally to educate their membership into an understanding of these issues;

2   in the face of growing urbanisation all over the world to make urgent provision for the training of lay and pastoral leadership in urban mission and to concentrate the use of their personnel and financial resources ecumenically in order to minister to the growing number of urban people with little hope or freedom of choice.

We recommend that greater attention be paid to the work already being done by agencies both within and outside the Churches, that provision be made for communicating their findings in appropriate forms, and that greater use be made of the specialist skills of our lay members to inform the Church's decision-making on social, economic, and technological issues.

Third, we call upon members to exercise their rights as citizens of their respective countries:

1   to create a moral climate which enables governments to act for the benefit of the world community rather than sectional interests;

2   in situations where the interests of minorities are in conflict with large-scale development schemes to give consideration to the needs of persons rather than economic advantage;

3   to review their life-style and use of the world's resources so that the service and wellbeing of the whole human family comes before the enjoyment of over-indulgent forms of affluence.

Resolution 3: Human rights
The Conference regards the matter of human rights and dignity as of capital and universal importance. We send forth the following message as expressing our convictions in Christ for the human family world-wide.

We deplore and condemn the evils of racism and tribalism, economic exploitation and social injustices, torture, detention without trial and the taking of human lives, as contrary to the teaching and example of our Lord in the Gospel. Man is made in the image of God and must not be exploited. In many parts of the world these evils are so rampant that they deter the development of a humane society. Therefore,
1   we call on governments to uphold human dignity; to defend human rights, including the exercise of freedom of speech, movement, and worship in accordance with the United Nations Declaration of Human Rights; the right to be housed, freedom to work, the right to eat, the right to be educated; and to give human value and worth precedence over social and ethnic demarcations, regardless of sex, creed, or status;
2   we thank God for those faithful Christians who individually and collectively witness to their faith and convictions in the face of persecution, torture, and martyrdom; and for those who work for and advocate human rights and peace among all peoples; and we assure them of our prayers, as in penitence and hope we long to see the whole Church manifesting in its common life a genuine alternative to the acquisitiveness and division which surround it, and indeed penetrate it;
3   we pledge our support for those organisations and agencies which have taken positive stands on human rights, and those which assist with refugee problems;
4   we urge all Anglicans to seek positive ways of educating themselves about the liberation struggle of peoples in many parts of the world;
5   finally we appeal to all Christians to lend their support to those who struggle for human freedom and who press forward in some places at great personal and corporate risk; we should not abandon them even if the struggle becomes violent. We are reminded that the ministry of the Church is to reveal the love of God by faithful proclamation of his Word, by sacrificial service, and by fervent prayers for his rule on earth.

Resolution 4: Economic development and minority cultural groups
The Conference believes that a caring Church must be ready to resist and oppose the unheeding advance of economic development where it treats minority cultural groups as disposable.

Resolution 5: War and violence
1   Affirming again the statement of the Lambeth Conferences of 1930 (Resolution 25), 1948, and 1968 that 'war as a method of settling international disputes is incompatible with the teaching and example of our Lord Jesus Christ', the Conference expresses its deep grief at the great suffering being endured in many parts of the world because of violence and oppression. We further declare that the use of the modern technology of war is the most striking example of corporate sin and the prostitution of God's gifts.
2   We recognise that violence has many faces. There are some countries where the prevailing social order is so brutal, exploiting the poor for the sake of the privileged and trampling on people's human rights, that it must be termed 'violent'. There are others where a social order that appears relatively benevolent nevertheless exacts a high price in human misery from some sections of the population. There is the use of armed force by governments, employed or held in threat against other nations or even against their own citizens. There is the worldwide misdirection of scarce resources to armaments rather than human need. There is the military action of victims of oppression who despair in achieving social justice by any other means. There is the mindless violence that erupts in some countries with what seems to be increasing frequency, to say nothing of organised crime and terrorism, and the resorting to violence as a form of entertainment on films and television.
3   Jesus, through his death and resurrection, has already won the victory over all evil. He made evident that self-giving love, obedience to the way of the cross, is the way to reconciliation in all relationships and conflicts. Therefore the use of violence is ultimately contradictory to the Gospel. Yet we acknowledge that Christians in the past have differed in their understanding of limits to the rightful use of force in human affairs, and that questions of national relationships and social justice are often complex ones. But in the face of the mounting incidence of violence today and its acceptance as a normal element in human affairs, we condemn the subjection, intimidation, and manipulation of people by the use of violence and the threat of violence and call Christian people everywhere:
    (a) to re-examine as a matter of urgency their own attitude towards, and their complicity with, violence in its many forms;
    (b) to take with the utmost seriousness the questions which the

teaching of Jesus places against violence in human relationships and the use of armed force by those who would follow him, and the example of redemptive love which the cross holds before all people;
(c) to engage themselves in non-violent action for justice and peace and to support others so engaged, recognising that such action will be controversial and may be personally very costly;
(d) to commit themselves to informed, disciplined prayer not only for all victims of violence, especially for those who suffer for their obedience to the Man on the Cross, but also for those who inflict violence on others;
(e) to protest in whatever way possible at the escalation of the sale of armaments of war by the producing nations to the developing and dependent nations, and to support with every effort all international proposals and conferences designed to place limitations on, or arrange reductions in, the armaments of war of the nations of the world.

Resolution 6: Prayer
Since prayer, both corporate and personal, is central to the Christian life, and therefore essential in the renewal of the Church, the fulfilling of the Christian mission, and the search for justice and peace, the Conference gives thanks for all who are endeavouring to increase and strengthen the companionship of prayer throughout the world, and joins in calling the whole Christian community to share personal prayer daily and corporate services of prayer on regular and special occasions.

We also invite all who desire and labour for justice and peace in this world to join with us each day in a moment of prayerful recollection of the needs for a just peace among all people.

Resolution 7: The Holy Spirit and the Church
1   The Conference rejoices at the abundant evidence from many parts of the world that there is renewed awareness of the power and gifts of God's Holy Spirit to cleanse, sustain, empower, and build up the Body of Christ.
2   We have seen increased instances of parish life being renewed, of individual ministries becoming effective agencies of God's power to heal and reconcile, of witness to the faith and proclamation of the Gospel with converting power, and of a deeper involvement in the sacramental life of the Church.
3   We rejoice at the prompting of God's Spirit within the many expressions of ecumenicity among Christians, for the new forms of Christian communal life springing up and for Christian witness on behalf of world peace and the affirmation of freedom and human dignity.

4   The Conference, therefore, recalls the entire Anglican Communion to a new openness to the power of the Holy Spirit; and offers the following guidance to the Church, in the light of the several ways this Spirit-filled activity may be best understood and represented in the life of the parish.

(a) We all should share fully and faithfully in the balanced corporate and sacramental life of the local parish church. Informal services of prayer and praise need this enrichment in the same way as the sacramental life needs the enrichment of informal prayer and praise.

(b) We all should ensure that reading and meditation of the Bible be part of the normal life of the parish and be accompanied by appropriate study of scholarly background material so that the Scripture is understood in its proper context. Those who search to understand the scholarly background material in their reading of the Bible should ensure that they do so under the guidance of the Holy Spirit, so that the Scripture is understood in its proper context.

(c) We all should search out ways to identify with those who suffer and are poor, and be involved personally in efforts to bring them justice, liberation, healing, and new life in Christ.

(d) We should remember always that the power of the Spirit is not to be presented as either an exemption from suffering or a guarantee of success in this life. The road from Palm Sunday to Pentecost must pass through Good Friday and Easter. It is at the cross that new life through the Holy Spirit is found, and in the shadow of the cross that Christians must pray 'Come, Holy Spirit.'

Resolution 8: The Church's ministry of healing
The Conference praises God for the renewal of the ministry of healing within the Churches in recent times and reaffirms:

1   that the healing of the sick in his name is as much part of the proclamation of the Kingdom as the preaching of the good news of Jesus Christ;

2   that to neglect this aspect of ministry is to diminish our part in Christ's total redemptive activity;

3   that the ministry to the sick should be an essential element in any revision of the liturgy (see the Report of the Lambeth Conference of 1958, p 2.92).

Resolution 9: Stewardship
1   The Conference calls for continuing emphasis on stewardship teaching and practice. We urge all Anglicans, especially in the western world, to review their value systems, so that life-styles may become related to necessities rather than affluence and consumerism. We commend the biblical principle of tithing as a guide for normal Christian living.

2   In the opinion of the Conference, the scriptural injunction 'he who would be chief among you, let him be the servant of all' requires bishops to reject pretentious life-styles and by example to lead their clergy and people in the wise use of their personal resources and also those of the Church.

3   We ask that dioceses should increasingly share their financial resources (by a specific amount each year) and skilled persons with those whose resources are more slender.

Resolution 10: Human relationships and sexuality

The Conference gladly affirms the Christian ideals of faithfulness and chastity both within and outside marriage, and calls Christians everywhere to seek the grace of Christ to live lives of holiness, discipline, and service in the world, and commends to the Church:

1   The need for theological study of sexuality in such a way as to relate sexual relationships to that wholeness of human life which itself derives from God, who is the source of masculinity and femininity.

2   The need for programmes at diocesan level, involving both men and women,

(a) to promote the study and foster the ideals of Christian marriage and family life, and to examine the ways in which those who are unmarried may discover the fullness which God intends for all his children;

(b) to provide ministries of compassionate support to those suffering from brokenness within marriage and family relationships;

(c) to emphasise the sacredness of all human life, the moral issues inherent in clinical abortion, and the possible implications of genetic engineering.

3   While we reaffirm heterosexuality as the scriptural norm, we recognise the need for deep and dispassionate study of the question of homosexuality, which would take seriously both the teaching of Scripture and the results of scientific and medical research. The Church, recognising the need for pastoral concern for those who are homosexual, encourages dialogue with them. (We note with satisfaction that such studies are now proceeding in some member Churches of the Anglican Communion.)

Resolution 11: Issues concerning the whole Anglican Communion

The Conference advises member Churches not to take action regarding issues which are of concern to the whole Anglican Communion without consultation with a Lambeth Conference or with the episcopate through the Primates Committee, and requests the primates to initiate a study of the nature of authority within the Anglican Communion.

Resolution 12: Anglican conferences, councils, and meetings
The Conference asks the Archbishop of Canterbury, as President of the Lambeth Conference and President of the Anglican Consultative Council, with all the primates of the Anglican Communion, within one year to initiate consideration of the way to relate together the international conferences, councils, and meetings within the Anglican Communion so that the Anglican Communion may best serve God within the context of the one, holy, catholic, and apostolic Church.

Resolution 13: Lambeth Conferences
In order that the guardianship of the faith may be exercised as a collegial responsibility of the whole episcopate, the Conference affirms the need for Anglican bishops from every diocese to meet together in the tradition of the Lambeth Conference and recommends that the calling of any future Conference should continue to be the responsibility of the Archbishop of Canterbury, and that he should be requested to make his decision in consultation with the other primates. While recognising the great value which many set on the link with Canterbury, we believe that a Conference could well be held in some other province.

Resolution 14: The Wider Episcopal Fellowship
The Conference requests the Archbishop of Canterbury:
1   in consultation with the primates, to convene a meeting of Anglican bishops with bishops of Churches in which Anglicans have united with other Christians, and bishops from those Churches which are in full communion with Anglican Churches; and to discuss with them how bishops from these Churches could best play their part in future Lambeth Conferences;
2   to recognise the deep conviction of this Lambeth Conference that the expressed desire of both the Lusitanian and Spanish Reformed Churches to become fully integrated members of the Anglican Communion should receive both a warm and a positive response.

Resolution 15: Partners in Mission
The Conference commends the 'Partners in Mission' process to the member Churches of the Anglican Communion and asks them to plan future consultations in accordance with the principles set out in Resolution 27 of the second (Dublin, 1973) meeting of the Anglican Consultative Council and Resolution 17 of its third (Trinidad, 1976) meeting, and in recommendations 1–8 below:
1   The consultation process is concerned with the meaning of mission as well as its implementation. This point is made clear in the Trinidad report (p 57, para. 2(b)(ix)), but has not yet been widely

received. PIM consultations may be weakened or confused by the failure to recognise that their purpose is to bring about a renewed obedience to mission and not simply to make an existing system efficient. We therefore recommend that each province seek to educate Anglicans in the meaning of the PIM process and of the significant reorientation of mission strategy which is involved.

2   One way of achieving this is to encourage the Church to experience the PIM principle at many levels of its life: e.g. between provinces in large national Churches, between dioceses, between a group of parishes, or between parochial and sector ministries.

3   We draw attention to the weakness of the ecumenical dimension in many past consultations and urge the correction of this in the future. Anglicans in any place cannot undertake mission effectively without consulting and planning with fellow Christians.

4   Churches should not be content with inviting partners only from those areas which share a natural or racial affinity with them. The insights of other cultures, and of various understandings of mission, are vital to growth in a true and balanced theology of mission, and to ensuring the possibility of a creative exchange of resources both personal and material.

5   Representatives of partner Churches do not always have long enough in the host Church and country before the consultation begins. We believe that a period of two weeks, or even longer, would be helpful and appropriate in most situations. Forward planning should allow invitations to be sent out well in advance.

6   We believe the PIM process can help all of us to catch the vision of an interdependent world as well as an interdependent Church. To this end we underline how essential it is that, where possible, the key secular issues should also be well presented in each consultation and by those in society who understand them best.

7   PIM has helped us to develop the concept of sharing rather than of some giving and others receiving. Yet there is an ever-present danger of lapsing into the 'shopping list' way of thinking. At the same time we are sure that consultations should always contain the opportunity for the frank stating of specific needs.

8   Within the Anglican Communion as a whole, thought needs to be given to follow-up as well as co-ordination of response to PIM consultations. We recommend that the ACC gives particular attention to this matter.

Resolution 16: Sharing resources
The Conference asks the Anglican Consultative Council to assist the member Churches to develop a more effective system for responding

to needs identified in Partners in Mission consultations, including the sharing of resources, both of people and of material things.

Resolution 17: New dioceses
The Conference urges that, when a new diocese is created,
1   adequate financial support should be underwritten by the member Churches concerned, and/or by the Partners in Mission of the new diocese, to insure against unforeseen financial difficulties;
2   adequate provision should be made for the stipend of the bishop, preferably through the creation of an episcopal endowment fund;
3   when, owing to unforeseen circumstances, a new diocese is faced with financial problems and deficits, it should be aided financially by the member Church concerned and/or by the Partners in Mission of the new diocese;
4   these matters be referred for the consideration of the Anglican Consultative Council at its earliest convenience.

Resolution 18: Public ministry of the bishop
The Conference affirms that a bishop is called to be one with the Apostles in proclaiming Christ's resurrection and interpreting the Gospel, and to testify to Christ's sovereignty as Lord of lords and King of kings. In order to do this effectively, he will give major attention to his public ministry. Reflecting the ministry of the prophets, he will have a concern for the wellbeing of the whole community (especially of those at a disadvantage) not primarily for the advantage or protection of the Church community. The bishop should be ready to be present in secular situations, to give time to the necessary study, to find skilled advisers and to take sides publicly if necessary (in ecumenical partnership if at all possible) about issues which concern justice, mercy, and truth. Members of the Church should be prepared to see that the bishop is supported in such a ministry.

Resolution 19: Training for bishops
The Conference asks each member Church to provide training for bishops after election in order more adequately to prepare them for their office; and to provide opportunities for continuing education.

Resolution 20: Women in the diaconate
The Conference recommends, in accordance with Resolution 32(c) of the Lambeth Conference of 1968, those member Churches which do not at present ordain women as deacons now to consider making the necessary legal and liturgical changes to enable them to do so, instead of admitting them to a separate order of deaconesses.

Resolution 21: Women in the priesthood

1   The Conference notes that since the last Lambeth Conference in 1968, the Diocese of Hong Kong, the Anglican Church of Canada, the Episcopal Church in the United States of America, and the Church of the Province of New Zealand have admitted women to the presbyterate, and that eight other member Churches of the Anglican Communion have now either agreed or approved in principle or stated that there are either no fundamental or no theological objections to the ordination of women to the historic threefold ministry of the Church.

We also note that other of its member Churches have not yet made a decision on the matter. Others again have clearly stated that they do hold fundamental objections to the ordination of women to the historic threefold ministry of the Church.

2   The Conference acknowledges that both the debate about the ordination of women as well as the ordinations themselves have, in some Churches, caused distress and pain to many on both sides. To heal these and to maintain and strengthen fellowship is a primary pastoral responsibility of all, and especially of the bishops.

3   The Conference also recognises
(a) the autonomy of each of its member Churches, acknowledging the legal right of each Church to make its own decision about the appropriateness of admitting women to Holy Orders;
(b) that such provincial action in this matter has consequences of the utmost significance for the Anglican Communion as a whole.

4   The Conference affirms its commitment to the preservation of unity within and between all member Churches of the Anglican Communion.

5   The Conference therefore
(a) encourages all member Churches of the Anglican Communion to continue in communion with one another, notwithstanding the admission of women (whether at present or in the future) to the ordained ministry of some member Churches;
(b) in circumstances in which the issue of the ordination of women has caused, or may cause, problems of conscience, urges that every action possible be taken to ensure that all baptized members of the Church continue to be in communion with their bishop and that every opportunity be given for all members to work together in the mission of the Church irrespective of their convictions regarding this issue;
(c) requests the Anglican Consultative Council
(i) to use its good offices to promote dialogue between those member Churches which ordain women and those which do not, with a view to exploring ways in which the fullest use can be made of women's gifts within the total ministry of the Church in our Communion; and

(ii) to maintain, and wherever possible extend, the present dialogue with Churches outside the Anglican family.

6 Consistent with the foregoing, this Conference

(a) declares its acceptance of those member Churches which now ordain women, and urges that they respect the convictions of those provinces and dioceses which do not;

(b) declares its acceptance of those member Churches which do not ordain women, and urges that they respect the convictions of those provinces and dioceses which do.

(c) With regard to women who have been ordained in the Anglican Communion being authorised to exercise their ministry in provinces which have not ordained women, we recommend that, should synodical authority be given to enable them to exercise it, it be exercised only

(i) where pastoral need warrants and

(ii) where such a ministry is agreeable to the bishop, clergy, and people where the ministry is to be exercised and where it is approved by the legally responsible body of the parish, area, or institution where such a ministry is to be exercised.

7 We recognise that our accepting this variety of doctrine and practice in the Anglican Communion may disappoint the Roman Catholic, Orthodox, and Old Catholic Churches, but we wish to make it clear

(a) that the holding together of diversity within a unity of faith and worship is part of the Anglican heritage;

(b) that those who have taken part in ordinations of women to the priesthood believe that these ordinations have been into the historic ministry of the Church as the Anglican Communion has received it; and

(c) that we hope the dialogue between these other Churches and the member Churches of our Communion will continue because we believe that we still have understanding of the truth of God and his will to learn from them as together we all move towards a fuller catholicity and a deeper fellowship in the Holy Spirit.

8 This Conference urges that further discussions about the ordination of women be held within a wider consideration of theological issues of ministry and priesthood.

Voting: For 316; Against 37; Abstentions 17.

Resolution 22: Women in the episcopate
While recognising that a member Church of the Anglican Communion may wish to consecrate a woman to the episcopate, and accepting that such member Church must act in accordance with its own constitution, the Conference recommends that no decision to consecrate

be taken without consultation with the episcopate through the primates and overwhelming support in any member Church and in the diocese concerned, lest the bishop's office should become a cause of disunity instead of a focus of unity.

Resolution 23: Liturgical information
The Conference welcomes and commends the adoption of a common structure for the Eucharist as an important unifying factor in our Communion and ecumenically. We ask provincial liturgical committees to continue to keep in touch with one another by circulating work in progress to the chairmen of the other liturgical committees through the good offices of the Secretary General of the Anglican Consultative Council.

Resolution 24: A common lectionary
The Conference recommends a common lectionary for the Eucharist and the Offices as a unifying factor within our Communion and ecumenically; and draws attention to the experience of those provinces which have adopted the three-year eucharistic lectionary of the Roman Catholic Church.

Resolution 25: An Anglican doctrinal commission
The Conference endorses the proposal suggested in Resolution 8 of the third (Trinidad, 1976) meeting of the Anglican Consultative Council, to set up an inter-Anglican theological and doctrinal advisory commission, and asks the Standing Committee of the ACC to establish the commission with the advice of the primates, and the primates and provinces, by whatever means they feel best, to review its work after a period of not more than five years.

Resolution 26: An association of French-speaking dioceses
The Conference gives thanks to God for the special role and witness of the French-speaking dioceses of our Communion. We learned with deep interest of the emergence of a French-speaking province in Central Africa. We recognise the special difficulties of French-speaking dioceses in communication, in the production of literature, and in training for the ministry. We call for the active encouragement, under the Partners in Mission scheme, for all forms of support from the dioceses of our Communion to French-speaking provinces and dioceses.

Resolution 27: Service in the world-wide Church
The Conference requests that in order to encourage world-wide service by the clergy and lay servants of the Church, all member Churches be asked to make adequate provision for the future service of those returning to their home province after a term of duty elsewhere, and

also to ensure that ultimate retirement and other relevant provisions are fully protected, either in their home country or in the country of service.

Resolution 28: Ecumenical relationships

The Conference:

1   reaffirms the readiness of the Anglican Communion as already expressed in Resolution 44(c) of the Lambeth Conference of 1968 (with reference to the Uppsala Assembly of the World Council of Churches), to 'work for the time when a genuinely universal council may once more speak for all Christians';

2   acknowledges the pressing need stated by the Nairobi Assembly of the WCC that we should develop more truly sustained and sustaining relationships among the Churches, as we look towards the time when we can enjoy full conciliar fellowship (see *Breaking Barriers: Nairobi 1975*, p 60);

3   encourages the member Churches of the Anglican Communion to pursue with perseverance and hopefulness the search for full communion and mutual recognition of ministries between themselves and other world confessional families and the Methodist and Baptist Churches both internationally and locally, on the basis of the Lambeth Quadrilateral and the counsel offered by successive meetings of the Anglican Consultative Council;

4   calls on member Churches of the Anglican Communion to review their commitment to ecumenical structure as well as bilateral conversations at various levels with a view to strengthening the common advance by all Churches to the goal of visible unity;

5   notes that many Christians belong to Churches not members of the World Council of Churches and wishes to develop the opportunities for dialogue and common action with these Churches when appropriate. In particular, the Conference welcomes the participation of Anglican lay persons, priests, and bishops in the Lausanne Congress on World Evangelism of 1974 and subsequent meetings, in which many of these Churches are represented.

Resolution 29: The World Council of Churches

The Conference urges that, in this thirtieth anniversary year of the World Council of Churches, all Churches of the Anglican Communion reaffirm their support and strengthen their understanding of this body, which is not only the most comprehensive expression of the ecumenical movement, but also the chief vehicle of world-wide ecumenical co-operation and service. It also asks the World Council of Churches to accept the guidance given through Section 3 of the Conference, considering war and violence:

(1) to re-examine our complicity with violence in its many forms;
(2) to take with the utmost seriousness the question which the teaching of Jesus places against *all* violence in human relationships.

Resolution 30: Inter-Church relations: definitions of terms
The Conference requests the Anglican Consultative Council, in consultation with other Churches, to formulate appropriate definitions of terms used in inter-Church relations.

Resolution 31: Relations with Lutheran Churches
The Conference encourages Anglican Churches together with Lutheran Churches in their area:
1   to study the report entitled 'Anglican–Lutheran International Conversations' (the Pullach Report, 1972), Resolution 2 of the second meeting (Dublin, 1973) and Resolution 5 of the third meeting (Trinidad, 1976) of the Anglican Consultative Council;
2   to give special attention to our ecclesial recognition of the Lutheran Church on the basis of these reports and resolutions; and
3   to seek ways of extending hospitality and of engaging in joint mission.

Resolution 32: Relations with united Churches
The Conference requests that those member Churches that have placed limitations on the ministry among them of episcopally ordained clergy from united Churches with which they are in communion be asked to reconsider these restrictions so that the same courtesy might be accorded to the clergy of those Churches as to those of other Churches in communion with us.

Resolution 33: The Anglican–Roman Catholic International Commission
The Conference:
1   welcomes the work of the Anglican–Roman Catholic International Commission which was set up jointly by the Lambeth Conference of 1968 and by the Vatican Secretariat for Promoting Christian Unity;
2   recognises in the three Agreed Statements of this Commission* a solid achievement, one in which we can recognise the faith of our Church, and hopes that they will provide a basis for sacramental sharing between our two Communions if and when the finished Statements are approved by the respective authorities of our Communions;
3   invites ARCIC to provide further explication of the Agreed Statements in consideration of responses received by them;
4   commends to the appropriate authorities in each Communion

further consideration of the implications of the Agreed Statements in the light of the report of the Joint Preparatory Commission (the Malta Report received by the Lambeth Conference 1968—see p 134 of its Report), with a view to bringing about a closer sharing between our two Communions in life, worship, and mission;

5 asks the Secretary General of the Anglican Consultative Council to bring this Resolution to the attention of the various synods of the Anglican Communion for discussion and action;

6 asks that in any continuing Commission, the Church of the South and the East be adequately represented.

* 'Eucharistic Doctrine' (the Windsor Statement, 1971), 'Ministry and Ordination' (Canterbury, 1973), and 'Authority in the Church' (Venice, 1976).

Resolution 34: Anglican–Roman Catholic marriages
The Conference welcomes the report of the Anglican–Roman Catholic Commission on 'The Theology of Marriage and its Application to Mixed Marriages' (1975).

In particular we record our gratitude for the general agreement on the theology of Christian marriage there outlined, and especially for the affirmation of the 'first order principle'* of life-long union (i.e. in the case of a breakdown of a marriage). We also welcome the recognition that the differing pastoral practices of our two traditions do in fact recognise and seek to share a common responsibility for those for whom '*no* course *absolutely* consonant with the first order principle of marriage as a life-long union may be available'.

We also endorse the recommendations of the Commission in respect of inter-Church marriages:

(1) that, after joint preparation and pastoral care given by both the Anglican and Roman Catholic counsellors concerned, a marriage may validly and lawfully take place before the duly authorised minister of either party, without the necessity of Roman Catholic dispensation;

(2) that, as an alternative to an affirmation or promise by the Roman Catholic party in respect of the baptism and upbringing of any children, the Roman Catholic parish priest may give a written assurance to his bishop that he has put the Roman Catholic partner in mind of his or her obligations and that the other spouse knows what these are.

We note that there are some variations in different regions in the provisions of Roman Catholic directories on inter-Church marriages. We nevertheless warmly welcome the real attempts of many Roman Catholic episcopal conferences to be pastorally sensitive to those problems arising out of their regulations, which remain an obstacle to the continued growth of fraternal relations between us. In particular, we note a growing Roman Catholic understanding that a decision as to the baptism and upbringing of any children should be made within the unity of the marriage, in which the Christian conscience of both partners must be respected. We urge that this last development be encouraged.

The problems associated with marriage between members of our two Communions continue to hinder inter-Church relations and progress towards unity. While we recognise that there has been an improved situation in some places as a result of the *Motu Proprio*, the general principles underlying the Roman Catholic position are unacceptable to Anglicans. Equality of conscience as between partners in respect of all aspects of their marriage (and in particular with regard to the baptism and religious upbringing of children) is something to be affirmed both for its own sake and for the sake of an improved relationship between the Churches.

* See *Anglican–Roman Catholic Marriages* (London, CIO 1975) p 21, para. 49.

Resolution 35: Anglican–Orthodox theological dialogue
The Conference:
1   welcomes the achievement of the Anglican–Orthodox Joint Doctrinal Commission as expressed in the Moscow Agreed Statement of 1976, and believes that this goes far to realise the hopes about Anglican–Orthodox dialogue expressed at Lambeth 1968;
2   requests the Anglican–Orthodox Joint Doctrinal Commission to continue to explore the fundamental questions of doctrinal agreement and disagreement in our Churches; and to promote regional groups for theological dialogue which would bring to the Commission not only reactions to their work, but also theological issues arising out of local experience;
3   requests that all member Churches of the Anglican Communion should consider omitting the Filioque from the Nicene Creed, and that the Anglican–Orthodox Joint Doctrinal Commission through the Anglican Consultative Council should assist them in presenting the theological issues to their appropriate synodical bodies and should be responsible for any necessary consultation with other Churches of the Western tradition.

Resolution 36: Cultural identity
The Conference recognises with thanksgiving to God the growth of the Church across the world and encourages every particular Church to strengthen its own identity in Christ and its involvement with the community of which it is part, expressing its faith through the tradi-

tions and culture of its own society except where they are in conflict with the essentials of the Gospel.

Resolution 37: Other faiths: Gospel and dialogue

1   Within the Church's trust of the Gospel, we recognise and welcome the obligation to open exchange of thought and experience with people of other faiths. Sensitivity to the work of the Holy Spirit among them means a positive response to their meaning as inwardly lived and understood. It means also a quality of life on our part which expresses the truth and love of God as we have known them in Christ, Lord and Saviour.

2   We realise the lively vocation to theological interpretation, community involvement, social responsibility, and evangelisation which is carried by the Churches in areas where Hinduism, Buddhism, Taoism, Confucianism, and Islam are dominant, and ask that the whole Anglican Communion support them by understanding, by prayer, and where appropriate, by partnership with them.

3   We continue to seek opportunities for dialogue with Judaism.

1988

Resolution 1: The ordination or consecration of women to the episcopate

This Conference resolves:

1   That each province respect the decision and attitudes of other provinces in the ordination or consecration of women to the episcopate, without such respect necessarily indicating acceptance of the principles involved, maintaining the highest possible degree of communion with the provinces which differ.

2   That bishops exercise courtesy and maintain communications with bishops who may differ, and with any woman bishop, ensuring an open dialogue in the Church to whatever extent communion is impaired.

3   That the Archbishop of Canterbury, in consultation with the primates, appoints a commission:

(a) to provide for an examination of the relationships between provinces of the Anglican Communion and ensure that the process of reception includes continuing consultation with other Churches as well;

(b) to monitor and encourage the process of consultation within the Communion and to offer further pastoral guidelines.

4   That in any province where reconciliation on these issues is necessary, any diocesan bishop facing this problem be encouraged to seek continuing dialogue with, and make pastoral provision for, those clergy and congregations whose opinions differ from those of the bishop, in order to maintain the unity of the diocese.

5   Recognises the serious hurt which would result from the questioning by some of the validity of the episcopal acts of a woman bishop, and likewise the hurt experienced by those whose conscience would be offended by the ordination of a woman to the episcopate. The Church needs to exercise sensitivity, patience and pastoral care towards all concerned.

Voting: For 423; Against 28; Abstentions 19.

(See further paras 132-150 of the Report on 'Mission and Ministry'.)

[Resolution 2 failed]

Resolution 3: 'Baptism, Eucharist and Ministry': Report of the Faith and Order Commission of the World Council of Churches

This Conference:

1   Welcomes the text *Baptism, Eucharist and Ministry* (BEM) as a contribution of great significance in the search for the visible unity of the Church and notes that the ecumenical climate has already been much improved by it in many places. It recognises this text to be one part of a wider agenda in which the Faith and Order Commission of the World Council of Churches is engaged. It values the consonance between BEM and the bilateral and other multilateral dialogues in which Anglicans are engaged and the fact that BEM enables us to see a convergence towards substantial agreement in faith and practice between many Communions.

2   Endorses the view of the provincial responses that Anglicans can recognise to a large extent in the text *Baptism, Eucharist and Ministry* 'the faith of the Church through the ages'.

3   Considers that Anglicans can draw important consequences from *Baptism, Eucharist and Ministry* for their relations with other Churches, particularly with those Churches which also recognise the text as an expression of the apostolic faith.

4   Recommends that provinces take guidance from the text for their worship, educational, ethical and spiritual life and witness.

5   Encourages the Faith and Order Commission of the World Council of Churches to pursue its work to develop the convergences of *Baptism, Eucharist and Ministry* and the study on 'Towards Com-

mon Expression of the Apostolic Faith Today' within the context of the study on 'Unity and Renewal'. Anglicans urge the Faith and Order Commission to resume its work on structures of authority and decision-making in order that the work of the bilateral dialogues may be seen in a broader context.

6   Recommends that formal response be sought from those provinces that have not yet replied to the World Council of Churches; asks the Anglican Consultative Council to find ways of promoting a continuing reception of the BEM text in all provinces of the Anglican Communion; and hopes that sufficient finances and personal resources will be set aside for this to be carried out effectively.

EXPLANATORY NOTE
The Four BEM Questions
The Faith and Order Commission of the WCC asked the Churches to prepare an official response to BEM at the highest appropriate level of authority. Four questions were to be answered:
1 *the extent to which your Church can recognise in this text the faith of the Church through the ages.*
In the light of the provincial responses it is clear that Anglicans can recognise to an impressive degree the faith of the Church through the ages. BEM is found to be a positive document, balanced and comprehensive, in the subjects it treats. In each of the three areas of baptism, eucharist and ministry we look forward to an even greater development of the convergence. In the area of baptism more work needs to be done on the inter-relationship of the various parts of the initiation process and the strengthening of the theme of covenant in relation to baptism. In the area of eucharist we should like to ensure that the *anamnesis* of the mighty acts of God in Christ remains focused upon his saving death and resurrection, and that while at every eucharist the true president is Christ, an ordained priest ought to preside. In the area of ministry we look for a fuller treatment of the ministries of all the baptized and clarification of the nature of priesthood and the respective roles of bishops, presbyters and deacons. In particular we think it important to develop work on the personal, collegial and communal forms of ministry exercised at every point in the Church's corporate life. It would be helpful to Anglicans if work on the ordination of women to the priesthood was developed in the context of the multilateral dialogue.

The responses from the provinces detect three underlying issues of a more general nature that need continuing exploration: the relation between Scripture, Tradition and traditions; the nature of the sacraments, their efficacy and their relation to the word; the ecclesiology implicit in the text of BEM.
2 *the consequences your Church can draw from this text for its relations and dialogues with other Churches, particularly with those Churches who also recognise the text as an expression of the apostolic faith.*
We should like to develop the ecumenical consequences of the fact that our common baptism is a basic bond of unity. The responses of the provinces to BEM encourage us to take up specific matters with particular partners in dialogue: the theology and practice of baptism with those who practise only 'believers' baptism; the question of eucharistic hospitality with Churches with whom we have no eucharistic fellowship; the mutual recognition of ministries, and particularly the role of the episcopate as a sign of unity and continuity.

3 *the guidance your Church can take from this text for its worship, educational, ethical, and spiritual life and witness.*
We recognise that BEM brings to expression the fruits of recent liturgical revision in our Communion and in others. The text challenges Anglicans to reform their own lives and practice in the areas of: preparation for baptism, and the continuing nurture of the baptized; the eucharist as the centre from which Christians go out to work as reconcilers in a broken world; the theology and practice of the diaconate, the complementarity of women and men in ministry, and the exercise of episcopacy.
4 *the suggestions your Church can make for the ongoing work of Faith and Order as it relates the material of this text on* Baptism, Eucharist and Ministry *to its long-range research project 'Towards the Common Expression of the Apostolic Faith Today'.*
We look forward to the developing study on 'Towards the Common Expression of the Apostolic Faith Today'. In light of the work of the bilateral dialogues on authority, Anglicans encourage the Faith and Order Commission to resume as soon as possible the earlier study 'How does the Church Teach Authoritatively Today?' The study on the 'Unity of the Church and the Renewal of Human Community' will help to locate the search for the visible unity of the Church in the proper context of God's mission to the world for the sake of the Kingdom.
(See further paras 60-64 of the Report on 'Ecumenical Relations'.)

Resolution 4: Anglican–Lutheran relations
This Conference:
1   Receives with gratitude the *Cold Ash Report* (1983) of the Anglican–Lutheran Joint Working Group and approves its recommendations (see *Emmaus Report*, pp 82-84).
2   Welcomes the *Niagara Report* of the Anglican–Lutheran Consultation on *Episcope* (1987), recognises in it a substantial convergence of views, and commends it to the member Churches of the Anglican Communion for study and synodical reception.
3   Recommends that the permanent body already established by the Anglican Consultative Council and the Lutheran World Federation to co-ordinate and assess developing Anglican–Lutheran relationships (the Anglican/Lutheran International Continuation Committee) be renamed as the Anglican–Lutheran International Commission, and asked to undertake the following tasks in addition to its existing terms of reference:

(a) to integrate in a broader document the theological work already accomplished in international, regional and local dialogues;
(b) to explore more thoroughly the theological and canonical requirements that are necessary in both Churches to acknowledge and recognise the full authenticity of existing ministries (see *Niagara Report,* para. 94);
(c) to advise with sensitivity on the actual pastoral practices of our Churches in regard to the celebration of God's word and sacraments, especially the Holy Eucharist;
(d) to produce a report which will indicate the degree of conver-

gence of views on the ordained ministry of bishops, presbyters and deacons.

4 Recognises, on the basis of the high degree of consensus reached in international, regional and national dialogues between Anglicans and Lutherans and in the light of the communion centred around word and sacrament that has been experienced in each other's traditions, the presence of the Church of Jesus Christ in the Lutheran Communion as in our own.

5 Urges that this recognition and the most recent convergence on apostolic ministry achieved in the *Niagara Report* of the Anglican-Lutheran Consultation on *Episcope* (1987) prompt us to move towards the fullest possible ecclesial recognition and the goal of full communion.

6 Recommends to member Churches, subject to the concurrence of the Lutheran World Federation, that:

(a) Anglican and Lutheran Churches should officially establish and encourage the practice of mutual eucharistic hospitality—if this is not already authorised—where pastoral need exists and when ecumenical occasions make this appropriate;

(b) The provinces of our Communion should make provision for appropriate forms of 'interim eucharistic sharing' along the following lines:

(i) They should by synodical action recognise now the member Churches of the Lutheran World Federation as Churches in which the Gospel is preached and taught;

(ii) They should encourage the development of common Christian life throughout their respective Churches by such means as the following proposals of the *Niagara Report*:

(a) eucharistic sharing and joint common celebration of the Eucharist;

(b) meetings of Church leaders for regular prayer, reflection and consultation, thus beginning joint *episcope*;

(c) mutual invitation of Church leaders, clergy and laity, to synods, with a right to speak;

(d) common agencies wherever possible;

(e) exploring the possibility of adjusting boundaries to assist local and regional co-operation;

(f) covenants among Church leaders to collaborate in *episcope*;

(g) joint pastoral appointments for special projects;

(h) joint theological education and training courses;

(i) sharing of information and documents;

(j) joint mission programmes;

(k) agreed syllabuses for Christian education in schools, joint materials for catechesis and adult study;

(l) co-operation over liturgical forms, cycles of intercession, lectionaries and homiletic materials;

(m) welcoming isolated clergy or diaspora congregations into the life of a larger group (see ALERC *Helsinki Report*, 5);

(n) interchange of ministers to the extent permitted by canon law;

(o) twinning (partnership) between congregations and communities;

(p) joint programmes of diaconal ministry and reflection on issues of social responsibility;

(q) joint retreats and devotional materials.

(iii) They should affirm by synodical action now on the basis of the consensus documents of Anglican–Lutheran International Conversations that the basic teaching of each respective Church is consonant with Scripture and that Lutheran teaching is sufficiently compatible with the teachings of the Churches of the Anglican Communion so that a relationship of interim sharing of the Eucharist may be established between these Churches under the guidelines appended.

APPENDIX

GUIDELINES FOR INTERIM SHARING OF THE EUCHARIST

(a) The Churches of the Anglican Communion extend a special welcome to members of the Lutheran Churches to receive Holy Communion on the understanding that the Lutheran Churches will do likewise. This welcome constitutes a recognition of eucharistic teaching sufficient for interim sharing of the Eucharist.

(b) Bishops of dioceses of the Anglican Communion and bishops/presidents of Lutheran districts and synods may by mutual agreement extend their regulations of church discipline to permit common, joint celebration of the Eucharist within their jurisdictions according to guidelines established by respective synods.

In this case:

When a joint Eucharist is held in an Anglican church an Anglican bishop or priest should preside, using an Anglican liturgy, with the Lutheran preaching; when a joint Eucharist is held in a Lutheran church a Lutheran should preside using a Lutheran liturgy, with the Anglican preaching. This is not concelebration, nor does it imply rejection or final recognition of either Church's eucharist or ministry. The liturgical arrangements, including the position of the ministers in relation to the altar, should take into account local circumstances and sensitivities.

(See further paras 72-78 and para. 82b of the Report on 'Ecumenical Relations'.)

Resolution 5: Anglican–Oriental Orthodox relations

This Conference:

1 Warmly welcomes the renewal and development of relationships between the Anglican Communion and the Armenian Apostolic, Coptic Orthodox, Ethiopian Orthodox, Syrian Orthodox and Indian Orthodox Churches.

2   Warmly welcomes the renewal of relationships between the Anglican Communion and the Holy Apostolic Catholic Assyrian Church of the East.

3   Particularly welcomes the presence of more observers from these Churches than at any previous Lambeth Conference, thus regaining the momentum of the Conferences of 1908 and 1920.

4   Notes with satisfaction the visits to these Churches made before and since the WCC Assembly at Vancouver in 1983 by Bishop Henry Hill, the meeting of the Anglican–Oriental Orthodox Forum held at St Albans in 1985 and the subsequent publication of the symposium *Light from the East*, as well as the meetings between the Archbishop of Canterbury and the Patriarchs of these Churches, including that with Pope Shenouda III in 1987 resulting in their Joint Declaration.

5   Affirms our friendship with these two families of Churches, and recognises the severe difficulties and challenges faced by them through war and persecution, through the growth of secularism and militant atheism, and also recognises the challenge presented by the interface with Islam.

6   Recognises that we are present together in many parts of the world, and offers our hopes for the development of friendship, fellowship and support wherever we find ourselves side by side.

7   Values greatly the rich contribution that these Churches have made to the spirituality of the Church as a whole throughout the centuries.

8   Affirms and supports the work of the Anglican–Oriental Orthodox Forum, and commits itself to the task of the forum in developing areas of possible co-operation, particularly:

(a) The development of dialogue on matters of common theological interest and concern.

(b) The establishment of theological scholarships mainly for post-graduate study for students who have completed their basic training in their own institutions and the possibility that some Anglican students spend some time in Oriental Orthodox theological institutions and monasteries as part of their regular training for the ministry.

(c) The hope that theological seminaries of the Oriental Orthodox Churches can be assisted, especially in the building up of libraries, in the supply of new books, and in subscriptions to scholarly journals, with journals and magazines published by the Churches of the two Communions being exchanged on a more systematic basis.

(d) The need for regional co-ordinating bodies for promoting understanding and co-operation among the Churches especially in the USA and Canada, in the Middle East, in Australia and New Zealand, and in the United Kingdom.

9   Desires that in view of the importance of Anglican–Oriental Orthodox relations, the Anglican Consultative Council enter into consultation with the relevant Oriental Orthodox authorities with a view to the Forum being upgraded to a formally recognised commission.
(See further para. 57 of the Report on 'Ecumenical Relations'.)

Resolution 6: Anglican–Orthodox relations
This Conference:
1   Remembers with gratitude the long history of cordial relations between Anglicans and Orthodox, not only in Europe but throughout the world, and records our sense of privilege at sharing in the celebrations of the Millennium of the Baptism of Kievan Rus, and the enrichment of the Conference by the presence of Orthodox consultants and observers who have shared with us in our life and worship; and values the dialogue between our Communions not only because it transcends East–West divisions (theological, cultural and political) but also because it stimulates and aids our own internal reflection on important issues.
2   Warmly welcomes the Dublin Agreed Statement of 1984 as an important successor to the Moscow Agreed Statement of 1976 and notes with particular pleasure the measure of theological agreement which the Dublin Statement records, the honesty with which it expresses divergences of outlook, and its special emphasis on prayer and worship as the context in which doctrinal discussion must be pursued.
3   Commits itself to drawing the attention of all the provinces of our Communion to the contents of the Dublin Agreed Statement, hoping to see it given the serious discussion which it deserves, especially in those provinces where there is a strong Orthodox presence and where there has hitherto been too little fraternal contact, and asks further all the provinces to submit to the Secretary General of the ACC, by a date to be specified by that body, their responses to the Dublin Statement, such responses as far as possible to be expressed after conversation with local Orthodox Christians.
4   Welcomes the resumption of the Anglican–Orthodox Joint Doctrinal Discussions (AOJDD) and encourages the work of that Commission towards the restoration of that unity for which Christ prayed, particularly noting its intention to address the question of ecclesiology which it is hoped will include the increasingly significant concept of 'reception', the issue of ecclesial diversity and the inter-relationship between faith and the culture in which it is expressed, believing that these are pressing issues which affect both our Communions; and at the same time urging that the AOJDD take into its consideration other

dialogues in which both Anglicans and Orthodox separately are involved.

5   Asks that further thought be given to the Filioque clause, recognising it to be a major point of disagreement, (a) recalling Resolution 35.3 of the Lambeth Conference 1978 and the varied, and on the whole positive, response from those provinces which responded to ACC-4's request to consider the removal of this clause from liturgical texts, (b) noting that the Report of the Faith and Order Commission of the WCC 'Ecumenical Explication of the Apostolic Faith as expressed in the Niceno-Constantinopolitan (381) Creed' bases itself on the original text, (c) believing that it may be possible to achieve unity of action on the part of all the 'Western Churches' to adopt the original form of the Creed without any betrayal of their theological heritage, (d) recommending to the provinces of the Anglican Communion that in future liturgical revisions the Niceno-Constantinopolitan Creed be printed without the Filioque clause.

6   Noting the forthcoming Pan-Orthodox Consultation on Women and Ordination, requests that the results of its deliberations be circulated to the provinces of the Anglican Communion and urges that ecumenical theological dialogue ensue on this issue.

7   Notes with gratitude to God the increasing openness towards the Orthodox Churches in the Soviet Union and encourages the provinces of the Anglican Communion:

   (a) to explore increased contact, co-operation and exchanges;
   (b) to offer such theological literature and other aid as may be practicable.

8   Welcomes the various international exchange programmes and study visits that are taking place between Anglicans and Orthodox and hopes that more such opportunities will be created.

9   Welcomes the many examples of friendship, hospitality, co-operation and participation in each other's worship that already exist at the local level and urges the Churches of the Anglican Communion to be more active in such endeavours, noting with particular thanksgiving the influence of Orthodox spirituality and iconography on contemporary Anglicanism and asking Anglicans to share with Orthodox their experience of witness and ministry in secular contexts.

(See further paras 57 and 59 of the Report on 'Ecumenical Relations'.)

Resolution 7: Anglican–Reformed dialogue

This Conference:

1   Impressed by the insight of the Report of the Anglican–Reformed Conversations, *God's Reign and our Unity*, particularly of the way in which the unity and mission of the Church and the quest for human

201

unity are set within the context of the Kingdom of God, commends this text for widespread study and synodical reception throughout the Anglican Communion.

2   Notes with satisfaction that the dialogue helps both Anglicans and Reformed to recover together a reformed pattern of the three-fold ministry; and that Anglicans are challenged to consider the expression of diaconal ministry, the Reformed the expression of the personal dimension of oversight (*episcope*) at the regional level.

3   Endorses the stress on the need for personal, collegial and communal expressions of ministry exercised at every level of the Church's life.

4   Recommends that the ACC collects from the provinces responses to the dialogue and any implications that have resulted; and requests the ACC to consult with the World Alliance of Reformed Churches (Presbyterian and Congregational) over the setting up of a small continuation committee to encourage wider study and implementation in life of the insights of this dialogue as a contribution towards growth in unity.

5   Acknowledging that this is the only dialogue which deals at any length with the ordination of women to the threefold order, notes that it is suggested that 'it is clearly impossible for Churches which exist in the same geographical area but which take different stands on this issue to enter into complete union'; recommends further study on this issue in the light of the remaining differences of opinion and practice in both traditions.

6   Affirms the concept promoted in this dialogue that orthopraxis (right action) is as important in ecumenical conversations as orthodoxy (right belief), and therefore urges that adequate attention be given to orthopraxis in all ecumenical dialogue.

(See further paras 59, 61, 64 and 70 of the Report on 'Ecumenical Relations'.)

Resolution 8: Anglican–Roman Catholic International Commission (ARCIC)

This Conference:

1   Recognises the Agreed Statements of ARCIC I on 'Eucharistic Doctrine, Ministry and Ordination', and their Elucidations, as consonant in substance with the faith of Anglicans and believes that this agreement offers a sufficient basis for taking the next step forward towards the reconciliation of our Churches grounded in agreement in faith.

2   Welcomes the assurance that, within an understanding of the Church as communion, ARCIC II is to explore further the particular issues of the reconciliation of ministries; the ordination of women;

moral questions; and continuing questions of authority, including the relation of Scripture to the Church's developing tradition and the role of the laity in decision-making within the Church.

3   Welcomes 'Authority in the Church' (I and II), together with the Elucidation, as a firm basis for the direction and agenda of the continuing dialogue on authority and wishes to encourage ARCIC II to continue to explore the basis in Scripture and tradition of the concept of a universal primacy, in conjunction with collegiality, as an instrument of unity, the character of such a primacy in practice, and to draw upon the experience of other Christian Churches in exercising primacy, collegiality and conciliarity.

4   In welcoming the fact that the ordination of women is to form part of the agenda of ARCIC II, recognises the serious responsibility this places upon us to weigh the possible implications of action on this matter for the unity of the Anglican Communion and for the universal Church.

5   Warmly welcomes the first Report of ARCIC II, 'Salvation and the Church' (1987), as a timely and significant contribution to the understanding of the Churches' doctrine of salvation and commends this Agreed Statement about the heart of Christian faith to the provinces for study and reflection.

EXPLANATORY NOTE

This Conference has received the official responses to the *Final Report* of the Anglican–Roman Catholic International Commission (ARCIC I) from the member provinces of the Anglican Communion. We note the considerable measure of consensus and convergence the Agreed Statements represent. We wish to record our grateful thanks to Almighty God for the very significant advances in understanding and unity thereby expressed.

In considering the *Final Report* the Conference bore two questions in mind:
(i) Are the Agreed Statements consonant with Anglican faith?
(ii) If so, do they enable us to take further steps forward?

Eucharistic Doctrine

The provinces gave a clear 'yes' to the Statement on 'Eucharistic Doctrine'.

Comments have been made that the style and language used in the Statement are inappropriate for certain cultures. Some provinces asked for clarification about the meaning of *anamnesis* and bread and wine 'becoming' the body and blood of Christ. But no province rejected the Statement and many were extremely positive.

While we recognise that there are hurts to be healed and doubts to be overcome, we encourage Anglicans to look forward with the new hope which the Holy Spirit is giving to the Church as we move away from past mistrust, division and polarisation.

While we respect continuing anxieties of some Anglicans in the areas of 'sacrifice' and 'presence', they do not appear to reflect the common mind of the provincial responses, in which it was generally felt that the Elucidation of 'Eucharistic Doctrine' was a helpful clarification and reassurance. Both are areas of 'mystery' which ultimately defy definition. But the Agreed Statement on the Eucharist *sufficiently* expresses Anglican understanding.

Ministry and Ordination

Again, the provinces gave a clear 'yes' to the Statement on 'Ministry and Ordination'.

The language and style have, however, been a difficulty for some provinces, especially in the Far East. Wider representation has also been called for from Africa. Though this has now been partially remedied in ARCIC II, there is still currently no representation from Latin America, a subcontinent with very large Roman Catholic populations.

An ambivalent reply came from one province which has traditionally experienced a difficult relationship with the Roman Catholic Church. This seems to reflect the need for developing deeper links of trust and friendship as ecumenical dialogue goes forward.

While some provinces asked for a clarification of 'priesthood' the majority believed this had been dealt with sufficiently—together with the doctrine of the eucharist—to give grounds for hope for a fresh appraisal of each other's ministries and thus to further the reconciliation of ministries and growth towards full communion.

Authority in the Church

The responses from the provinces to the two Statements on 'Authority in the Church' were generally positive.

Questions were, however, raised about a number of matters, especially primacy, jurisdiction and infallibility, collegiality, and the role of the laity. Nevertheless, it was generally felt that 'Authority in the Church' (I and II), together with the Elucidation, give us real grounds for believing that fuller agreement can be reached, and that they set out helpfully the direction and agenda of the way forward.

(See further paras 59, 64, 80, 85-89 of the Report on 'Ecumenical Relations'.)

Resolution 9: Methodist Church

This Conference:

1   Gives thanks to Almighty God for the 250th anniversary of the conversion of John and Charles Wesley, and for the influence and witness of the Methodist Church.

2   Recognises with regret that at this time there is no international theological dialogue between the Anglican Communion and the World Methodist Council.

3   Requests the Anglican Consultative Council to initiate conversations with the World Methodist Council with a view to the beginning of such a dialogue.

Resolution 10: Baptist World Alliance

This Conference:

1   Gives thanks for the many dialogues which are taking place between the Anglican Communion and other Christian Churches and for the closer fellowship which these dialogues have enabled between us.

2   In the light of the growing reception of *Baptism, Eucharist and Ministry*, believes that the time is ripe for a dialogue between the Anglican Communion and the Baptist World Alliance.

3   Requests the Anglican Consultative Council to initiate conversations with the Baptist World Alliance with a view to the beginning of such a dialogue.

Resolution 11: Pentecostal Churches
This Conference notes the rapid growth of Pentecostal Churches in many parts of the world, and encourages where possible the initiation of personal contact and theological dialogue with Pentecostal Churches especially at the local level.

Resolution 12: United Churches in full communion
This Conference:
1   Expresses its gratitude for the presence of bishops from the Church of South India, the Church of North India, the Church of Bangladesh and the Church of Pakistan, acknowledging that their presence reminds us that our commitment as Anglicans is to the wider unity of the Church.
2   Affirms the request of ACC-7 (Resolution 17) that all United Churches with which the Churches of the Anglican Communion are in full communion be invited to accept full membership in the Lambeth Conference and the Primates Meeting (as is already the case with the Anglican Consultative Council).
3   Welcomes the proposals entitled *Ministry in a Uniting Church* of the Covenanted Churches in Wales, and insofar as the Welsh proposals are similar to the North India and Pakistan Scheme, sees no difficulties in relation to the question of full communion if such proposals are brought to fruition.
4   Encourages the development of similar proposals in other parts of the world.

EXPLANATORY NOTE
The term 'united Churches in full communion' is used of those Churches where Anglicans have entered into union with Christians of other traditions. These Churches are in full communion with the Churches of the Anglican Communion.
(See further paras 3, 51, 93-97 of the Report on 'Ecumenical Relations'.)

Resolution 13: Unity: Locally, nationally and internationally
This Conference:
Acknowledging that the withdrawal of Anglicans from several previous covenanting proposals and schemes of unity with Methodist, Reformed and other Churches is a cause for sorrow and repentance, nevertheless is encouraged by
1   the continuing unity conversations in the Consultation on Church Union (USA) and the Welsh covenanting proposals;
2   the developing partnership in oversight of ecumenical ventures which is being shared by bishops with the leaders of other Churches;
3   the local unity developing in various countries such as the co-operating parishes in New Zealand, the 'shared ministries' in Canada

and the local ecumenical projects (with the proposed new canons) in England.

4   Recognises the special pastoral needs of inter-Church families and wishes to express its support and encouragement for the work of associations of inter-Church families and all forms of work locally and internationally which seek to help them.

(See further paras 2-9 and 102-108 of the Report on 'Ecumenical Relations'.)

Resolution 14: Councils of Churches

This Conference:

1   Recognises the World Council of Churches as a special instrument of God in bringing into fuller unity and mission those Churches that confess 'the Lord Jesus Christ as God and Saviour according to the Scriptures, and therefore seek to fulfil together their common calling to the glory of the one God, Father, Son and Holy Spirit', and in expressing their commitment to justice, peace, and the integrity of creation.

2   Encourages the provinces of the Anglican Communion to fuller commitment to the work of the WCC as well as other councils.

3   Recommends that all such councils be as inclusive of the baptized as possible and that all Churches be encouraged to contribute to the life and witness of such councils as fully as possible.

4   Expresses the hope that, through the councils, the Churches are helped to function as closely as possible in accordance with the Lund Principle, viz. that Churches should do together all those things that deep differences of conviction do not compel them to do separately.

(See further paras 101 and 102 of the Report on 'Ecumenical Relations'.)

Resolution 15: Local ecumenism

This Conference:

1   Believes that the significance and value of the bilateral and multilateral conversations which Anglicans continue to have with other Churches depend in large part on a parallel movement of growth in unity at the local level, and therefore commits itself to work at this at provincial, diocesan and parish level, and in particular to share in fellowship, discussion, study, worship, mission and action with fellow Christians of other traditions, in order that the unity which our Lord has given to all who believe in him may be more generally experienced and more visibly realised.

2   Requests that special attention be given to the ways in which bishops may share with the leadership of other Churches in the pastoral oversight of all Christians in ecumenical projects.

(See further paras 102-108 of the Report on 'Ecumenical Relations'.)

Resolution 16: Theological education

This Conference notes with gratitude the numerous experiments in joint education with other Churches which are being made all over the world, and recommends the extension of such work beyond the training of those who are to be ordained both in order to meet the needs of the whole people of God for a better understanding and fuller knowledge of their faith, and to foster the development of ecumenical theology and catechetics.

Resolution 17: Steps towards unity

This Conference recognises that the growth of Christian unity is a gradual and costly process in which agreement in faith, sharing in prayer, worship and pastoral care, and co-operation in mission all play their part and recommends to the Churches in their own particular situations that they progress from mere coexistence through to co-operation, mutual commitment or covenant and on to full visible unity with all their brothers and sisters in Christ.

(See further paras 80-108 of the Report on 'Ecumenical Relations'.)

Resolution 18: The Anglican Communion: Identity and authority

This Conference:

1   Resolves that the new Inter-Anglican Theological and Doctrinal Commission (or a specially appointed inter-Anglican commission) be asked to undertake as a matter of urgency a further exploration of the meaning and nature of communion; with particular reference to the doctrine of the Trinity, the unity and order of the Church, and the unity and community of humanity.

2   (a) Urges that encouragement be given to a developing collegial role for the Primates Meeting under the presidency of the Archbishop of Canterbury, so that the Primates Meeting is able to exercise an enhanced responsibility in offering guidance on doctrinal, moral and pastoral matters.

(b) Recommends that in the appointment of any future Archbishop of Canterbury, the Crown Appointments Commission be asked to bring the primates of the Communion into the process of consultation.

3   Resolves that the Lambeth Conference as a conference of bishops of the Anglican Communion should continue in the future, at appropriate intervals.

4   Recommends that regional conferences of the Anglican Communion should meet between Lambeth Conferences as and when the region concerned believes it to be appropriate; and in the event of these regional conferences being called, it should be open to the region con-

cerned to make them representative of clergy and laity as well as bishops.

5   Recommends that the ACC continue to fulfil the functions defined in its Constitution (developed as a consequence of Resolution 69 of the 1968 Lambeth Conference) and affirmed by the evaluation process reported to ACC-6 (see *Bonds of Affection*, pp 23-27); in particular to continue its consultative, advisory, liaison and communication roles within the Communion (and to do so in close co-operation with the Primates Meeting).

6   Requests the Archbishop of Canterbury, with all the primates of the Anglican Communion, to appoint an advisory body on Prayer Books of the Anglican Communion. The body should be entrusted with the task of offering encouragement, support and advice to Churches of the Communion in their work of liturgical revision as well as facilitating mutual consultation concerning, and review of, their Prayer Books as they are developed with a view to ensuring:

(a) the public reading of the Scriptures in a language understood by the people and instruction of the whole people of God in the scriptural faith by means of sermons and catechisms;

(b) the use of the two sacraments ordained by Christ, Baptism with water in the threefold name, and Holy Communion with bread and wine and explicit intention to obey our Lord's command;

(c) the use of forms of episcopal ordination to each of the three orders by prayer with the laying-on of hands;

(d) the public recitation and teaching of the Apostles' and Nicene Creeds; and

(e) the use of other liturgical expressions of unity in faith and life by which the whole people of God is nurtured and upheld, with continuing awareness of ecumenical liturgical developments.

EXPLANATORY NOTE

On 1 above If there is the possibility of ordination of women bishops in some provinces, it will throw into sharper focus the present impaired nature of communion. It is a matter of urgency that we have a further theological enquiry into and reflection on the meaning of communion in a trinitarian context for the Anglican Communion. Such an enquiry should relate to ecumenical discussions exploring similar issues. This, more than structures, will provide a theological framework in which differences can be handled.

On 2 above We see an enhanced role for the primates as a key to a growth of inter-dependence within the Communion. We do not see any inter-Anglican jurisdiction as possible or desirable; an inter-Anglican synodical structure would be virtually unworkable and highly expensive. A collegial role for the primates by contrast could easily be developed, and their collective judgement and advice would carry considerable weight.

If this is so, it is neither improper nor out of place to suggest that part of the consultative process prior to the appointment of a future Archbishop of Canterbury should be in consultation with the primates.

On 3 above We are convinced that there is considerable value in the bishops of the Anglican Communion meeting as bishops, both in terms of mutual understanding and as an effective agent of interdependence.

On 4 above Regional issues need regional solutions. Regional conferences can also provide for wider representation.

On 5 above We value the present work of the ACC. We do not see, however, that it ought to move beyond its present advisory role.

On 6 above Concern for how the Church celebrates the sacraments of unity and with what consequences is a central expression of episcopal care and pastoral oversight in the Church of God. As bishops of the Anglican Communion we have a particular responsibility for securing those elements in worship which nurture our identity and unity in Christ and which therefore have an authority for us as Anglicans. (A parallel but significantly different resolution has been proposed by the Anglican Consultative Council: Resolution 12 of ACC-7.)

(See further paras 113-152 of the Report on 'Dogmatic and Pastoral Concerns'.)

Resolution 19: Draft Common Declaration

This Conference resolves that the Inter-Anglican Theological and Doctrinal Commission consider paragraph 20 of the paper 'Instruments of Communion and Decision-Making' (Draft Common Declaration) and report to the Primates Meeting.

(See further para. 129 of the Report on 'Dogmatic and Pastoral Concerns' and Appendix 5.)

Resolution 20: Inter-faith dialogue

This Conference commends dialogue with people of other faiths as part of Christian discipleship and mission, with the understanding that:

(1) dialogue begins when people meet each other;

(2) dialogue depends upon mutual understanding, mutual respect and mutual trust;

(3) dialogue makes it possible to share in service to the community;

(4) dialogue becomes a medium of authentic witness.

Acknowledging that such dialogue, which is not a substitute for evangelism, may be a contribution in helping people of different faiths to make common cause in resolving issues of peacemaking, social justice and religious liberty, we further commend each province to initiate such dialogue in partnership with other Christian Churches where appropriate.

(See further paras 55-58 of the Report on 'Dogmatic and Pastoral Concerns'.)

Resolution 21: Inter-faith dialogue: Jewish/Christian/Muslim

This Conference:

1   Commends the document *Jews, Christians and Muslims: The Way of Dialogue* for study and encourages the Churches of the Anglican Communion to engage in dialogue with Jews and Muslims on the basis of understanding, affirmation and sharing illustrated in it.

2   Recommends that the Anglican Consultative Council gives consideration to the setting up of an inter-faith committee, which committee, in the interest of cost and in practical pursuance of our commitment to ecumenism, would work in close co-operation with the Inter-Faith Dialogue Committee of the WCC; and that this committee, amongst its other work, establishes a common approach to people of other faiths on a Communion-wide basis and appoints working parties to draw up more detailed guidelines for relationships with Judaism and Islam and other faiths as appropriate.

3   Recommends that provinces initiate talks wherever possible on a tripartite basis, with both Jews and Muslims.

4   Urges provinces to support those institutions which are helping Christians towards a more informed understanding of Judaism and Islam.

(See further paras 63 and 64 of the Report on 'Dogmatic and Pastoral Concerns' and Appendix 6.)

Resolution 22: Christ and culture

This Conference:

(a)   Recognises that culture is the context in which people find their identity.

(b)   Affirms that God's love extends to people of every culture and that the Gospel judges every culture according to the Gospel's own criteria of truth, challenging some aspects of culture while endorsing and transforming others for the benefit of the Church and society.

(c)   Urges the Church everywhere to work at expressing the unchanging Gospel of Christ in words, actions, names, customs, liturgies, which communicate relevantly in each contemporary society.

(See further paras 23-40 of the Report on 'Dogmatic and Pastoral Concerns'.)

Resolution 23: Freedom of religious activity

This Conference calls upon all governments to uphold religious freedom, including freedom of worship and freedom to teach and evangelise, as a fundamental human right, the denial of which threatens all other liberties.

EXPLANATORY NOTE

We are concerned for minority religious groups, but have a special concern for those in Islamic states.

(See further para. 68 of the Report on 'Dogmatic and Pastoral Concerns'.)

Resolution 24: Palestine/Israel

This Conference, saddened by the present suffering in the West Bank and Gaza Strip:

1   Affirms the importance of the Church in the exercise of its

prophetic role by standing on the side of the oppressed in their struggle for justice, and by promoting justice, peace and reconciliation for all peoples in the region.

2   Affirms the existence of the state of Israel and its right to recognised and secure borders, as well as the civic and human rights of all those who live within its borders.

3   Affirms the right of the Palestinians to self-determination, including choice of their own representatives and the establishment of their own state.

4   Supports the convening of an international conference over Palestine/Israel under the auspices of the UN and based on all the UN resolutions in relation to this conflict, to which all parties of the conflict be invited.

5   Commits itself to continued prayer for Israelis and Palestinians, for Muslim, Jew and Christian, for the achievement of justice, peace and reconciliation for all.

(See further paras 36 and 48 of the Report on 'Christianity and the Social Order'.)

Resolution 25: Iran
This Conference, recognising the positive development of recent events in Iran, and in the light of a declared policy of religious tolerance in that land, respectfully requests the Islamic Republic of Iran to facilitate a positive response to the many requests, sent on behalf of the Diocese of Iran, the Primates of the Anglican Communion, and the President Bishop of the Episcopal Church in Jerusalem and the Middle East, concerning all the claims of the Church in Iran.

Resolution 26: Church and polygamy
This Conference upholds monogamy as God's plan, and as the ideal relationship of love between husband and wife; nevertheless recommends that a polygamist who responds to the Gospel and wishes to join the Anglican Church may be baptized and confirmed with his believing wives and children on the following conditions:

(1) that the polygamist shall promise not to marry again as long as any of his wives at the time of his conversion are alive;

(2) that the receiving of such a polygamist has the consent of the local Anglican community;

(3) that such a polygamist shall not be compelled to put away any of his wives, on account of the social deprivation they would suffer;

(4) and recommends that provinces where the Churches face problems of polygamy are encouraged to share information of their pastoral approach to Christians who become polygamists so that the most appropriate way of disciplining and pastoring them can be

found, and that the ACC be requested to facilitate the sharing of that information.

Resolution 27: War, violence and justice
This Conference:
1   (a) reaffirms the statement of the 1930 Lambeth Conference that war as a method of settling international disputes is incompatible with the teaching and example of our Lord Jesus Christ;
     (b) affirms also that there is no true peace without justice, and reformation and transformation of unjust systems is an essential element of our biblical hope;
2   (a) supports those who choose the way of non-violence as being the way of our Lord, including direct non-violent action, civil disobedience and conscientious objection, and pays tribute to those who in recent years have kept before the world the growing threat of militarism;
     (b) understands those who, after exhausting all other ways, choose the way of armed struggle as the only way to justice, whilst drawing attention to the dangers and injustices possible in such action itself; and
3   encourages provinces and dioceses to seek out those secular and religious agencies working for justice and reconciliation, and to make common cause with them, to ensure that the voice of the oppressed is heard and a response is made so that further violence is averted.

(See further paras 98-126 of the Report on 'Christianity and the Social Order'.)

Resolution 28: Sexual abuse
This Conference:
1   Expresses deep concern about the frequency of domestic violence and the sexual abuse of children.
2   Asks Christian leaders to be explicit about the sinfulness of violence and sexual abuse whether of children or adults, and to devise means of providing support for the victims and perpetrators of such exploitation to enable them to break the cycle of abuse.
3   Reaffirms the traditional biblical teaching on the value of the human person who, being made in the image of God, is neither to be exploited nor abused.

(See further paras 156-160 of the Report on 'Christianity and the Social Order'.

Resolution 29: Acquired Immune Deficiency Syndrome (AIDS)
This Conference, recognising (a) that the disease AIDS poses a catastrophic threat to every part of the world, and (b) that unless preven-

tative measures are taken, the disease can spread rapidly (though the long latency period may mask its presence, thus giving a false sense of security), asks bishops to accept their responsibility to witness to Christ's compassion and care, in response to this crisis, by giving a lead in:

1   The promotion of, and co-operation with, educational programmes both of Church and state concerned with the cause and prevention of the disease, in a loving and non-judgemental spirit towards those who suffer.

2   The development of diocesan strategies:
   (a) to train and support pastoral helpers;
   (b) to give direct personal support to those living with AIDS;
   (c) to identify and try to resolve the social problems leading to and arising from the disease;
   (d) to reaffirm the traditional biblical teaching that sexual intercourse is an act of total commitment which belongs properly within a permanent married relationship.

3   The need to work together:
   (a) to encourage global co-operation between Churches, governments and non-government agencies in the fight against the disease;
   (b) to develop ways in which the Churches can share information and resources;
   (c) to press where necessary for political action;
   (d) to promote prayer for all concerned, not forgetting those active in research to discover a cure.

(See further paras 161-194 of the Report on 'Christianity and the Social Order'.)

Resolution 30: Conscientious objection

This Conference, recalling Resolution 8 of the Lambeth Conference 1968 to 'uphold and extend the right of conscientious objection', and learning of the jail sentences given to David Bruce and to Dr Ivan Toms, both young South Africans, who on grounds of conscience refuse to serve in the South African Defence Force:

1   sends them greetings and assures them of our prayers;
2   calls on the South African government
   (a) to repeal the sentences given to these persons,
   (b) to provide a more comprehensive non-military alternative to compulsory military service,
   (c) to review its legislation regarding conscientious objection.

Resolution 31: Voiceless minority

This Conference, conscious of the work in many dioceses with deprived minorities in developed, affluent countries, such as native Americans and Canadians, Australian aborigines and islanders, ethnic Koreans in Japan, and black urban communities in Britain, asks the relevant Anglican provinces to support work among such minorities who have difficulty in making their plight known in national and world forums.

(See further paras 55-65 of the Report on 'Christianity and the Social Order'.)

Resolution 32: World peace
This Conference:
1   Welcomes recent new directions in Soviet policy as a constructive contribution to world peace.
2   Urges the leaders of the western nations to review their foreign and defence policies to allow for new opportunities for co-operation with the Soviet Union.
3   Appeals to all governments with nuclear forces to cease the production of nuclear weapons and to plan together an international programme for the dismantling of such weapons.
4   Urges the major world powers to recognise and respect the self-determination of smaller states and not to penalise them when their decisions conflict with the foreign policies of these major powers.

(See further paras 122-126 of the Report on 'Christianity and the Social Order'.)

Resolution 33: Human rights
This Conference:
1   Endorses the UN Universal Declaration of Human Rights, and asks the provinces of the Anglican Communion to support all who are working for its implementation.
2   Commends to all Churches the good practice of observing 'One World Week' in proximity to United Nations Day, 24 October, as a means of highlighting human interdependence and the need to eliminate exploitation.
3   Urges the Church to speak out against:
(a) torture, used as a cruel, inhuman and degrading treatment of prisoners, burning down of people's homes, granaries, and the confiscation of livestock and denial by governments of supplies of medical facilities and relief food by international organizations to people in areas of armed conflict;
(b) all governments who practise capital punishment, and encourages them to find alternative ways of sentencing offenders so that the divine dignity of every human being is respected and yet justice is pursued;
(c) the incarceration of prisoners of conscience, challenging governments to search for treatment and punishment of convicted persons in accordance with internationally accepted standards;

(d) any denial of the principle that a person is innocent until proven guilty by due, fair and impartial procedures of law.

4   Commends the work of various international human rights organisations campaigning to support the freedoms set out in the Universal Declaration of Human Rights, and their work on behalf of human rights activists throughout the world who are persecuted for their defence of those fundamental freedoms.

(See further paras 36-50 of the Report on 'Christianity and the Social Order'.)

Resolution 34: Marriage and family

This Conference:

1   Reaffirming the 1978 Lambeth statement on marriage and the family, calls the Churches of the Anglican Communion to ministries that prepare couples for marriage, sustain them throughout their lives together with the spiritual, pastoral, and community life of the Church and, in the face of increasing stresses, encourage and support them with the resources of the Church as an extended family.

2   Recognises that the same range of pressures no less affect clergy marriages and families and recommends that each diocese identify some means of providing confidential counselling and support services for clergy families;

3   Noting the gap between traditional Christian teaching on pre-marital sex, and the life-styles being adopted by many people today, both within and outside the Church:

(a) calls on provinces and dioceses to adopt a caring and pastoral attitude to such people;

(b) reaffirms the traditional biblical teaching that sexual intercourse is an act of total commitment which belongs properly within a permanent married relationship;

(c) in response to the International Conference of Young Anglicans in Belfast, urges provinces and dioceses to plan with young people programmes to explore issues such as pre-marital sex in the light of traditional Christian values.

4   Recognising the political, economic and social pressures on family life:

(a) affirms the family in its various forms, as the fundamental institution of human community;

(b) calls our Churches to the development of support systems for families at every level within the Church and to the advocacy of public policies supportive of family life;

(c) commends in particular the developing Family Network inaugurated by the Anglican Consultative Council and encourages participation in the continuing educational and pastoral work of the Network;

(d) recognises that these pressures serve to diminish the economic wellbeing and status of women, welcomes the World Council of Churches 'Decade for Solidarity with Women', and encourages dioceses to consider how they might through their theological, structural and pastoral approaches help to achieve a fuller recognition of the contribution and status of women in the Church and society.

5   Affirms that effective ministries to families and to individuals, who are thereby enabled to experience the Church as an extended family, are signs of life and hope and are central to evangelism that proclaims and models the oneness that Christ wills for all people.

(See further paras 127-152 of the Report on 'Christianity and the Social Order'.)

Resolution 35: Concerns of South Pacific islands

This Conference, noting that in Churches of the South Pacific there is deep pain and anxiety in many tiny island sovereign nations in the region regarding the abuse and exploitation of their lands and seas by powerful external political and economic forces:

1   Affirms the desire of many indigenous peoples in the region to self-determination and to be in control of their own affairs and especially of the use of the vital resources of their lands and seas.

2   Supports them in their opposition to the testing of nuclear weapons, the dumping of nuclear waste and the establishment of further military bases in the region, and calls on France and the superpowers to cease these activities forthwith.

3   Further supports them in their resistance to all those powerful states and multinational corporations who, for immediate economic and political gain, rape and destroy the forests, fisheries and mineral deposits in the region.

4   Wishes to be identified with the stand of the Churches in Australia, New Zealand and Japan in support of these concerns and requests the member Churches of the Anglican Communion to make these matters known in their own countries and congregations as a matter of urgency, to pray for them and to press their governments for action.

(See further para. 50 of the Report on 'Christianity and the Social Order'.)

Resolution 36: Poverty and debt

This Conference:

1   Calls attention to the life-and-death urgency of the problems of world poverty.

2   Salutes the courage and solidarity of poor people who, at great personal cost, are struggling to achieve their own liberation from poverty and oppression.

3   Calls for an international, co-operating settlement, negotiated by both industrial and developing countries, that will establish policies to reduce interest charges and the level of indebtedness, based on shared responsibility for the world debt and in accordance with Christian and humanitarian principles of economic justice and social and ecological interdependence.

4   Calls on national governments, transnational corporations, the International Monetary Fund and the World Bank together, to re-examine all principles governing trade relationships, the transfer of technology and resources and all loan and aid policies in order to improve the economic viability and local autonomy of developing countries.

5   Requests these bodies to consider these and other creative ways of involving the global economy over time by:

(a) (i) correcting demand imbalances;
    (ii) reducing protectionism;
    (iii) stabilising exchange rates;
    (iv) increasing resource transfers;

(b) offering relief from debt incurred with commercial banks in ways that will not leave debtor economies vulnerable to foreign manipulation, by
    (i) lending directly to developing countries at reduced and subsidised interest rates;
    (ii) improved rescheduling of existing debt repayments;
    (iii) debt conversion arrangements;
    (iv) establishing a multilateral body to co-ordinate debt relief;

(c) offering relief from official debts incurred with the World Bank and the International Monetary Fund through
    (i) improved rescheduling of existing debt repayment;
    (ii) lending on conditions oriented to development objectives;
    (iii) refraining from making demands on debtor countries which would endanger the fabric of their national life or cause further dislocation to their essential human services.

(See further para. 73 of the Report on 'Christianity and the Social Order'.)

Resolution 37: Latin America

This Conference:

1   Affirms that self-determination is a fundamental human right based on the freedom which God has given to us, and to which every person, nation and region is entitled.

2   Commends and supports the Church in Latin America as it seeks ways and means of helping their people to develop a higher standard of living and to motivate their governments to provide greater freedom and justice for their people.

3   Urges those governments whose military policies inhibit self-determination to refrain from unjust political manipulation of Latin American countries and from military interference in their lives.

4   Urges the lifting of the sanctions imposed upon Nicaragua, Panama and Cuba by the United States of America.

5   Urges the industrial countries of the world to cease all military aid to combatants in Latin American countries and to give them economic and humanitarian assistance so as to end the suffering of the people.

6   Commends the peace effort of the Central American countries and the support given by other Latin American nations.

Resolution 38: Namibia

This Conference, bearing in mind the tenth anniversary of the United Nations Resolution 435, and being deeply aware of the protracted suffering of the Namibian people at the hands of the South African regime:

1   Expresses support for the people in their struggle for independence, and pays tribute to the Anglican Diocese and the Council of Churches in Namibia for their courageous witness.

2   Calls on the South African government (a) to withdraw from Angola; (b) to implement Resolution 435.

3   Asks the Anglican provinces of Canada, the United Kingdom and the United States of America to press their governments to fulfil their obligations as members of the Contact Group of nations.

Resolution 39: South Africa

This Conference:

1   Reaffirms its belief that the system of apartheid in South Africa is evil and especially repugnant because of the cruel way a tyrannical racist system is being upheld in the name of the Christian faith.

2   Condemns the detention of children without just cause.

3   Calls upon the Churches to press their governments to
(a) bring the maximum pressure to bear on the South African regime in order to promote a genuine process of change towards the establishment of democratic political structures in a unified state;
(b) institute forms of sanction calculated to have the maximum effect in bringing an end to the evil dispensation, and in establishing a just peace among all citizens;
(c) give direct aid to anti-apartheid organisations within South Africa particularly with a view to assisting the unemployed and persecuted;
(d) give effective practical support to the Frontline States in order to ensure their economic survival and welfare, as well as their military protection from the threat of South African aggression;

(e) push for the release of Nelson Mandela and all other political prisoners and detainees in South Africa, and the unbanning of organisations like the African National Congress and the Pan Africanist Congress which represent the majority of citizens;

(f) give direct moral and humanitarian support to such organisations in the pursuit of a just order which reflects Gospel values, and urges the Churches to ensure that none of their own financial resources is used to support the present regime in South Africa and for this purpose to disinvest from all corporations which have a significant financial stake in South Africa (ACC-7, Resolution 24).

4   Believes that to work for a just peace in South Africa is to work for the true liberation of all peoples of the region, black and white.

NOTE
The Lambeth Conference agreed to the request by Bishop D. Sengulane (Diocese of Lebombo, Mozambique) that he be dissociated from this motion.

Resolution 40: Environment, militarism, justice and peace

This Conference:

1   Identifies four interrelated areas in which the misuse of people or resources poses a threat to the life system of the planet, namely (a) unjust distribution of the world's wealth, (b) social injustice within nations, (c) the rise of militarism, (d) irreversible damage to the environment; and therefore

2   Calls upon each province and diocese to devise a programme of study, reflection and action in which the following elements should play a part:

(a) as a matter of urgency, the giving of information to our people of what is happening to our environment, and to encourage them to see stewardship of God's earth for the care of our neighbours as a necessary part of Christian discipleship and a Christian contribution to citizenship;

(b) actively to support by public statement and in private dialogue, the engagement of governments, transnational corporations, management and labour in an examination of what their decisions are doing to our people, and our land, air and water;

(c) opposition to the increase in the arms trade, questioning both excessive expenditure of scarce resources on weapons and trade policies which look upon arms sales as a legitimate source of increased export revenue;

(d) the encouragement of Christians to re-examine the currently accepted economic policies which operate to the disadvantage of those with less bargaining power at every level from international to personal, and to use God's gifts of technology for the benefit of all;

(e) the critical examination of the exercise of power, first within congregations and all other Church bodies, and then in secular institutions which affect the lives of all. Insofar as the aim is to achieve a just and sustainable society world-wide, priority must be given to those modes which nurture people's gifts and evoke responsible participation rather than those which dominate and exclude.

3　(a) Commends, in general, the participation by every province in the WCC's programme for 'Justice, Peace and the Integrity of Creation';

(b) Urges Churches, congregations and individual Christians to actively support all other agencies which share this urgent concern. In particular we commend a widespread study of the United Nations report *Our Common Future* and a participation by Church bodies in the local responses it requires;

(c) Recommends that, in view of the resolutions passed by ACC-7, information concerning local needs and initiatives be shared throughout provinces, possibly by extending the terms of reference for the existing Peace and Justice Network;

(d) Encourages people everywhere to make changes, personal and corporate, in their attitudes and life-style, recognising that wholeness of living requires a right relationship with God, one's neighbour, and creation.

EXPLANATORY NOTE

Some effects, like famine, can be recognised immediately; some, like pollution, are a creeping crisis which is nonetheless deadly. These major threats to the earth's future cannot be averted by action in one region of the world alone, nor by focusing on a single issue. Everything connects.

(See further paras 36-50, 81-97 and 122-126 of the Report on 'Christianity and the Social Order'.)

Resolution 41: Training of bishops

This Conference:

(a)　congratulates African provinces for having made provisions for the training of newly consecrated bishops as recommended by Lambeth 1978 (Resolution 19);

(b)　resolves that every province implement programmes of initial preparation and in-service training for the episcopate, and accordingly that:

(1) A duration of one month, at least, be set aside for preparation, which should include instruction regarding the tasks and functions of a bishop, finance and management control; such training being in the language and culture of the bishop concerned.

(2) After six years in office, all bishops should be encouraged to have a period of sabbatical leave for study and refreshment; and

that financial support for such a period should be available from appropriate sources within the province concerned.

(3) Where appropriate, preparation, training and support should also be made available to the spouse.

(4) In view of the stress factor within the life of the bishop, bishops should present themselves for a medical examination at least once a year.

(See further paras 160-174 of the Report on 'Mission and Ministry'.)

Resolution 42: Ministry of lay people

This Conference recommends that provinces and dioceses encourage, train, equip and send out lay people for evangelism and ministry.

(See further paras 87-110 of the Report on 'Mission and Ministry'.)

Resolution 43: Decade of Evangelism

This Conference, recognising that evangelism is the primary task given to the Church, asks each province and diocese of the Anglican Communion, in co-operation with other Christians, to make the closing years of this millennium a 'Decade of Evangelism' with a renewed and united emphasis on making Christ known to the people of his world.

(See further paras 14-23 of the Report on 'Mission and Ministry'.)

Resolution 44: Evangelism in the Anglican Communion

This Conference:

1   calls for a shift to a dynamic missionary emphasis going beyond care and nurture to proclamation and service; and therefore

2   accepts the challenge this presents to diocesan and local church structures and patterns of worship and ministry, and looks to God for a fresh movement of the Spirit in prayer, outgoing love and evangelism in obedience to our Lord's command.

(See further paras 10-13 of the Report on 'Mission and Ministry'.)

Resolution 45: Mission and ministry of the whole Church

This Conference:

1   acknowledging that God through the Holy Spirit is bringing about a revolution in terms of the total ministry of all the baptized, thus enriching the Church and making Christ known to men and women as the hope of the world;

2   urges each bishop with his diocese to take the necessary steps to provide opportunities, training and support to ensure that this shared style of ministry becomes a reality.

(See further paras 70-75 of the Report on 'Mission and Ministry'.)

Resolution 46: Ministry of all bishops

This Conference resolves that each province re-examine the position and work of all bishops active in full-time diocesan work, including those known in the various provinces as suffragan, assistant, assisting, area or regional bishops, to ensure that all bishops have a true *episcope* of jurisdiction and pastoral care and are seen as belonging fully to the local college of bishops.

(See further paras 156 and 157 of the Report on 'Mission and Ministry'.)

Resolution 46A: Ministry of all bishops

This Conference resolves that each province re-examine the principle that all bishops active in full-time diocesan work be made full members, with seat, voice and vote, of all provincial, national and international gatherings of Anglican bishops.

(See further para. 157(b) of the Report on 'Mission and Ministry'.)

Resolution 47: Liturgical freedom

This Conference resolves that each province should be free, subject to essential universal Anglican norms of worship, and to a valuing of traditional liturgical materials, to seek that expression of worship which is appropriate to its Christian people in their cultural context.

(See further paras 181-186 of the Report on 'Mission and Ministry'.)

Resolution 48: Mission to youth

This Conference:

1   Encourages every diocese to conduct an evaluation of existing mission and ministry among its youth*, as far as possible in co-operation with other Churches, which should include an examination of the current nature and extent of youth involvement in the life of the diocese and provinces and at every level.

2   Suggests that this should include the following questions to be investigated:

(a) What occasions or venues for meeting are provided for young people who have no contact whatever with the Church or the Christian faith?

(b) What proportion of diocesan and parish budgets is set aside for youth ministry, compared with other activities?

(c) What relationships exist between the diocese and its clergy on the one hand, and the local schools and state education authorities on the other, if any?

(d) How are the dioceses and parishes making use of the skills and gifts of local Christian teachers, youth leaders, young people who have a ministry among their peers, and what opportunities for encouragement and training in Christian witness are being provided?

* Known elsewhere as a 'mission audit'; see [Report of] ACC-6, Resolution 11, p 60, for suggested guidelines.

(See further paras 32-35 and 75 of the Report on 'Mission and Ministry'.)

Resolution 49: Support for French-speaking dioceses

This Conference draws the attention of the whole Anglican Communion to the problems faced by the Province of Burundi, Rwanda and Zaire and other French-speaking dioceses, so that they can be supported by their Partners in Mission and other parts of the Communion with an aim of helping them to obtain self-sufficiency in fulfilling their mission in terms of training manpower, transport and financial support.

(See further para. 159 of the Report on "Mission and Ministry".)

[Resolution 50 failed]

Resolution 51: Election and retirement of bishops and archbishops

This Conference:

1   Urges all provinces to ensure that their provincial provisions for election and retirement of bishops and archbishops are unambiguous and are adhered to.

2   Recommends that, where problems arise regarding implementation of such provisions, and such problems cannot be solved at the provincial level, the regional conferences of primates should be called upon to advise, and if such conferences fail to solve the problem, the matter is referred to the Meeting of the Primates of the Anglican Communion.

Resolution 52: Primates Meeting and ACC

This Conference requests the Primates Meeting and the Anglican Consultative Council to give urgent attention to implementing the hope expressed at Lambeth 1978 (and as confirmed by recent provincial responses) that both bodies would work in the very closest contact.

Resolution 53: Anglican communications

This Conference:

(a)   Directs the ACC to explore the establishment of a telecommunication network linked to every province in order to improve the communication and consultation process throughout the Anglican Communion and to ensure that accurate information is available to the Churches.

(b)   Urges the creation of a telecommunication centre for the Communion through the sharing of resources between provinces and building on the experience of the Inter-Anglican Information Network (IAIN).

Resolution 54: Inter-Anglican budget

This Conference, recognising that there is a common secretariat for meetings of the primates, the Lambeth Conference, and the ACC, endorses the concept of an inter-Anglican budget and requests the ACC to consult with the provinces about the best way in which this is to be achieved.

EXPLANATORY NOTE

Resolution 34 of ACC-7 asks for a response from the Lambeth Conference on the subject of an inter-Anglican budget about which provinces are being consulted. In addition resolutions will be passed by the Lambeth Conference which have financial consequences and it is desirable to remind the Conference that when they ask for work to be done the consequential bill falls upon the provinces.

Resolution 55: Conference translation

This Conference warmly appreciates arrangements made for simultaneous translation of Conference deliberations into French, Spanish, Japanese and Swahili, and requests that the final Conference report be translated into these Conference languages.

Resolution 56: Refugees

This Conference commends to the members of the Communion the Report of the ACC Refugee and Migrant Ministry Network meeting held at Harare for study and action.

(See further paras 40 and 41 of the Report on 'Mission and Ministry'.)

[Resolution 57 failed]

Resolution 58: Civic and land rights for indigenous people of the Americas

This Conference supports all efforts being made for the procuring of land and civic rights for native indigenous people of the Americas, specially in the light of the forthcoming celebrations of the 500th anniversary of the arrival of Columbus in the New World in 1992.

EXPLANATORY NOTE

In 1992 a great celebration is being proposed to commemorate the arrival of Europeans and their culture, specially the Spanish conquest. That arrival meant the destruction of many indigenous cultures and peoples as the Spanish, British, French, Portuguese and Dutch colonisers arrived. Efforts are being made to highlight this suffering. Traditionally Anglicans have taken the side of the Indians throughout the Americas and a lot of our work has been to improve their lot.

This Resolution is backed by:

The Primate of the Southern Cone of South America, The Bishop of Honduras (ECUSA), The Bishop of Guatemala (ECUSA), The Bishop of Western Mexico (ECUSA), The Bishop of South Dakota (ECUSA), The Right Revd Robert Townshend, Suffragan Bishop of Huron (Canada), The Primate of Brazil, and The Right Revd Martiniano Garcia-Montiel, Suffragan Bishop of South and Central Mexico (ECUSA).

(See further paras 40 and 92 of the Report on 'Christianity and the Social Order'.)

Resolution 59: Extra-provincial dioceses
This Conference requests the Primates Meeting and ACC to give urgent consideration to the situation of the extra-provincial dioceses, that they may be fully part of the structures of the Anglican Communion.

Resolution 60: Recognition of saints
This Conference:
1   welcomes the proposal by Africa Region that the Anglican Communion should recognise men and women who have lived godly lives as saints by including them in the calendars of the Churches for remembrance; and
2   recommends that the Anglican Consultative Council discusses this matter and advises the provinces on the procedure to follow in recognition of such saints.

Resolution 61: Islamic fundamentalism
This Conference:
1   Expresses concern that the emergence of Islamic religious fundamentalism has resulted in serious violation of fundamental human rights, including the right of religious belief, practice and propagation, as well as destruction of property of Christian Churches in such places as Northern Nigeria and the Sudan.
2   Urges the ACC to find ways and means of bringing these concerns to international Islamic organisations and the United Nations, and encourages dialogue with countries where pursuit of Islamic religious fundamentalism has led to such violations of human rights.
EXPLANATORY NOTE
This is a real issue in Sudan and Nigeria.

Resolution 62: Peace in the Sudan
This Conference:
1   commends the effort of the Christian Churches in the Sudan in seeking peace and reconciliation between southern and northern Sudan,
2   urges the government of the Sudan to take the initiative in beginning negotiations with the Sudan People's Liberation Army as a first step towards peace in the Sudan, and further

3   urges the Sudanese government to consider accepting a third party to initiate peace talks, e.g. World Council of Churches and the All Africa Conference of Churches.

Resolution 63: Sharî'a law in the Sudan
This Conference:
1   Notes with great concern that the government of the Sudan wishes to reintroduce Sharî'a Law and impose it upon the people of the Sudan.
2   Respectfully requests the government of the Sudan to reconsider its decision on this matter and replace Sharî'a Law with some other more humane legislation for punishing offenders.

Resolution 64: Human rights for those of homosexual orientation
This Conference:
1   Reaffirms the statement of the Lambeth Conference of 1978 on homosexuality, recognising the continuing need in the next decade for 'deep and dispassionate study of the question of homosexuality, which would take seriously both the teaching of Scripture and the results of scientific and medical research'.
2   Urges such study and reflection to take account of biological, genetic and psychological research being undertaken by other agencies, and the socio-cultural factors that lead to the different attitudes in the provinces of our Communion.
3   Calls each province to reassess, in the light of such study and because of our concern for human rights, its care for and attitude towards persons of homosexual orientation.
(See further paras 153-155 of the Report on 'Christianity and the Social Order'.)

Resolution 65: Missions to Seamen
This Conference thanks God for the world-wide Missions to Seamen, which began its work in 1856. It supports and endorses the remarkable way in which the society has adapted its ministry to changed circumstances, acknowledging the fact that there is no part of the Church which has greater ecumenical involvement and experience; that it is deeply involved in dialogue with people of other faiths every day; and that through the Centre for Seafarers' Rights and through almost every member of staff, it is daily involved in issues of social justice. The Conference, encouraged by the appointment of liaison bishops throughout the Anglican Communion, accepts the ministry and mission of the society as the mission of the Church to all seafarers, regardless of creed, class or colour.

Resolution 66: Handbook of Anglican sources

This Conference encourages the publication of the proposed handbook of Anglican sources, which will reflect the catholicity of our tradition from the beginning and the concerns of the world-wide Anglican Communion today.

EXPLANATORY NOTE
Plans are in hand for SPCK to publish such a handbook*, to be edited by J. Robert Wright and G.R. Evans, with a consultative editorial board drawn from the Anglican provinces. It will involve no cost to the Church. It will be useful for encouraging understanding of Anglicanism, both among Anglicans and people of other traditions.

* [*The Anglican Tradition* (SPCK, 1991)]

Resolution 67: Youth Network

This Conference:
1   Endorses the recent developments that have taken place concerning the youth of the Anglican Communion, particularly the establishment of a Youth Network and the holding of the first International Conference of Young Anglicans in Belfast in January 1988.
2   Urges each diocese to ensure that the momentum created by these developments is continued.

Resolution 68: The Gulf and Lebanon

This Conference:
1   views with grave concern the continued conflict between Iran and Iraq, with its very dangerous consequences not only for all the Gulf states and for the Middle East as a whole, but also for the world at large;
2   welcomes Iran's acceptance of Security Council Resolution 598 and looks to Iraq to honour its commitment to do so, and calls upon all countries which have influence to use it to bring an end to the conflict on that basis;
3   condemns the use of chemical weapons in any circumstances and urges that any further use by any country should immediately be met by punitive sanctions; and calls upon the international community to take steps to prevent the sale and supply of such chemical weapons;
4   urges that all countries involved should respect property rights and contractual obligations;
5   recognises that the grief of the families of hostages is universal, knowing no boundaries of religion or nationality;
6   conveys its deep sympathy to the families of all hostages and to all the people of Lebanon who have suffered for so long the brutal savagery of civil war;

7   calls upon all states with influence to use their good offices to secure the release of all hostages in Lebanon of whatever nationality; and
8   prays earnestly for peace and tranquillity in the region.

Resolution 69: Admission to communion

This Conference requests all provinces to consider the theological and pastoral issues involved in the admission of those baptized but unconfirmed to communion (as set out in the Report of ACC-7), and to report their findings to the ACC.

EXPLANATORY NOTE

This Resolution does what ACC-7 expected to be done, and is in line with a draft statement from 'Mission and Ministry'. Whilst it comes as a private member's Resolution, it comes with the goodwill of the 'Mission and Ministry' Section.

(See further para. 194 of the Report on 'Mission and Ministry'.)

[Resolution 70 failed]

Resolution 71: 1988 Lambeth Call to Prayer

This Conference calls upon individuals, prayer groups, congregations, devotional organisations, and religious communities to give renewed emphasis to the work of prayer. We call upon the bishops of the Anglican Communion to give a strong lead in the ministry of prayer in all its forms, so that we may know God's will for our time and be empowered for the mission of the Lord Jesus Christ.

EXPLANATORY NOTE

A Call to Prayer has been issued by the last two Lambeth Conferences. This encouragement for prayer is even more essential as we meet the challenges of the coming years in the Anglican Communion.

Resolution 72: Episcopal responsibilities and diocesan boundaries

This Conference:
1   reaffirms its unity in the historical position of respect for diocesan boundaries and the authority of bishops within these boundaries; and in light of the above
2   affirms that it is deemed inappropriate behaviour for any bishop or priest of this Communion to exercise episcopal or pastoral ministry within another diocese without first obtaining the permission and invitation of the ecclesial authority thereof.
3   Urges all political and community leaders to seize every opportunity to work together to bring about a just and peaceful solution.

EXPLANATORY NOTE

With the number of issues that could threaten our unity it seems fair that we should speak of our mutual respect for one another, and the positions we hold, that serves as a sign of our unity.

Resolution 73: Northern Ireland

This Conference:

1   Expresses solidarity with fellow Anglicans and with all the people of Northern Ireland in their suffering.

2   In the circumstances of Northern Ireland condemns all violence.

3   Urges all political and community leaders to seize every opportunity to work together to bring about a just and peaceful solution.

Index

Abortion xxv; 1908:42,43; 1930:16; 1978:10.

Academic degrees and awards 1897:61,62; 1908:6; 1958:98.

Adult education 1948:33.

Adultery xxv; 1888:4; 1908:39,40.

Affluence *See* Wealth.

African National Congress 1988:39.

African peoples and Christianity 1930:4.

Aged *See* Elderly.

Agriculture 1968:19.

Aid *See* Relief, international.

AIDS (Acquired immune deficiency syndrome) 1988:29.

Alcohol xxv; 1888:1; 1897:23; 1920: 6,79; 1930:23.

Alexandria, Patriarch of 1930:33.

All Africa Conference of Churches 1988:62.

Amsterdam Assembly (WCC) 1948:76.

Anglican Communion i-xv,xx-xxii; 1930:48,49; 1988:18,66. Central college 1948:86; 1958:95-99. Consultation within 1897:1,5; 1948:81; 1958:63,69; 1978:11,12. External relations 1888:11-14; 1897:33; 1930:40; 1948:54,75; 1958:23,46, 55; 1968:60,62,64. Structure 1897: 9; 1920:43; 1988:59.

Anglican Congress xxxv,xxxvi; 1948: 87; 1958:68. *See also* Pan-Anglican Congress.

Anglican Consultative Council xiii-xv; xxxvii; 1968:69. Communications role 1968:18, 36-38; 1978:23; 1988:26,53,60. Finance 1988:54. Inter-Anglican relations 1968:39,63; 1978:12,15, 17,21,25; 1988:12,18,34,40,52,56, 59. Inter-Church relations 1968:62; 1978:28,30,33; 1988:3,5,6,9,10. Inter-faith relations 1988:21. *See also* Lambeth Consultative Body.

Anglican Cycle of Prayer xxxviii; 1958:69,101.

Anglican-Lutheran International Commission 1988:4.

'Anglican-Lutheran International Conversations' xxxvii; 1978:31.

Anglican-Oriental Orthodox Forum 1988:5.

Anglican-Orthodox Joint Doctrinal Discussions (AOJDD) 1978:35; 1988:6.

Anglican-Roman Catholic International Commission (ARCIC) xxxix; 1968:53; 1978:33; 1988:8.

Anglican Tradition, The 1988:66.

Anglican Youth Network 1988:67.

Angola 1988:38.

Animals, human stewardship of 1968:6.

Anointing xxii; 1908:36; 1920:63; 1930:73.

Apartheid xl; 1988:39.

Apostles' Creed xxi; 1888:11; 1920:9; 1988:18.

Apostolic succession 1888:19.

Appeal court 1878:8,9; 1930:51.

'Appeal to all Christian People' 1920:9,10; 1930:31,43; 1948:56.

Arbitration, international 1878:8; 1897:41-43; 1930:27.

Archbishops 1897:7,8; 1988:51. *See also* Metropolitans; Primates Meeting.

Archbishops' Commission on Christian Doctrine 1968:43.

Area bishops 1988:46.

Armaments xxvi; 1948:10,11; 1958: 106; 1968:8; 1978:1,2,5; 1988:37, 68.

Armenian Church xxiii; 1920:20; 1948:68; 1988:5.

Arms trade 1930:28; 1968:8; 1978:1, 2,5; 1988:40,68.

Art and the Christian message 1948: 39; 1958:10.

Asian peoples and Christianity 1930:4.

Assistant bishops 1968:40; 1988:46.

Assyrian Church xxiii; 1920:20; 1930: 36; 1948:68; 1988:5.

Athanasian Creed *See* Quicunque Vult.

Atheism 1948:25; 1968:11,12.

Doctrine (cont'd)
Catholic 1930:35; 1948:67; Orthodox 1897:36; 1930:33; 1948:66;
1958:40; 1968:57; 1978:35; Presbyterian 1958:28. Book of Common
Prayer xix; 1897:46; 1958:74,76.
And Church unity 1888:19; 1908:
77,78; 1948:56. Doctrinal Commission 1978:25; 1988:18. Teaching
1930:6-8. Thirty-nine Articles 1968:
43. United Churches 1930:40;
1958:33. *See also* Theology.
Drama 1958:10,62.
Drink *See* Alcohol.
Drugs xxv; 1908:51; 1920:6; 1930:30;
1958:126.
Drunkenness *See* Intemperance.
Dublin Statement (1984) 1988:6.
Dutch Reformed Church *See* Netherlands Reformed Church.

'Eames Commission' 1988:1.
East Africa, Church of the Province
of xxxvi; 1930:58; 1948:79.
Eastern Churches Committee 1920:
19; 1948:66.
Eastern (Separated) Churches 1908:
63,64; 1920:20,21; 1930:36; 1948:
68; 1958:35,42-45; 1968:57; 1988:5.
Economic policy 1920:74; 1930:17,
29; 1948:14,23,26; 1968:11,19-21;
1978:1,2,4; 1988:35,36,40.
Ecumenical Councils i,ii,xx-xxii.
Ecumenism *See* Inter-Church relations; Non-Anglican Churches;
Unity, Christian; World Council
of Churches; etc.
Education 1897:53,63; 1908:11; 1948:
35,43,46; 1978:1,3. Church policy
1908:17; 1920:77; 1948:27,30;
1968:19. Church schools 1908:15;
1948:29. Of clergy 1897:61,62;
1908:6,7; 1930:63; 1958:83-86. Co-
operation in 1878:3; 1930:7; 1988:
4,48. Sunday schools 1908:14. *See
also* Nurture, Christian; Schools
and Colleges; Training; Universities.
Elderly 1958:124.
Emigration *See* Migration.
Employers, responsibilities of 1888:6;
1908:49.

Employment 1948:43; 1958:93; 1978:
1,3; 1988:39.
Encyclicals, papal xxxi, xxxiii, xxxiv,
xxxvii; 1930:32; 1968:22
Encyclicals of the Lambeth Conference *See* Pastoral letters.
Energy, alternative sources of 1978:
1,2.
England, Church of iii,xix,xxiii;
1867:12; 1878:3; 1897:9; 1930:44;
1948:75; 1958:29; 1988:13,31,38.
Environment 1968:2,6,7; 1978:1,2;
1988:35,40.
Ephesus, Council of xxi.
Episcopal endowment funds 1978:17.
Episcopate iii-v,xii,xvi,xvii; 1888:11;
1968:39-41; 1988:4,7. And Church
unity 1908:75; 1920:9. General
consultation 1948:74; 1958:16,52;
1968:65; 1978:14. And religious
communities 1897:11; 1908:57.
Consecration of women 1978:22;
1988:1. *See also* Archbishops;
Bishops.
Episcopi vagantes 1920:28; 1958:54.
Equality of opportunity 1930:21;
1948:43.
Established Churches xvi.
Estonia, Evangelical Lutheran
Church of 1948:71; 1958:48.
Etchmiadzin (Armenia) 1948:68.
Ethics xiii,xxv; 1978:2; 1988:3,8.
Ethiopian Church 1988:5.
Eucharist *See* Holy Communion.
Europe, Anglican ministry in 1867:
12; 1878:12; 1968:60.
Evangelical Free Churches of
England 1930:44; 1948:61.
Evangelism vi; 1897:14,16,17; 1930:1,
2,46; 1948:20,35-37,42,80,82,84;
1958:7,58,60,65,67,71; 1968:19,28,
30,64; 1978:28,37; 1988:4,20,23,34,
42-45. *See also* Missionary work.
Evening Prayer 1930:70.
Examinations in Divinity, Board of
1897:62.
Exchange rates 1988:36.
Excommunication of J.W. Colenso
vii.
Executive Officer of the Anglican
Communion xiii,xxxvi,xxxvii.
Extra-marital intercourse 1930:18,19.

Motherhood 1948:48.
Multinational corporations 1988:35,
36,39,40.
Music 1958:10.
Mutual Responsibility and Interdependence (MRI) 1968:67. *See
also* Partners in Mission.

Nairobi Assembly (WCC) 1978:28.
Namibia 1988:38.
Nandyal (South India) 1948:55;
1958:19.
Natal, Diocese of vi,vii,xviii;
1867:6,7.
National Churches 1878:1; 1908:8;
1930:49,52. *See also* Local
Churches.
Nature *See* Environment.
Neill, Bishop S.C. xxvii.
Nestorian Christians *See* Assyrian
Church.
Netherlands, Old Catholics in the
1888:15; 1908:68; 1920:26;
1958:47.
Netherlands Reformed Church
1958:50.
New Churches 1888:19; 1908:69.
New dioceses 1878:11; 1897:54; 1930:
56; 1978:17.
New provinces 1920:43; 1930:53,54.
Newspapers 1958:62.
New Testament 1920:50; 1930:68;
1958:2.
New Zealand, Church of the Prov-
ince of iii,vi; 1978:21; 1988:13.
Niagara Report xl; 1988:4.
Nicaragua 1988:37.
Nicaea, Council of xx,xxi.
Nicene Creed xxi,xxii; 1888:11,18;
1920:9; 1978:35; 1988:6,18.
Nigeria 1968:14; 1988:61.
Nigeria, Church of the Province of
xxiii; 1948:65; 1958:31.
Nippon Sei Ko Kai (NSKK) xxx;
1930:57; 1948:89-91; 1988:31,35.
Non-Anglican Churches xxii,xxiii;
1897:27; 1908:66; 1920:9,10,16;
1958:14,15; 1968:36; 1968:46,47.
Co-operation in evangelism 1908:
23; 1930:46; 1948:50; 1988:43.
Episcopal consultation 1948:74;
1958:16; 1968:65; 1978:14. *See also*

Inter-Church relations; Unity,
Christian.
Non-Christian faiths 1897:15; 1920:
41,55-65; 1968:10-12; 1978:37;
1988:20,21,65.
North America, indigenous land
rights in 1988:58.
Northern Ireland 1988:73.
North India, Church of xxiii; 1948:
63; 1958:24; 1968:49; 1988:12.
Norway, Church of 1948:72;
1958:49.
Nuclear energy 1948:11; 1958:107;
1978:1,2.
Nuclear waste, dumping of 1988:35.
Nuclear weapons xxvi; 1958:106;
1968:8; 1988:32.
Nursing 1920:62.
Nurture, Christian 1897:48; 1948:30,
104. *See also* Children; Education.

Obedience, canonical 1897:9,10;
1920:43; 1930:54.
Oecumenical Patriarch xiv; 1888:17;
1930:33; 1958:40; 1968:10.
Old Catholic Churches xi,xii,xxiii;
1888:15; 1897:28,29; 1908:68,69;
1920:26,27; 1930:35; 1948:67;
1958:46; 1978:21.
Old people *See* Elderly.
Old Testament 1958:2.
One World Week 1988:33.
Opium 1908:51; 1930:30.
Oppression of colonial peoples
1897:60.
Orders, Holy 1897:37-39; 1930:59,63,
65; 1948:38; 1958:88. Women in
1920:48; 1930:67; 1978:21; 1988:1.
Ordinal 1958:74; 1968:32.
Ordination xxiii; 1908:5,71; 1920:12;
1930:65; 1948:73; 1968:43; 1988:
18. Deaconesses 1920:50,51; 1930:
68. Standards for candidates 1908:
6,7; 1948:85. *Sub conditione* 1920:
27,28,31; 1958:54.
Organic union schemes 1948:57,58.
Oriental Orthodox Churches *See*
Eastern Churches.
Oriental religions 1897:15.
Orthodox Churches v,xii,xxii,xxiii;
1888:17; 1897:36; 1908:61,62;
1920:18,19,23; 1930:33; 1948:66;

Orthodox Churches (cont'd)
1958:35,39-41; 1968:56-58; 1978:
21,35; 1988:6. *See also* Greek
Orthodox Church; Russian Orthodox Church.
Orthopraxis 1988:7.

Pacific regional councils 1948:79;
1958:66.
Pain 1908:33,34; 1920:59.
Pakistan, Church of xxiii; 1958:20,
24; 1968:49; 1988:12.
Palestine xxvii; 1948:16; 1988:24. *See
also* Israel.
Pan-Africanist Congress 1988:39.
Panama 1988:37.
Pan-Anglican (review) 1958:70.
Pan-Anglican Congress 1908:26.
Pan-Orthodox Consultation on
Women and Ordination 1988:6.
Pantheism (Christian Science)
1920:59.
Papacy ii,xi,xii; 1988:8.
Pardo, Dr (UN delegate) 1968:7.
Parents 1908:4,19; 1920:71; 1930:12,
14,61; 1948:38,104,107; 1958:112,
115; 1968:22. *See also* Children;
Family.
Parish 1948:37; 1958:100; 1968:44;
1978:7; 1988:13,15,71.
Partners in Mission 1978:15-17,26;
1988:49.
Pastoral care xxiii; 1897:59; 1948:36,
93,95; 1958:114; 1988:13,17,26,34,
46,64.
Pastoral letters (Lambeth Confer-
ence) xviii; 1867:3.
Pastoral visiting 1948:36.
Paul VI, Pope 1968:10,22.
Pay *See* Remuneration.
Peace and Justice Network 1988:40.
Peace and war xxvi; 1897:43; 1908:
52; 1930:25-29; 1948:9,10,12; 1958:
106,107; 1968:8,10,13,14; 1978:3,5,
6,29; 1988:24,27,32,62,68,73.
Pensions (clergy and church workers)
1908:8; 1930:60,72; 1948:88;
1978:27.
Pentecostal Churches 1988:11.
Persecution ii,xxiii; 1920:17,20; 1930:
34,36; 1988:5,39.

Persia, Church in 1930:41; 1948:64.
See also Iran, Diocese of.
Philippine Independent Church xxxi;
1958:53.
Pius IX, Pope v,vii.
Polish National Catholic Church
1948:67.
Politics xxvi-xxviii; 1908:44; 1920:75;
1948:17,19,39; 1958:102-104; 1968:
17-19,21.
Pollution of the environment 1968:6;
1978:1; 1988:40.
Polygamy xii,xxvi; 1888:5; 1920:39;
1958:120; 1968:23; 1988:26.
Pope *See* Papacy; Paul VI; Pius IX;
Shenouda III.
Pornography xxv; 1920:70.
Portugal 1897:32; 1888:15.
Portuguese Episcopal Church *See*
Lusitanian Church.
Post-ordination training 1958:87;
1968:42.
Poverty 1948:14; 1958:105; 1968:21;
1978:1,2,7; 1988:36.
Power, political 1948:17; 1968:17;
1978:1,2.
Prayer xxiv; 1908:33,35; 1920:61;
1948:37; 1958:69,121,122; 1968:4;
1978:6; 1988:71. For Christian
unity 1878:6; 1897:35,40; 1908:59,
77. On other subjects 1908:3;
1948:100; 1958:100,101,103,107,
108,120; 1978:5. Leadership 1920:
52,53.
Prayer Books 1968:43; 1988:18. *See
also* Book of Common Prayer.
Preaching xxiv,xxv; 1920:12,24,53;
1930:6,64,70; 1958:7,100; 1968:38;
1988:18.
Prejudice *See* Discrimination, racial.
Presbyterian Churches 1958:25-28,31.
See also Reformed Churches; Scotland, Church of.
Presiding bishops *See* Metropolitans.
Press, secular and religious 1958:62.
Priesthood 1968:31; 1978:21. *See
also* Clergy; Women, ministry of.
Primacy, universal 1988:8.
Primates 1897:8,10.
Primates Meeting xiv; 1978:11,12;
1988:12,18,25,51,52,54,59.

The Gift that is in You

A model for wholeness in ministry

Barry Valentine

A practical and sensitive design for the ministry of teaching, evangelism, administration, spirituality, pastoral care, and worship in a parish. Who does it? How is it organized? Where does responsibility lie? What are the priorities for people, time, money? Bishop Valentine identifies and examines the basic elements of parish life, and proposes a pattern of effective and integrated ministry for both lay people and clergy.

"I heartily commend this book for careful study and consideration. It will undoubtedly enhance understnding and provide practical assistance in parish ministry" — RICHARD JOHNS, former Personnel Resources Officer, Anglican Church of Canada.

Anglican Book Centre
93 pages, paper $9.95

Order Form

Please send _____ copies of **The Gift that is in You** @ *$9.95*

☐ Payment enclosed (please add 10% for shipping and handling)

☐ ABC Account # _____

☐ VISA/MasterCard/American Express

_____

Exp. Date _____

Signature _____

Name _____

Address _____

_____

_____

Send order form to:

Anglican Book Centre
600 Jarvis Street
Toronto, Ontario
M4Y 2J6
(416) 924-9192 or 924-1332
Fax: (416) 968-7983

Toll order line (Over $20.00 please)
Canada: 1-800-268-1168
Ontario Customers only: 1-800-668-9950

Price subject to change without notice/Apr.'92

Workers 1888:6; 1897:44; 1908:49;
1920:54,78; 1930:23; 1948:21,22,
36,47; 1958:127; 1968:33.
World Alliance for Promoting International Friendship 1930:26.
World Alliance of Reformed
Churches 1988:7.
World Bank 1988:36.
World Council of Churches (WCC)
xiv; xxxv; 1948:76; 1958:15,55;
1968:44,62; 1978:28,29; 1988:3,14,
34,40. Developing countries 1968:
19-21; Inter-faith dialogue 1968:12;
1988:21. And world peace 1958:
109; 1968:10,14-16; 1988:62.
Refugees 1958:56,128.
World Methodist Council 1988:9.
World War I xii; 1920:20.
World War II xxiii; 1948:12.
Worship i,xix,xx; 1878:7; 1888:13;
1897:45,46; 1920:52; 1958:6,74,
121,122; 1968:38; 1988:3. Corpor-
ate 1930:8; 1948:32,36,37; 1958:84.
Freedom of 1948:8; 1958:67; 1988:
23. *See also* Book of Common
Prayer; Liturgical revision;
Liturgy; etc.
Writing as a Christian vocation
1958:72.

Young Anglicans, International Con-
ference of xl; 1988:34,67.
Youth 1930:75; 1948:30,47; 1958:114;
1968:28,29; 1988:48,67. *See also*
Children; Schools and colleges;
Universities.

Printed in Canada

ST. BARNABAS' EPISCOPAL CHURCH
22 W 415 BUTTERFIELD ROAD
GLEN ELLYN, ILLINOIS 60137